# Dysfunctional humans

## Atheists, Christians and other liars

by

### Philippe Boucard

# Dedication

I dedicate this book, #13, in memory of my Taino and black ancestors, who endured the cruel fate of being burned alive or hanged in groups of thirteen, as a twisted "tribute" to Jesus and his twelve apostles.

To all who face adversity, yearn for true justice and a natural desire for a better life.

Books by Philippe Boucard (available on Kindle e- books and paperback at Amazon.com)

My journey into reality

Deadly Faith

Willy's garden

Spiritual Mess

Sinful Deception

Incestuous Savior

The Church of the Tasty Griot

The Lost books of the Tasty Griot

2 burgers and a beer (available on paperback only)

My little homestead

World super predators

Papa time

Dysfunctional humans

# Table of Contents

# Akwaaba

Anything is better than lies and deceit. (Leo Tolstoy)

To the naked eye, the large patch of pedosphere looks like an inert static piece of material. For the longest conceivable time, planet Earth has been doing what it does best; life has been flourishing over every inch of ground. Hidden from view, minerals, organic matter, gases, liquids, and countless organisms are hard at work keeping Mother Nature healthy and beautiful. Upon a closer inspection of the soil, we can admire the business of life in all its wonder. The seniors, in the form of myriads of micro-organisms, are still moving fine, the same way they did 13.5 trillions years before the dinosaurs came along. An earthworm nonchalantly hurries to feed on live or decaying organic matter. The early worm gets the humus, the yummiest carbon flavored humus. A few inches above, a family of ants is rushing to excavate the sand, grain by grain, to build their nest and maybe get to the earthworm, like their ancestors did 99 millions years before. It would be an easy and quick lunch if the roots of the ever growing olive trees were not slowing down the insects.

Above ground, under the lingering altocumuli, there is a multitude of bigger creatures going about the same business of life. Everyone is expected to play by the long ago established rules of Mother Nature. Clouds decorate the blue sky, volcanoes spew their lava, birds sing to their heart's content, plants display their flowers, bees collect nectar, deers munch on plants, carnivores munch on deer, while the gentle breeze caresses everything...

Today is the day she had been dreaming of, since they first met on that beautiful moment when the shy boy gathered the courage to say "hi" to her. She remembers the first exciting date, the first tender embrace, the first passionate kiss, the long romantic walks, the many wishful and ambitious talks full of hope for the future, while watching the sunset. They always held hands as they professed their love for each other every chance they met. They talked about the life they want and hope for, their future dream house, and the children they will have. Today is day one, finally day one of the new chapter, the official beginning of the materialization of their dream together.

Over the years, the shy boy has grown into a wonderful man. Right now, he is a handsome groom waiting in his tuxedo, as his teary-eyed mom proudly and gently turns him around to straighten his tie and makes sure her beloved son is at his best. His dad can not hide his pride to see his youngest son following the tribal traditions, on his way to becoming a father, like himself. He remembers the day of his own wedding, when he couldn't control the sweat dripping down his temples or the beat of his racing heart. Oh! The memories of that beautiful day when he, himself, joined his blushing bride in the blissful arms of sweet and exquisite matrimony. Together, they have poured a lot of love, nurturing, caring, sacrifice, and devotion into their children. And this wonderful son is one of the many gifts they were fortunate enough to receive from Mother Nature.

Her jet black hair is a lot longer now than a few years ago when she started dating him. She had matured into a graceful head turning lady with an amazing smile that could brighten any day. Thoughts of him created the sweetest melody that caused her smile to go on for miles. Right now, she is looking in the mirror, admiring the details of her white flowing wedding dress that have required so many hours of painstakingly arduous work. It was well worth it. It is absolutely unique and amazingly beautiful. Just like her. Today, standing on the high heels of her gem encrusted satin white sandals, is the day she will read her vows; the moment of truth has arrived for her, a gorgeous bride in all her classy grace, ready to wow her new husband and the many friends who have lovingly gathered to express their support and admiration. Laughter and joy are the order of the day.

Time grows scarcer as everyone move toward the cars that will take them to a pre-selected place overflowing with flowers, music, ample food, neatly arranged chairs, banquet style tables, and the festive atmosphere of a carnival. Boom! Body parts are ejected in all directions. The contagious laughter is no more, the smiles are frozen. The groom is nowhere to be found. One man grimaces before taking his last breath. The bride lays lifeless, as the details of her white flowing wedding dress that have required so many hours of painstakingly arduous work are covered in blood and chunks of flesh. Only one of her gem encrusted satin white sandals still adorns her horribly mangled foot. Gone are the sweet kisses, the hugs, the dreams, the innocent lives, the families, the pastoral scene... in an instant.

Blood on the hot sand, blood on the olive trees, blood on the green leaves, blood on the houses, bloody dusty clots raining over a newly formed crater, twisted bloody wreckage everywhere... bloody dark bodies shredded to pieces, bulging eyes where a tender gaze and a smile lived a few seconds earlier... and the ample food, so meticulously prepared, will sit uneaten at the pre-selected place overflowing with flowers, music, neatly arranged chairs, banquet style tables, as the festive atmosphere of a carnival turns into a tearful requiem.

Half way across the globe, they hastily arranged a press conference for the tail-wagging media: "Today, we have to confess to a terrible mistake. A drone strike, carried out on al-Qaida operatives, accidentally killed all the members of a wedding party, who were concealed at the site." That's all, folks! That was all the ink and saliva devoted to the ending of the lives of innocent people who have gathered to celebrate their love, as more pressing arguments were being made. This is the war on terrorism!

Newspapers, like sharks in a feeding frenzy, quickly

dispatch any unwanted responsibility for the grim "accident". A few articles explain to an uncaring public that the "failure is in the intelligence about who it is that we are killing, and not necessarily in the program itself." A top US national security aide explains on BBC Radio 4: "The military is not there to reflect America. They are there to kill people and blow stuff up." Questions, like whoever provided the false information or how they collected the erroneous intelligence in the first place, will never see the light of day or enter the dead brain cells of "experts" who line up in front of the cameras of various networks, to convince anyone listening and peddle "the hope this event allows us, at last, to have an honest dialogue about the drone program." Others deplore the obvious fact that people make many decisions "often unsure about who will die."

Many keyboard warriors report for duty, hurriedly rush online and don't waste any time to express their idiotic racist xenophobic feelings, as they rejoice at the slaughter, demanding more of the same. One comment echoes the next: "these people are terrorists, they deserve to die."

Just another human day on the planet... The hamburgers are on the grill, the ice cold beers are in the cooler. Life goes on.

Meanwhile, the FBI defines terrorism, according to U.S. law, specifically 18 U.S.C., section 2331, which defines terrorism, both domestic and international, as any activity that is violent, or dangerous to human life, which violates federal or state law, and appears to be intended to: Intimidate or coerce a civilian population.

This book will tackle the state of a planet in which too many have been suffering and dying needlessly, for a long time, needlessly over hyped up paranoid ideologies. Hopefully, it will grab the attention of those who truly want to make the world a better place, starting with their home, street, neighborhood, and moving on to the town, city, state, country. And when we join the different parts of a better world, we will have a decent planet to live in.

THANK YOU! I would like to thank everyone who reads this book. Thanks once again for your support. I appreciate it. In particular, I would like to thank my son, who patiently devoted as much needed time to edit and publish these books on Create Space.

I still promise you, the readers: "I will tell you what you don't want to hear, because anyone can tell you what you want to hear." I wish you peace and many wonderful discoveries on your journey.

# THE TICKING CLOCK

How did we get to the point of murdering two people in love... along with their families and friends?

Carl Sagan provided the answer: "The earth is a very small stage in a vast cosmic arena. Think of the endless cruelties visited by the inhabitants of one corner of this pixel on the scarcely distinguishable inhabitants of some other corner, how frequent their misunderstandings, how eager they are to kill one another, how fervent their hatreds. Think of the rivers of blood spilled by all those generals and emperors so that, in glory and triumph, they could become the momentary masters of a fraction of a dot."

The above scenario could have produced the same or worse consequences, in another account, in another time, and another place. The murderers could have easily been chasing and killing millions of unbelievers in Dorylaeum or Nicaea during the Crusades; in Spain, Italy or Portugal during the Inquisition. They could have held the torches, ready to burn heretics, alive at the stakes. They could have been Catholic priests sodomizing little boys. They could have been the indoctrinated and radicalized murderers following and supporting the new Hitler on the West Bank. They could have been arranging marriages to minors, blowing up abortion clinics, oppressing women and homosexuals, conducting ethnic cleansing or flying planes into buildings. They could have been King Leopold II of Belgium, and his clique butchering 60 millions Africans in the Congo. They could have been Generation Identity conducting its operation Defend Europe. They could have been the racist criminals of the Golden Dawn in Greece. They could have been the genocidal murderers onboard the Santa Maria, the Nina, the Pinta, or the Mayflower. They could have been the descendants of the white pirates slaughtering the dark-skinned pirates of Somalia. They could have been the white supremacists pursuing their agenda to control negroes in Niger and other parts of Alkebulan. They could have been the suicide bombers, conducting a jihad or obeying a fatwa. They could have been raiding the coasts of Kemet, to kidnap, castrate and sell young black men or enslaving black women in their harems. They could have been offering a human sacrifice to their fairy god, or following the esteemed tradition of honor rape or honor killing. They could have been the pilots of bombers dropping their heavy concentrations of ordnance on targeted civilian villages or towns. They could have been the soldiers who gamble their lives to please a richer so-called elite. They could have been the evangelists fleecing the poor and collecting millions of tax-free dollars while spreading ignorance all over the planet. They could have been the publicity-seeking atheists challenging the greedy and holy religious con-men while fleecing the uneducated and collecting tax-free donations. They could have been the rich demented genocidal cowards hiding behind fake charities to infect dark-skinned people with tainted vaccines. They could have been anyone, everywhere. Such is the state of a planet in which too many have been suffering and dying needlessly for a long time. Needlessly.

And it is no longer reserved for so-called third world countries populated by perceived savage cannibals. Everywhere, the game remains the same as they always place squarely the blame on the victims and never the true culprits. Human suffering is now the greatest world exported commodity. Few on the planet seem aware of the deterioration of human values, as the lust for money has overpowered everyone's brain, at the expense of reason and common sense.

BLACK MONSTER Sometimes, something so horrible happens it leaves most of us speechless and deeply troubled. They have charged a Georgia woman with two counts of murder after cops say she killed her two young sons by placing them in an oven. According to authorities in Fulton County, the bodies of 1-year-old Jakarter Penn and 2-year-old Keyounte Penn were found in their apartment over the weekend. WWJD... What was Jesus doing?

Their mother, 24-year-old Lamora Williams, told authorities she had left the boys in the care of a family member at the time of their deaths. However, affidavits say the father of the boys called the cops to the home after Williams contacted him via video chat to show him the crime scene. "After I seen what I seen, you know I called the police," the father Jameel Penn told the Atlanta Journal-Constitution.

Investigators say they found the boys with burns on their bodies. They also removed an oven from the home, CBS reports. The arrest warrant alleges Williams put her sons in the oven sometime last week, between Thursday and Friday (10/19th - 20th/2017). Family members said Lamora Williams suffered from mental health issues all her life and was suffering from post-partum depression at the time of the alleged murders. "Mora wasn't right", said Williams' mother, Brenda Williams. "She hasn't been right and what happened three months ago that the kid's father left her? I told him something tragic is going to happen. She's going to do something to those kids, she's going to do something to herself". They charged Williams with two counts of murder and one count of cruelty to children in the first degree.

A black woman suffering from mental illness coupled with an absentee black father to produce four children. Another Negro adding to the already full list of stereotypical trash heaped on blacks. No intervention or help from any "sane" family member; now two of the children are dead. This is not a rare case, it's the reality of many black families in the US. Whatever happened to the black BS "it takes a village to raise a kid?"

WHITE MONSTERS On October 27, 2017, authorities announced they have captured Joshua Gurto, a 37-year-old white Ohio man, in the Franklin Park area. On October 13, they spotted him buying groceries at a convenience store in Girard, Pa. and evaded police. The arrest happened 3 weeks after he raped and murdered the 13 months old daughter of his girlfriend Kelsie Blankenship. A 13 months old baby, raped and murdered by a 37 years old white supremacist.

On 11/03/2017, a tragedy happened in Mabank, a town 55 miles southeast of Dallas. Sheriff Botie Hillhouse announced they took Sarah Nicole Henderson, a 29-year-old North Texas woman, into custody. That's after her husband, Jacob Henderson, who is not the biological father, called 911 to report that his wife had shot her 2 little girls, ages 5 and 7. WWJD... What was Jesus doing? Sarah had planned the killing for weeks and wanted to shoot the husband before taking her own life.

NATURE. Where does all that destructiveness come from? Violence and pacifism are encrusted, embedded in all, they derive from Mother Nature. The ocean can be calm or stormy; the wind can be a gentle breeze, a tornado or a hurricane; lightning can be a beautiful display of lights or deadly. Since the beginning of time, it seems that humans have been cursed with the malevolent desire to kill one another. Our large brain was supposed to dull the propensity to eliminate our own kind. It's not working.

While fulfilling a definite purpose in the natural world, or directly related to survival in other animals, violence can be exacerbated by human ignorance and racism, while religion may be the alcoholic excuse needed to remove any inhibition, or disguise the real intention of a person. Right now, humanity is a dysfunctional mess, subjected to many genocides conducted in the name of just about anything... just one bloodbath after the last. Murder has become an art form, and many have become talented artists.

The desire to murder has escalated to where it is now an acceptable and socially sought after trait and endeavor.

Malice aforethought is a thing of the past, as the greatness of a country can now be judged by the number of deaths it can inflict on its citizens or other nations for any inane reason. Even the descriptions of deadly events are getting a lot more sophisticated, to increase the experience. Human killers are now more settled in their cavalier ways to dispose of others, thru annihilation, assassination, bloodshed, carnage, butchery, crime, death, destruction, dispatching, foul play, hit, homicide, liquidation, one-way ticket, rub out, slaying, shooting, taking out, offing, etc... Natural selection is sometimes invoked, with many assumptions from evolutionary psychology about the modular functioning of the human brain.

It's safe to say that the planet can and will never recover from the amount of human putridity soiling its beauty; the only way to redemption and renewal is to get rid of the fecal waste called humanity.

OUR DECAY. We are about to run out of countries and people to destroy. The world is being bullied by a gang of morons who are getting more daring with each feat. The planet is in serious trouble when a "democratic" nation, like the US, outlaws cockfighting, yet eggs Africans on to fight and kill each other. All the present wars between the African states are not of religious cause, but the result of the racist western destabilization for better control and theft of African resources. It requires very little effort to hate a man whom you have wronged.

The war in Afghanistan has never been about 9/11. It has always been about wrestling the opium trade from Afghani farmers who make more money growing poppies than conventional crops. We also known Afghanistan to have vast reserves of oil, gas, copper, cobalt, gold and lithium. This campaign of corruption has now evolved into a full collaboration between the US and the selected, hand-picked Afghan administration.

Screwed by their corrupt government on one side and the US vultures on the other side, the Afghan people are the pawns of the new and improved imperialistic game. It requires very little effort to hate a man whom you have wronged.

In Palestine, the daily slaughter in Gaza is about Benzion Mileikowski and Israhell cashing and collecting its Rothschild loans from an indebted Britain; unfortunately, the Palestinians are in the way. Or is it? Could it also be a foothold, like South Africa was, for the future invasion of Africa? Either way, Israhell is nothing but an invading, apartheid, racist, genocidal gang of terrorists led by the deranged Polish-born butcher of the West Bank. President Trump told U.N. Secretary General Antonio Guterres that Zionist Prime Minister Benjamin Netanyahu was more of an obstacle to peace efforts in the Middle East than Palestinian Authority President Mahmoud Abbas, according to news hound Haaretz. Trump reportedly made the comments during a meeting with Guterres at the United Nations General Assembly in New York City, last September 2017. A Western diplomat who had been briefed on the meeting told the publication that Trump had acknowledged both leaders were being "problematic", but the Israeli leader was "the bigger problem." They murder Palestinian women and children every single day and the world sits idly by, watching another genocide. It requires very little effort to hate a man whom you have wronged.

Around our world, there are a lot of venues that tried to legitimize the conduct of predators regarding the treatment accorded and reserved for the destruction of other humans. Just like the lip service to the victims of cancer "research" from companies which infected them with cancer in the first place?

From the so-called compassionate, civilized elite dealing everything from injustice and racism to modern-day slavery, a select few are imposing their will on the "rest of them" who are too afraid to defend themselves. The masses have made gods of their masters; so when shit rains on them, they better call it blessed manna and feel happy. Now that paranoia has fertilized and taken over the withered brains of the richest decision makers, nothing is off the table.

The sins of the past have not yet been expunged, and the dossier keeps piling up. While some have blamed religion, progress, technology, the industrial revolution, or dark-skinned people themselves, few will expose the true and real culprit that is racism. It is still a taboo subject, better left out of any real public or social debate, a prickly anathema better reserved for "some other time," so the conversation can be used stealthily in practice, in-like-groups.

THE "N"-WORD. We can observe and verify the above fact when ever an offended person publicly or loudly pushes back against a racist comment or act, or simply when someone uses the mysterious acronymic N-word* that almost everyone is afraid to spell or pronounce entirely, while not too shy and afraid to use the word nigger among close friends.

(Note*: N is not a word, but a consonant, the 14th letter of the alphabet.)

The offending parties will usually either cope with a conciliatory tone to avoid escalating the problem, or do the opposite to satisfy their original intention to show the hatred for their "counterparts." In the same line, white supremacist morons are always quick to tell blacks to go back to Africa, but are never ready to go back themselves to their icy caves of the Caucasus mountains. Racism is a blend of hatred and ignorance.

Once in a great while, a few will dare venture out of the racist closet, momentarily, to defend their Freudian slip by saying that blacks use the word all the times. Blacks did not separate people by skin color, the white folks did. Let's not kid ourselves, even white people with black friends, are racists. Of course, there is the inevitable reply that blacks can also be racists. For people who are still too busy to research or understand what racism is: prejudice with power. Blacks don't have any power. They took away it from them, a long, very long time ago. And the American Negro still does not understand that real power, you don't ask or beg for; you take it.

This book doesn't plan on skipping or tripping over the truth, but kicking it out in the open for all to see and stop the denial.

Its intended mission is to start a dialogue, find and destroy absurdities, fight ignorance and educate. It will expose and shed the light on many given silly reasons for the state of our planet. I also meant this book to rectify many lies about the true historical facts being altered every day. I wrote it to lend a voice, however small but nevertheless audible, to the bullied, intimidated, downcast, disheartened, maltreated, mistreated, but not the hopeless.

To save time, I will limit the observations to the most aggravating contributing factors, such as organized religion, and the planned, legalized terrorist genocide of Negroes, which started in 550 AD. I will exempt wrongly classified Eastern "religions" because they are truly philosophies, mislabeled by people hell bent on avoiding to credit African spirituality where they emerged and were "borrowed" from. Moreover, they have not caused any devastating harm to humankind.

While some people offer the words progress, advancement of technology, and industrial revolution as causes for exacerbating human suffering, we can dismiss them summarily. We will need only a few words and examples in this chapter to discard them quickly. Only then will we be left with more time to deal with the real culprits of organized religion, revised and tainted history, and the virulent racism affecting specific tribes from the self-proclaimed better, superior specimens of humanity.

INTERNATIONAL ABSCESS. There are a few words that most people use as an excuse or try to readily avoid in a public discussion. While everyone is familiar with the true meaning, they are described differently depending on the intended impact: bias, discrimination, unfair treatment, prejudice, apartheid, bigotry, partiality, segregation, unfairness, social separation, Jim Crowism, Nazism, Zionism, injustice, race snobbery, eugenics, racialism, hatred, intolerance, white supremacy, skinhead, ethnocentrism, mono culturalism, xenophobia, klansperson, confederate ideal. Racism always describes the fuel behind the common corrupt behavior of a person in power.

William Pitt said: "Unlimited power is apt to corrupt the minds of those who possess it." All the destruction unleashed on other humans came from people after they have reached a certain unlimited level of power, given or taken. The Roman emperors declared themselves gods, Napoleon declared himself an emperor, Russia invaded Crimea, the Zionist gang invaded Palestine, Britain invaded Germany, the US invaded the world. Alphonse Lamartine said: "power corrupts and absolute power corrupts absolutely".

The offenders always claimed to be the ones who were offended when exercising power. That's why on the home front, Americans refuse to accept any responsibility for the discrimination they heap on non-whites every single day, at home and around the world. 60 to 64% of white male Southerners, from Alabama, Kentucky, Louisiana, Mississippi, South Carolina and Tennessee, mostly white evangelical Protestants, believe that blacks do not face a lot of discrimination. They have distanced themselves from many blacks who are not only Americans but also Southerners. Party affiliation also plays a role as 65% of republicans reject the idea that black Americans face a great deal of discrimination today, while 77% of Democrats agree blacks experience a great deal of discrimination. And different venues are responsible for dishing out all this racism, especially when they bring the supernatural into the equation.

The above consensus dictates that many I will dedicate pages in this book to the black tribe. Why? Western religion and institutional racism do not target other communities as much. Anyone who travels to China, Russia, Iran or North Korea with the slightest intention of spreading any racist religious manure is quickly baptized in reality. These countries know that religion is at the very beginning of the white supremacy doctrine. Humans, being shown the way to heaven and freedom, are treated to a world tour by various religious and political cults simmering in racism and corruption. Christianity is about a god, riding the waves of pre-creation nothingness, who is always pushing for a supremacist tribe over all other nations. Wherever corrupt politics are found, organized religion will also be present.

Sometimes, Mother Nature provides certain attributes that make a particular breed of animals more susceptible to be dominated. We can see everywhere it in the world, between hawks and pigeons, lions and impalas, Venus flytrap and flies, Spanish moss and oak trees. In all instances, the victims developed better ways of protecting themselves. The pigeons learn new aerial maneuvers; the impalas increase their speed and evasive techniques. Flies realize the trap and oak trees secrete a better deterrent in their sap.

Blacks only find more ways to increase their legendary resilience as they seem to take punishment peacefully all day long, while avoiding to find a solution to the problems, a way out. In 2017, they remain easy prey for religion or any other joker. After centuries of abuses, they will still believe anything. There is even a fake statement to that effect attributed to Georges Soros, who claimed that he can bring down the country by using Negroes, because the black community is easiest to manipulate.

BUZZWORDS. "It has become appallingly obvious that our technology has exceeded our humanity (Albert Einstein)."

Progress, technology, and the industrial revolution have captured everyone's attention, and we can find anywhere them everywhere on the entire planet. More so today, in the age of the internet. Yet the worst stereotypes and buzzwords, mostly directed toward dark-skinned people, continue to dominate many conversations and political decisions in our modern society.

The human ego has outgrown the human mind and is leading to many atrocious decisions and actions. Instead of the common good, people are dedicated to the worship of their own group, their own narrow-minded ideology. Every individual wants to be a despot, a ruler, an autocrat, a "do what I say" dictator. More and more on the planet, it is becoming apparent that every single person knows exactly, to the most minute detail, how everything should be done properly at all times. And the frosting on that delusion is that everyone else should fall in line and copy the proposed hallucination. In case of a refusal to "follow the stronger leaders", we allow slander, libel, curses, jokes and violence, as explanation, especially in the media, to save face and live to try again another time.

TABLOID TRASH. Tik-Tok is the new turnip truck. Countless of idiots and morons fall off it every single day

We have reached such a high level of intelligence and integrity as a species that the most important news, every day, deserving of the front page is: who is having sex with whom, who got pregnant, who is getting divorced or the latest teacher arrested for sex with underage students. Many times, the leading news headline is about a childish president who delights in mental masturbation and is fascinated with petty tweets. And we love every minute so much that, like the biblical bread and fish, the jokes keep multiplying ad nauseum.

The line between real and fake news is so blurred and non-existent that no one seems to pay attention to any of it. Normal good-natured and genuinely honest people react the same indifferent way to a priest raping a little boy, a politician getting caught in a scandal or a western military aggression against a poor black country. While caring parents can save the little boy, it's impossible to avoid a politician who is enacting laws that influence everyone. And the actions of our leaders are getting more sadistic every time. Much more about that later.

What the racist media propaganda can not hide when covering "other" news, especially the foreign news, is the bias that is clear and evident when the chosen examples to back statements could be easily categorized in two separate and unequal parts. Negative examples are to be found only in so-called third world black countries and communities, while they chose mainly idyllic ones from Aryan nations. The skin color of the people involved is always a deciding factor in the selective wording and how long or often the news will be blasted to the public.

For instance, please consider the paradigm of hand picked and selected newsfeed, shown by the western media, which depict Africa as a desolate and arid "continent" where a few gangs of half naked primitive savages still roamed the jungle, speaking in an incoherent mumbo-jumbo. Sometimes the selective locus classicus purports to show and warn about areas torn by tribal warfare, where AIDS infested, monkey eating, uncivilized, dumb, violent 12 years old blacks, toting AK-47s, are fighting under the leadership of an arrogant, savage, cruel, illiterate leader. And it's very hard to know who the "bad guys" are, because all Negroes look alike. Yet, other videos imply a land loaded with an ungodly amount of starving pot-bellied children, the victims of famine, poverty and political corruption, with the only hope that the western Santas will bring food next time, instead of guns and bombs.

News from European countries have selected "modern and technologically advanced or enhanced" backgrounds to show the civility of westerners, where well dressed they show European thugs going about their business in the most carefree manner and talking about how happy they are of their good fortune.

Their only worry is that dark-skinned illegals will try to muddy their lily white communities, or worse, take revenge for the wrongs they have done to them. That's why white leaders always have very good "logical" reasons for conducting far away military operations to protect the security of their respective nations and the way of life of their people. Unlike Negroes, these white folks know how to band together, a credit to them, to defend their Confederate ideals.

In reality, Africa boasts many modern cities and towns that rival the very best that make the pride of the western world. Of course, Africa has areas of low income dwellers just like the US, or Britain, or Russia, or China, or any other so-called western lily white wonderland. The question that begs an answer is, where would these Snow White palaces be today if they have suffered the same fate as Africa?

REALITY. All nations, on many levels, have taken part in the last developments of humanity. Mostly by choice, respect or obedience to different traditions and customs, several black tribes have discarded and ignored many would-be new progressive technological marvels of western industrialization.

More suffering, diseases, famine, deaths and misery came to Africa from western industrialization than any other human endeavor.

What one person in a specific location understands to be progress, may not be for the next customer at another spot. Case in point: how important could it be for a person living in Haiti to own a snowmobile or snow shoes? Is a sled that important to anyone in the Caribbean, beside the Jamaican national bobsleigh team? Should Africans use the deadly mercury vapor light bulbs? Should blacks buy so-called organic food from companies which just joined the natural health craze bandwagon, when their organic claim can not be verified?

Should blacks indulge in food designed to target and destroy their health? Should they enslave themselves to the sugar industry? Should blacks eat genetically modified corn, soy, rice, cotton-based food, papaya, tomatoes, rapeseed, potatoes, dairy products or peas? Should blacks pay a premium price for steaks and fillets of farm-raised salmon or catfish labeled "wild- caught"? Should Africans buy "baby carrots" knowing that they are not? Should Negroes feed their kids almond "milk", knowing it's just dirty water?

Should Africans discard their uplifting and liberating spirituality to enslave themselves in the western religions designed to dominate and control them in submission? Should Africans sterilize their young women to satisfy the ideals of the American Eugenics movement? Should Africans believe the false claim that the AIDS virus was contracted through simian sex and not from western tourists?

Should Africans joyfully work to develop poisons to infect their fellow humans with? Should Africans keep or divert money raised for victims of disasters?

Should law enforcement officials in black countries shoot white people living in their society?

Should Africans exchange their traditions, customs and values to transform their communities into virtual western prisons where an alarm is required in every car or house, and where any bank account is readily available to countless of hackers looking for easy money?

Should Africans settle in a community behind a gate which will not protect them, follow the dictates of pinhead city leaders who couldn't pass ninth-grade biology if their lives depended on it, retain lawyers interested in simply making money when they are not too busy chasing ambulances, and patronize doctors who have found a way to pay for a lavish lifestyle without opening a church?

Should African mothers stop breastfeeding their newborns to purchase crappy and deadly baby formula? Should African mothers abandon their infants in a crib, in front of a TV set, instead of directly nurturing the mother-child bond by holding them?

COMMON SENSE. If we really want to consider progress and technology, blacks have done many incredible things that whites can not even figure out with all their computers, industrialization and science. The pyramids are a good example. It is so confusing a task to the European world that they presently claim that Marvin, the Martian or little green aliens with oversized heads, built the pyramids.

We can sum the ignorance of Europeans up in one of their proudest achievements to date: Egyptology. Since when can a society become a science? Is there a: Americanology, Britishology, Franceology, Spainology, Polandology, or Germanyology? It is one thing to rob a people, and another to know and understand what to do with the stolen loot.

Europeans thieves hijacked the African car and the idiots don't know how to drive, and can't even figure out how to start the vehicle.

Being able to survive in a hostile environment when there was no one else around to help is another great black accomplishment. Blacks started humanity and are more resilient than any other group. Reduced to the ranks of commodities, enslaved in plantations, beaten, abused, mutilated, raped, subjected to the most savage atrocities from psychotic terrorists, black men, women and children found the strength to sing during their captivity and be creative.

HUSH KNOWLEDGE. Many other black accomplishments being sidelined and rushed into obscurity include, but are not limited to,

- Blacks mapped Antarctica.

- Africans were the first people to circumnavigate the entire globe.

- Everywhere a European "discovered" new land on the planet, there were already blacks there.

- There are many ancient castles, built in Ethiopia long before they introduced the white man to soap and water. These displays of black architecture have the Muqarnas, horseshoe arches, voussoirs, domes, crenellated arches, lancet arches, ogee arches, courtyards, and the decorative tile work being copied today. Yet blacks are still called stupid.

- Blacks built the world, yet they are still called lazy.

- the Egyptians invented and used music to heal the body. The classical genre is the real African soul music. Not the "Blues" which belongs only to the black American.

- The so-called greatest European artists copied the art of West Africa, art that western museums and auctions houses insisted was bad and worthless.

- They pretend to be so smart, yet still can not think of anything on their own, that's why they had to wait for #blacklivesmatter as an inspiration to copy and plagiarize in order to come up with "bluelivesmatter" and "whitelivesmatter." Monkey see, monkey do. Who is the ape now?

WANT MORE? Common sense sometimes gets in the way of accepting or rejecting so-called progress. Military drones, fighter jets and missiles are an example. Instead of fighting person to person, Europeans use these cowardly weapons, as often as, or in concert with cunning propaganda called diplomacy, to invade or terrorize other countries.

Does a peaceful African tribe, who is enjoying a so-called primitive life, have a need for an F-35 to settle an argument with another black tribe over who can rest under the Baobab tree?

Does a bushman (San people) in Africa have a need for a 150 million dollars mansion when a simple grass hut is what his heart desires? Would the bushman be happier, with a better enhanced everyday life, if he had a laptop? Is it a sign of third world savageries if an African villager doesn't use a cell phone to order a hamburger with mayo, lettuce, and no onion? What good would a microwave oven be in an African village where there is no electricity and water is most needed?

Should a Pygmy, Hadzabe, Akie, Maasai, Sambunu, Fulani, Toubou, Himba, be less intelligent because they enjoy a hunter gatherer's life? Should the Aka, Efe, and Mbuti, be deprived of the ability to genuinely decide their own future? Are their personal choices indicative of "savageries" or lower intelligence?

Should we subject entire tribes of people to discrimination, domination and marginalization because their culture differs from that of the more aggressive society? Should the self- proclaimed super powers threaten the traditions and ways of life of the black pastoralists and violate their human rights, just to make a profit and enrich themselves? The answers are the reasons western ideas can not take hold and are failing in Alkebulan and other black countries.

MIC DROP. Other times, customs and traditions dictate the correct proper way to proceed. Let's consider land ownership. A lot of conflicts around the world come from that perverted Caucasian delusion. Europeans believe they own the earth, and also heaven, by the way, can partition them and sell plots to enrich themselves. Africans know no one owns or can own the earth. We are here, like the other species, to enjoy and care for it.

True and real blacks also know that heaven is a shiny white man's gold. Keyboard drop!

LE PON GONGON. A great example can illustrate one hilarious failure of western ways. My hometown, in the Caribbean, didn't have a bridge over the local river that we crossed to leave or enter the town. Whenever foreign diplomats visited the town, they made it a habit of berating the local leaders and making fun that there was no bridge over the river and one would be a sign of "civilization and progress."

The foreigners had no clue that the most exciting part of the trip, when I was young, was to be forced sometimes to disembark the vehicles, when heavy rains swelled the river, and cross on foot. We held hands in a long line and headed up the rolling water, singing, tripping over rocks, giggling and laughing. We pretended to protect and save the hot-looking girls. We made fun of anyone who ended up in the drink, right before we joined them for an impromptu swim. Trust me, I know what the Israelites would have gone through if they really crossed the Red Sea.

The technologically advanced geniuses of l'Alliance Francaise, who couldn't handle the wet crossing, petitioned their government, and France gifted a bridge to the town. It was built with great fanfare, dedicated with speeches and was proudly added to the short list of French reparations or humanitarian contributions to the town. A few years later, during another heavy rainy season brought by a hurricane, the river swelled again, overran its banks, and made a fresh course. The bridge became useless. Now, when we hold hands during a crossing and head up the rolling water, singing, tripping over rocks, we giggle and laugh at the bridge and the French idiots.

NEW LINGO. The Europeans have improved a habit they inherited from the Roman thugs, to rename everything they steal. The native Americans had a well-deserved moniker for the white man: fork tongue devil. Renaming existing things carries a price, because stupidity is not free. For instance, it is ignorant to still refer to native Americans as "Indians" because one of your birdbrain ancestors wanted to land in India. No one aboard the Santa Maria, Nina or Pinta thought they were going to India.

Just as asinine, silly, unnatural, stupid and incorrect as Elizabeth Taylor playing Cleopatra.

In "Papa time," I questioned why Europeans dared to write about black history, something they know nothing about, don't understand, were not part of, and are still hell bent on defacing. Here is a little shot glass of reality for you to celebrate with me. Dale Jensen, "BS and MA in Geography, focused on Physical, Historical and Political Geography" (sic), wrote an article on July 19th, 2016 titled "What's Africa's original name?" The highlight of this momentous work came when he penned, "I don't know that that's a question with a knowable answer." Then, why write about something you know nothing about? My 2-year-old grandson can tell him the true original name of Africa is Alkebulan. Another name is Ethiopia; the Atlantic Ocean used to be called the Ethiopian Sea. Dale Jensen doesn't know that the name Africa resulted from

the Romans, the well-dressed thugs, changing the names of
everything.

These famous 15-minute celebrity seekers are why the world
has a new language problem. It's almost impossible for non-
Europeans to understand the new western rambling coupled with
the lack of reasoning. American English is no longer adequate
enough. Africans have to learn a brand new lingo to communicate
with the western world. Words like free, together, humanitarian
aid, financial help, respect, private, sovereignty, dignity, trust,
cooperation, voluntary and charity have totally new meanings. So
does this saying: "success is within the reach of anyone willing to
work hard for it". All evidence points out that the best western way
to succeed is to use the unpaid or cheaply paid labor of others.
How rational are the words tourist, foreign journalist, Peace Corps
volunteer, news anchors at foreign desks, war reporter, war
correspondent, missionary, aid worker, peace envoy, diplomat,
volunteer, friend, when all of them fall under the definition of spy?

POSTURING. The western world maintains that the Negro
is nothing but a commodity, 3/5 of a human, lazy, prone to riots
and arson, yet the Caucasian continues to rob Africa and steal even
the bones of dead Negroes.

Where was all that European posturing and bravado circa
711 AD? Before their humanitarian rescue by Africans, the kings
and queens of Europe lived in barns, with their animals running all
over the place. They never bathed and slept next to the dogs, goats,
sheep, cows, and chickens. The Moors, under the leadership of
black general Tariq ibn Ziyad, kicked the Visigoths off the North
African Coast, entered and educated Spain from 711 until they
were themselves kicked out of Grenada, Spain, on January 2nd,
1492, by king Ferdinand II and Isabella I. They are the black Moses
who repeated the African mistake of handing knowledge
(originally given from 1680 to 1280 BCE by the Egyptians) to the

treacherous white man and trained him to be what he is today. The Europeans hated us and have never been our friends.

Apparently, the Spaniards are still mad at the Moors. Can anyone understand the subliminal message behind the Spanish "bull fight"? A matador, dressed in a full drastically altered, over-the-top gold laced attire, taking his time to kill the black bull, which represents Africa. This is an idea that the Caucasians copied for their billiards.

TOOTH DECAY. Trust, on the other hand, can become a real thorny issue sometimes. Nigeria, for instance, has a population which is supposed to receive protection from its government. On March 29th, 2017, a merchant from Lagos tried to export a "world reknown" soda to the UK, to fill an order for a customer. The shipment was seized and destroyed, because, as a Nigerian judge found out later, the international company used different formulas for different countries. The level of benzoic acid, sunset yellow and ascorbic acid was higher in Nigeria than allowed in the UK. They deliberately formulated this product to rot the teeth of the Nigerian customers. That fact, which infuriated the public at large, went right over the head of the NAFDAC. To add insult to injury, as can be verified anywhere a corporation gets caught doing something racist, the offending company's VP for public affairs and communications Eurasia and Africa, issued the following statement: "For one of the most successful and global brands, the hope is that the backlash does not travel beyond Nigeria's borders." To this day, the company has not revealed why they made the soda with a rate of chemicals higher in Nigeria than the UK.

It is safe to say that this above mentioned product is not the only one altered to the detriment of African lives. Vaccines, for example, are a great medical discovery which can ease a lot of suffering and prevent many diseases. What if someone decided to add a little extra to the vaccines, say something that could sterilize young girls of a certain skin color, or maybe a lab created disease for the purpose of testing on or infecting people of a certain skin color?

SHITTY ICE. On July 20, 2017, Mark Braboy wrote the following article: If there were ever a reason to quit eating fast food, this would be the perfect one. An investigation from BBC One's watchdog team has revealed that they have found traces of bacteria from fecal matter in the ice served at McDonalds, Burger King and KFC in the U.K.

The Liverpool Echo reports scientists sampled the ice from ten random branches of each fast-food chain to determine whether the ice contained coli-forms that show contamination from bacteria. The disturbing results revealed that seven out of 10 KFC locations had fecal bacteria in its ice and six out of 10 Burger King restaurants revealed the same findings. It only gets worse for KFC and BK, as five and four of its locations, respectively, have "significant" amounts. Meanwhile, McDonald's had the lowest results, with only three out of the 10 tested locations had contaminated ice.

Tony Lewis, the Head of Policy and Education at the Chartered Institute of Environmental Health, gave his take on the findings in a statement given to the Echo. "It's extremely worrying. When we're finding the numbers we're finding here, you have to look at the people making the ice, handling the ice, which they then transfer into customers' drinks. And then you also have to look at hygiene failure with potentially the machines themselves: are they being kept clean?"

Representatives from KFC, Burger King and McDonald's each gave statements on the horrific findings.

"We are shocked and extremely disappointed by these results", said the KFC spokesperson. "We have strict procedures for the management and handling of ice, including daily and weekly inspections and cleaning of the ice machine and storage holds, as well as the routine testing of ice quality across our business".

"Cleanliness and hygiene are a top priority for the Burger King® brand," said the Burger King spokesperson. "The strict procedures we have in place are designed to ensure all guests have a positive experience each time they visit our restaurants. We are proactively working with our franchisees in the U.K. to reinforce these procedures. This report is an opportunity for us to emphasize our training procedures and ensure all operations and safety standards are upheld in all Burger King restaurants."

The McDonald's spokesperson stated, "We have robust procedures in place with regard to the production, storage and handling of ice in our UK restaurants. Nothing is more important than the safety of our customers and people and we will continue to review our procedures and training, working closely with our restaurant teams to ensure those procedures are adhered to at all times."

They added: "As the investigation highlights, there are no specific ice production standards in place, only those relating to unfrozen drinking water. We would therefore welcome the introduction of an agreed standard and would be happy to work with relevant industry bodies."

If it is this bad in the U.K., who knows what the bacteria count is like at these same restaurants in the United States, where no one cares?

SALAD IN A CUP. The menu at many fast-food chains offers salads. But that doesn't mean you could name much of what goes into one. How about propylene glycol? Many chains dust their salads with that chemical to keep the leaves crisp. It's considered safe for consumption and can also be found in antifreeze and sexual lubricants.

- Styrofoam cups can leach styrene, a neurotoxin that can cause depression and a loss of concentration.

- It is now reported that elderly patients taking Naproxen (Aleve) were found to have a 50% greater chance of suffering strokes or heart attacks than those taking a placebo.

JUST ASKING. So they left us with the inevitable questions: Is humanity better off today with progress, technology and the industrial revolution than it was 32.5 trillions years ago without them? 32.5 trillions years ago, when we were learning to survive together, co-exist and rely honestly on each other, when we were truly one race, on one Earth, with one goal. The perfect world order. After all, our basic primitive instincts and needs have not changed.

Are we better off today, armed to the teeth and still scared inside a house protected by a security firm? Records show that most murder victims knew their attackers. So we are basically arming ourselves for protection from our closet kin.

Are we better off today when our cars can be left nowhere without an alarm?

Are we better off today, when anyone, casually standing in a public street, can get shot by a drugged up idiot joyriding in a stolen car?

Are we better off today, living in a world where 99.99% of the people are on some kind of mind-altering drugs?

Are we better off today, coming out of a doctor's office feeling better but not getting better?

Are we better off today when a little baby is murdered by the very parents responsible for his/her protection?

Are we better off today, because we eat hamburgers cooked by a king or a clown, and a colonel fried our chicken?

MONEY, MONEY, MONEY. Let's digress for a minute for a special offer. A few years ago, I issued a TRILLION dollars challenge to the religious thieves, crooks and liars living high on the hog, any Christian, preacher, pastor, priest, evangelist, who can prove to me that s/he lives by the words of the bible. So far, not one of these holy deceivers has accepted the challenge. Still waiting patiently for one to dare.

I would like to issue another TRILLION dollars challenge to any company which can prove to me that its overpriced foods are truly organic and healthy. This is a chance to show you care about your customers. Any taker?

Let's move the daylight saving time clock ahead and save even more time.

# CREATION VS EVOLUTION

The massive waves that can capsize a boat and shape the rocky shores are not different by nature from the gentle ones that caress the feet of visitors on a sandy beach. Same salty water, same ocean. Humans are similar by chemical composition to any other life form in the universe. The only difference is that we seem to have mastered and made an art of stupidity. We have long forgotten that we are part of nature and a few geniuses among us are presently competing against it.

Instead of sharing ideas about a way to better ourselves and reach a creative understanding of spirituality, we are at a point where even civil conversations are no longer possible among people more interested in jamming their personal beliefs down someone's throat to gain material riches. So it happens that many are caught in the crosshairs of a battle; for example, when science attempts to warn the masses of an approaching tsunami, while religion tells them to stay put, because an invisible fairy living behind the clouds will protect them.

Another round in the fight between science and religion.

While science tries to take the high road sometimes, and wait for proof and evidence, few scarce scientific explanations of natural things only land limited acceptance of the findings and theories. Another problem arose when science failed to heed the warning from Carl Sagan: "We have also arranged so that almost no one understands science and technology. This is a prescription for disaster. We might get away with it for a while, but eventually, this combustible mixture of ignorance and power is going to blow up in our faces." To confirm this statement, please visit the comment section of any NASA press release and read what the average human has to say.

Today's scientists have forgotten how to relay information to the masses. Any new discovery or theorem usually ends up a conversation among the scientific community, with the public at large as bumbling eavesdroppers ready to crack a joke. It doesn't help when certain questions asked of the scientific community are merely relegated to the trash or the "forgotten projects" bin. But unlike religion, we must give credit to science, because it is not afraid to admit when something is not yet known, and will also amend any previous explanation, like it is now questioning the correct size of the sun, and Pluto's status as a planet.

SCIENCE-FICTION. Many statements from science have to be taken with a bit of water and more than a grain of salt. After all, the scientific "findings" are only general propositions which are not self-evident, but rather, proved by a chain of reasoning. They are truths established by means of accepted truths.

Scientists use the term "time span" to describe ten of millions of years, the same way if you tell a human there are a trillion stars in the heavens, s/he will readily believe you, because it's not feasible to count and verify that many stars and mainly because a human can not wrap his/her mind around such a number with that many zeros. As stated in my previous books, tell a human there are 108 trillions of Milky Ways in the universe and s/he will believe you; tell him/her you have just painted a bench and s/he will have to sit on it to believe you.

An example of established truth is when science advances that man and ape have a common ancestor, yet is not able to explain why there are no mid-level evolving species anywhere to be found. Was the cut that clean where all the transitional intra-species went extinct suddenly? Then, science presents that the Cambian rock layers revealed the appearance of many life forms. Really? Neatly arranged like a computer file for scientists to find out exactly what happened?

Instances also abound of "scientific" press releases that make absolutely no sense: someone is told that a certain product or a certain diet can "add" a definite amount of years to one's life; people who do "insert activity here" live an average of 5 years longer; to get between 7 and 9 hours of sleep every night; drink coffee; drink red wine; hold the butter; use soy milk instead of cow's milk. How can we measure and verify these claims? Of course many of these findings are downright wrong, and plain silly. And what can we say when science prostitutes itself for financial gain?

- Diets are alike microwaves and religion. Nothing good can come out of them. They do not work for the greater good, a comprehensive lifestyle regimen does. Paying for junk food from a company is just a foolish waste of health, time and money. As explained before, a balanced meal, coupled with normal activities, should never require someone to go to extremes or a fat farm for a healthy, comfortable life.

- In time, a salesperson convinced a fool that paying to walk or run on a treadmill was healthier than a free stroll on an outdoor natural path. Joining a gym should be only for bodybuilding, not a person looking for a casual, normal workout; unless you plan to pack some serious muscles with the help of a few designer "roids," protein, amino-acid, glutamine, creatine, testosterone booster, prohormone, hydroxy, methyl butylate, and ephedrine, among other things. There are plenty of free exercises we can enjoy every day, from playing with kids, walking, swimming, stretching, to gardening. Running should never be a regular daily exercise, the human body is not designed for that. We should reserve it for cases of flight when the adrenaline kicks in. Today, millions park their vehicles in front of a gym, to continue the legacy of James Fuller Fixx who started the America's fitness revolution. He died of a heart attack while jogging.

- It is quite ridiculous to tell anyone they need 7 to 9 hours of sleep every night. Most people can do well with 4 good hours or a bit more. The time of sleep is more important than the duration of sleep. The perfect time for a restful sleep is between 9-10pm and 2-3am. You have the option to take a good one-hour nap in the afternoon, between 1 and 2pm, if desired.

- Drinking coffee introduces caffeine that gives a jolt to the body. Coffee is addictive, stimulates production of hydrochloric acid, irritates the stomach and the lining of the small intestines, affects iron absorption, releases stress hormones, and can be carcinogenic because of the roasting of the beans. How good is that?

- How doctors can recommend drinking red wine or any alcoholic beverage is beyond comprehension. As I wrote in my previous books, there is absolutely no place in the human body for alcohol, period. Nevertheless, people have a tendency to do things that will adversely affect them, and they are free to do so in a world where the dumbest usually prevails.

- Real natural butter, made without commercial butterfat, is not the culprit, margarine is the killer. We can also make butter with milk from other farm animals like goat or sheep, llama, alpaca, etc... Once again, the misleading ads need some cleaning up, as a lot of Frankenfoods are polluting the supermarket shelves nowadays.

- No one should drink commercial cow milk after they are weaned; no other animal does it, except humans. As explained in my previous books, there are many reasons to drop and avoid the milk mustache, because milk doesn't do the body any good. From rBGH to the foot-and-mouth disease, to the many unregulated problems with the cattle industry, drinking a glass of commercial cow milk is like playing Russian roulette.

- And the recommendation for the soy milk replacement happens when money controls scientific results. There is no such thing as soy milk, because there is no soy cow; it's just dirty water, at best soy juice. Soy, the second largest GMO crop grown in the US, has been linked to brain damage and breast cancer. It contains glyphosate and aminomethylphosphoric acid and goes in the feed for cattle, which are butchered to provide beef for customers.

When science is soiled by special interests or controlled by mega-companies or corporations, consumers become patients. Why is the scientific community so quiet when it comes to the deliberate lies and blatant mis-informations released by corporations? Why are consumers told that eating fat contributes to heart attacks, and not sugar or sugary confections? Why are kids given lollipops after a visit to the dentist?

HOLY COW. The mere honesty of true science, waiting for sure and verifiable answers, makes it impossible for many to rely on. We are talking about people with the short attention span of a free range chicken; people who get very upset if their order at a drive-thru window is not ready in 2 minutes or less; if their pizza takes over 30 minutes to be cooked and delivered. They want the hamburgers ready for them to eat, 2 months before they place the actual order, when the various meats were still "mooing" in the warehouse with the assorted chemicals and fillers.

That's where religion steps in to fill in the blanks; it has an answer for everything under, above and behind the sun. It suffices to mention anything and religion will go to great delusional length to staple an undated instructional tag on it, without an ounce of proof or evidence. All that is required is a donation and religion will spit out an answer faster than Porky Pig can say "that's all, folks."

ROUND 10. Creation: where did the original inert matter come from? Evolution: Where did the creator come from? Atheism:

What creator?

I looked everywhere in a picture shared by NASA, even checked twice like Santa would, and still couldn't find or see the hand of the Christian God anywhere near the 30 Doradus nebula. Yet, Christians still maintain that their peeping fairy created everything. According to religion, which craves to be above criticism, humans did not go through a learning process. On the sixth day, right before he rested from the work he delegated to various "invisible helpers", the Christian God invented a man, called Adam, by using earth as his flesh, dew for his blood, the sun as his eyes, stones as his bones, clouds as his intelligence, grass from the earth as his hair, and wind as his soul. Adam was made in the image of his creator, knew how to talk, read, build stuff, and was void of reason and common sense, just like his daddy. Within 5 hours of being invented, he became a smart cookie who just couldn't resist apple sauce.

The biblical birth of Adam and Eve earned many more qualifications to the already omniscient, omnipotent, almighty and good Christian God. Among the most fitting virtues in his repertoire are: stupid, narcissistic, genocidal murderer, xenophobe, white supremacist, baby killer, woman hater, rapist, adulterer, liar, and many more for a morally bankrupt fairy who ended up looking worse that his supposed nemesis, Satan. And that's after God wrote a bible to confess to his heinous crimes against humanity. He is also guilty of many war crimes when he commanded his deranged lunatic followers to slaughter men, women, children, and even trees in many conflicts that he himself instigated for no other reason than to steal and plunder. 25 millions innocent lives snuffed out, just in the Old Testament. After all, he wants his hallucinating believers to think that he is a good God, even when he is hell bent on achieving a delusional superior tribe. And Hitler is the bad guy?

How could a God be omniscient without foresight? What

Christians cannot accept and understand is that five and a half hours after their creation, Adam and his wife Eve would be kicked out of the biblical garden of Eden because they listened to a talking snake which used to walk on all four, and would soon eat dust forever as a punishment from its creator. That's from an omniscient, omnipotent, almighty and good Christian God who created everything, knew everything and could do everything. A dust eating snake.

Genesis, chapter 3, verse 14 of the bible is like a melody that will not leave one's memory. Once you read it, it's impossible not to shake your head in disbelief. It's worth repeating I feel sorry for the losers who buy mice and rats to feed their pet snakes. If they read the bible, they would have known, all they need is a shovel of dirt to feed snakes. God said so, and he works in delirious ways.

GODDAMNIT. He loves us so much that he created the universe so he could have a personal relationship with us, and since that wasn't enough, he killed his one and only son, in sacrifice for us to himself. I bet the real reason for the Cruci-fiction of Jesus was that the father didn't like his bastard son.

We are so special, the very best in the universe, the only geniuses able to score 350 on the Aryan IQ test, yet stupid enough to be the morons who believe in flying reindeers, a 400 lbs drunk sliding up and down chimneys at Christmas, rabbit laying chocolate eggs and an omniscient fairy hiding behind the clouds to spy on us and find out what he doesn't know.

ADVANCED STUPIDITY. Today, all the sacred and secret knowledge of western religion still comes to humans in the form of a book written, some 2000 years ago, by a few ancient illiterate goat herders who presumably inspired a select group of pedophile monks to tell the world the story of their invisible leader.

The same humans who are so amazingly intelligent as to

build a sophisticated nuclear device, with a computerized guidance system, yet amazingly dumb enough to be unable to understand the process, the inner working of the brain used to accomplish such feats. We know a lot about what we are looking at, yet not much about ourselves.

But luckily, religion is here to let us know that a sky dwelling, cloud skating, darkness surfing, peeping fairy "inspired" us, by his grace, to build that explosive device for the greater good of his glory. Like very excited contestants on a game show, many will choose the zonk behind religious door number 2.

A MONKEY'S UNCLE. Western scientific culture has rejected the idea of mitochondrial DNA only because it came from Africa, which has always placed the woman on a pedestal. At the end of the day, western scientists are now forced to reconsider their contradictory racist decision which advocates for a patriarchal based, 200,000 years old lineage in humans.

Countless of scientists are tearing through various amounts of grant money to explain how humans and simians have a common ancestor, even when monkeys and apes are generally not ignorant creatures. That punctuated equilibrium theory would only explain the origin of some people, because so far, there is no picture of monkeys with nappy hair and thick lips.

Because of that flawed scientific utterance, white supremacist dimwits enjoy calling blacks anything from apes to monkey. Yet, insofar, no one has seen an ape or monkey with wooly hair.

Several Nat-Geo videos and films have also failed to produce any female monkey with big boobs and a generously plump butt. The sexy and talented models seen in countless jungle documentaries are all flat chested, with straight hair, thin lips and a flat derriere, just like the modern European primates.

ROUND 12. Creationists balked at scientists for advancing that the world came from nothing, yet snapped a finger for an instant god to come out of nowhere and talk the universe into existence. That's besides the total disregard of how much time has elapsed between the beginning of human life, the first expression of the human mind, and the ability to write thoughts and observations. Religion suggests that the biblical Adam and Eve were born with a complete knowledge of everything, until they got evicted from their first apartment, five and a half hours after they signed the original lease. If the creator had waited just one more minute, the kids could have been born with a laptop and a bible in their hands.

It's like a game, as religion thrives on getting the feeble-minded to believe the most outlandish stories that can be concocted.

And anything that religion can not fabricate, it will skip right over, like providing a year for the described biblical events, if Adam and Eve were born as babies or full-grown adults, who verified Mary's virginity claim, if Jesus could do the dog paddle or walk on water after the cruci-fiction.

FINAL ROUND. While science contends that humans evolved from simpler life forms, religion countered that humans were made of garden mud. On one side, many people are thrilled to replace mud with dust, so they can be seen as more "refined." On the other end, arguing that humans and apes have a common ancestor, doesn't put anyone at the top of the class, because people are incredulous at the prospect of being a monkey's uncle. If the teacher is fair and has any common sense, both will end up in the corner, with dunce hats firmly on. Both missed the correct answer about the origin of the universe and the evolution of species.

RELI-CIENCE. Science is not a specialized word, but a type of knowledge which people can communicate with each other and share. Religious belief, on the other hand, is an occurrence that can be found in nature. It's called a mirage. It is a tool created to perform a specific task, and it worked beautifully. Religion constantly trolls science as evangelists continue to assert that modern scientific discoveries verify the scriptures. According to the religiously ignorant, research on the edge of the solar wind, progress in human DNA, exoplanets, general relativity, red shifting and neutrinos, all that research confirms that the earth is just like described in the bible: flat, sitting on pillars, with 4 corners, and barely 6000 years old.

Religion is a branch of politics. It's not a mirror image, but a foul, stealthy and polluted copy of the government it serves. The religious teaching echoes that of the political regime the religions operate within. In the same way governments use the threat of violence and terrorism to subdue the populace and scare other nations, religion uses hell and damnation to oppress and keep the masses in abject submission.

Sometimes science and religion argue over things that have no effect on us. As stated in my previous books, at the end of the day, the knowledge of the origin of the universe is irrelevant, doesn't matter, because it will not make humans or the universe better. We just keep telling ourselves that it is important to know where we came from. It is not. And that's another major point of contention between science and religion, presently; a rift which can be mended if both sides decide to get rid of the childish posturing and admit the truth. We don't know what the heck we are talking about. We make it up as we go. Science and religion are alike two blind men arguing over which one can look more stylish driving a loaded bus off a cliff.

Even today, in the age of amazing discoveries, computers and alleged trips into space, we have a seriously hard time explaining and deciding a few basic things, like egg or chicken first, over easy or scrambled, paper or plastic, cash or charge, toilet paper over or under, Bugs Bunny or Daffy, toilet seat up or down.

Heck, we can't even figure out where to relieve ourselves. There shouldn't be any controversy or debate about transgender bathrooms. One bathroom is for people standing up to pee, the other is for people who have to sit down. If you pee out of a piece of pipe, you go to one side; if you pee out of a tuna can, you go to the other. It's simple: weiner on one side, meow on the other.

MY TAKE. In my previous books, I proudly proclaimed that I don't subscribe to creation or evolution, which are used to vainly pretend we are intelligent. We are not. All the bravado about carbon-14 dating, complete with bar isotopic fractionation and variations in the 14C/12C ratio, is just scientific hot air. The only proven reality is that no one knows how and when the universe was created, or how species truly evolved. No one knows what happened because we were not witnesses to the beginning and formation of the world. It happened soooo long ago, that it would be like guessing how many grains of sand on a beach, or blades of grass in a pasture we didn't even visit.

We can yap about it all we want and care for, but the reality remains the same: no one knows. After we hatched and came on the scene, trillions of years ago, we still didn't know squat until the Egyptians invented language and writing, just a few years ago. Much later, when records were being kept, we were stupid enough to destroy the documents that could have told us about our most recent past. Let's be honest, stupidity is our forte, ignorance is the dominant force that guides our lives, the precepts we live by, while religion is just the drug some of us need to dull the senses.

ENTERING PARADISE. The greatest historic mistake of the world was in embracing religion. God is the ultimate stinking, rotten egg. Dropping a rotten egg in the mix is enough to destroy a recipe and create a dish that no one should want to eat. The quadruple threat to the planet, namely Judaism (Zionism), Christianity, Islam and the newly born-again Atheism are the same European racist farce, just bastardized versions of African spirituality.

Ana-Baptist, Anglican, Apostolic, Atheist, First Baptist, Runner- up Baptist, Last Baptist, Christian, Episcopal, Evangelical, Jehovah's witness, Jew, Lutheran, Mennonite, Methodist, Mormon, Muslim, Nestorian, Non-denominational, Orthodox, Pentecostal, Protestant, Reformed, Restored, Roman, and the rest of the ingredients in the religious compost pile, try as they may to distance themselves from the "child molesting central command", these various religious cults are none the less parts of the same and one dead Christian empire. They are only masquerading as different sects; they all grew like mushrooms from the droppings of the Catholic beast; they all salute and bear allegiance to the same Christian institutionalized system of doctrines, racism, dogma, beliefs and practices. They are one religion.

A religion is nothing more than a sect or cult with bigger coffers that more fools can drop their money in.

I will use the word Christianity in this book to encompass all of them unless a specific sect requires special attention. There is no difference between the Torah, the holy Bible, and the noble Quran. All three came from the same group of traitors; and no one, in his right mind, should venture to read a passage from any of these books without being properly fitted with chest high waders.

As explained in my previous books, religion is a single enormous pile of steamy manure, and different denominations are different angles to look at the same pile of manure.

I would never dare tell anyone they can not believe in what they want; I always told everyone that it's not healthy to believe and talk to an invisible fairy which lives in your head when he is not hiding behind a cloud.

Does it make any sense, on one hand, to hate and despise Hitler who killed 2 millions people on his way to create a superior race and, on the other hand, worship a white supremacist God who murdered 25 millions innocent people on his way to create a superior tribe? The Nazi rampage ended around 1945; the Christian God, when he was not doing the butchering himself, commanded his followers to slaughter other nations until the end of times. And Hitler is the bad guy?

Christianity is what the four horses of the Apocalypse "left behind" in a world of deadly fantasy, belonging in the realm of hallucinating fiction and idiocy. Christians are not just idiots, they are cunning and murderous idiots. They are truly children of their god, with similar attributed mysterious intentions and thoughts. Granted that the god of the Old Testament confessed, in his own book, to be an idiot genocidal supremacist murderer, and the new and improved god of the New Testament turned out to be a liar and lunatic, it suffice to say that the neo- Christian religious belief, in its purest form, is the expression of human ignorance and criminal stupidity. There is no need or reason to sugarcoat it.

COMMON SENSE. If I was incapacitated in any way, shape or form, a Christian would be my very last choice of who could make decisions for me. I can not rely, take advices or expect any common sense, any kind of reasonable, rational or sane action from a person who talks to, receives prophetic messages and obeys mental directives from an invisible fairy in his/her head. If anyone disagrees with my above premise, please drop me a note to enlighten me.

PURPLE CLOWNS. And the religious manure keeps spreading. When clueless wanna-be black neo-Israelites came on the scene, suddenly stupidity was not stupid enough. It takes a special breed of IUIC morons to teach from a book they cannot read or understand. The bible is the most racist piece of literature available in the world, created in Europe, by Europeans, for Europeans, with the sole purpose of facilitating the enslavement of Negroes. Like the lunch counters at Woolworth, any Southern restaurant, the public water coolers, the American justice system, the Montgomery public transportation, the bible is reserved for whites only. No negro allowed.

What could have possibly happened that drove these brainless Negroes away from the Motherland into the arms of utter stupidity? What did they gain, besides the tax free donations, that truly enriched their lives? Is the money they are begging for and collecting worth the degradation, the lost dignity, the surrender of their humanity? That's why I made it an extended part of my mission to not only rebuke and counter their nonsense, but to expose them and prove how stupid they are. These purple idiots, with 2 drunk brain cells fighting over the couch, should also understand that hating white people is a waste of resources, time and money; there are plenty of better things to do for the benefit of the black community.

ISUPK. General Yahanna is neither an Obama supporter nor a white supremacist. Quite the opposite. Yahanna, whose real name is John Lightborne, is the leader of the Israelite School of Universal Practical Knowledge, an extremist "Hebrew Isarelite" group preaching hatred of white people, Jews and anyone else who doesn't embrace its radical lunatic black separatist ideology.

There are events so clear, so basic, so precise, so transparent, that it is a wonder some people cannot see or understand them.

It doesn't take a rocket scientist or a brain surgeon to understand that the bible is only the greatest story ever sold, a white fairytale, a black nightmare. Adam and Eve living in the Cave of Treasures, below the fictitious garden of Eden, attests to the fact that they were white, because no black man, woman or child ever lived in a cave. (First book of Adam and Eve 17:4)

Anyone with a pulse should be able to put two and two together to find out that the bible is also the written confession of a genocidal butcher, a demented murderer, hell-bent on world domination and the utopia of a perfect chosen race. It's not hidden behind parables and stupid allegories, they did it on top of Mount Sinai, where the chosen ones were smoking whatever they could find in the desert. We can find all the ideals of the American Eugenics movement in a book that prohibits a certain group of people from mingling with the rest of humanity, while commanding the same chosen ones to slaughter anyone who doesn't share their belief or skin color.

That's why American society placed the bible in government buildings. Do you need another sign?

To collect tax-free donations, the fools of IUIC joined the doomsday cults of Christianity (End time, second coming of Jesus, Antichrist, day of judgment, tribulation, rapture), Islam (Al-Masih ad-Dajjal, Yawm al-Qiyamah), and Judaism (Armilus). Maybe these domesticated Negroes need insurance money to pay their lawyers, in case we prosecute them for raping the women who joined their cult.

I am not willing to discard and trash my glorious history, heritage, integrity, dignity, the memory of my ancestors, the sweat, blood, tears and lives of my predecessors for a few bucks or to please anyone. I will fiercely defend what is rightfully mine, as long as I carry the legacy of Jean-Jacques Dessalines in my blood.

And something that could never penetrate their thick purple skulls: What would be the purpose of a god coming for a final and eternal judgment of the people in every nation, resulting in the glorification of some and the punishment of others, when said god, all along, never hid his hallucinating utopia of only one superior supremacist tribe over all others?

Please allow me to repeat this argument: what kind of justice and fairness can be expected of a God who continuously promoted one superior tribe and commanded that all other nations be destroyed when he was not doing the destruction himself? What good did God accomplish by killing 25 millions people just in the Old Testament? What good did God accomplish by killing Onan (Genesis 38:9)?

No one, other than an IUIC purple dumbbell, would dare dress like a hooker to hang around a street corner and tell passing Anglo-Saxons that negroes will kill them. But in the US, can any idiot, dressed in a purple robe, work the street corners and find countless of uncultivated other dumb negroes who can be convinced that they are the true Israelites of the bible. No amount of drugs or hard liquor could produce this level of stupidity. That's why the CIA had no problem bringing drugs in the ghetto. Many blacks have no problem discarding their natural connection to Alkebulan, the Motherland, and their rich history, to hallucinate into becoming the members of a fake tribe, a made up people, from a fictitious land, under the guidance of a demented fairy god.

It's safe to say that no other skin color would fall for anything that absurd. It's safe to say that no other skin color would fall for something that stupid. The extraordinary inane propaganda of IUIC plays the black people's gullibility. Why are Negroes the only people in the entire universe to believe any crappy story from a slew of idiots? Many blacks do not reason enough (or at all) to comprehend that the decision to affiliate oneself to a group should be from conviction, not obligation. That's why the American Negro will continue to be an animal for the white man, especially the European. Emancipated, yet still a commodity.

If blacks devoted 1/10 of the time they waste learning the white man's way, to learn about their own captivating history, they wouldn't sound as stupid as when they repeat the biblical crap someone brainwashed them with.

REPERCUSSIONS. My contention is that my great grandchildren may go back into slavery because of the stupid and ignorant choices of these Oreos. I assert the road, that these IUIC dunces are on right now, leads directly back to the Muzzie harems or the new cotton and sugar plantations. The black community doesn't need another Jonestown.

HELLO. My special message to blacks in general and black Christians in particular: one fact that you will never hear from an IUIC dolt is that the bible was created in 325 AD, mainly as a weapon to challenge and counter African spirituality in general and the teachings of Arius of Africa, in particular. I will reiterate what you will find in my other books, that the Christian bible, with nothing added to and nothing removed from, is the same book that was used to enslave our ancestors. Now, the same massas are using it on us and, like before, they have received help from a few "bougies."

The bible teaches an earth which is 6000 years old for a reason. So no one can ask what happened before the Romans. They don't want you to know.

The Bible contains chrono-genealogies from Adam to Abraham, listing the age at which each person in the genealogy gave birth to the next person in the list, thus allowing by simple addition a determination of how many years passed between Creation and Abraham. There are other chronological indications also, allowing that calculation to be extended into the times of the kings, when the dates can be correlated with other events in history for which the absolute date is known. By this means, in theory, one can calculate the date of creation.

When you allow preachers, crooks, pastors, thieves, priests, con- men, evangelists, or out-to-lunch male street hookers to select a biblical passage, read that passage to you, explain that passage to you in their words, tells you how to react to that passage, you are in fact accepting their dictate that you are not only willing to be a slave to their assumed superiority, but that you are basically too stupid to read and understand a biblical passage on your own, in your own language. You need them to do so for you, and you will accept whatever they tell you. That's not faith, but the best example of voluntary ignorance.

The above statement helped a young black woman exit the Jehovah's witness plantation. She repeated my words to herself and said with a smile: "You know, that makes sense". She had a painful epiphany about the absurdity of the cult she was in and quit.

BLACK KNOWLEDGE. People, especially blacks, should know that the stories from these four cults of the Apocalypse were stolen, copied and altered from the Egyptian story of Osiris, Isis*, Horus and Seth which remains the one basis, and precursor of all western religions, as understood even by the Europeans, who couldn't reach spirituality, even if it was explained or presented to them on a silver platter. Any black person should know that the 10 commandments were stolen, copied and altered from the Egyptian positive assertions. Any black person should know that atheism has co-existed peacefully with the other western religious sects since the beginning.

(Note*: The western assault on Africa continues, in 2017, as the white supremacist terrorists named their new adversaries in the Middle East, after the Egyptian God, Isis. The same was done, for the same reason, by the same white supremacists to the African Swastika.

With each feat, the bullies are getting more daring. Little by little, every chance they get, the white supremacy machine strikes harder against the black civilization they can not compete against.

Blind to reason, they are determined to stigmatize all African symbols, by association with their ideas of racism, hatred and mass murders, while seeking to destroy anything they will never understand and can never outperform.)

MY PARADISE. I declared in my previous books that I was neither a Christian, Muslim, nor atheist and certainly not a Zionist. Any organized religion is beneath what I expect of myself, as it should be beneath any black man or woman to join such cults.

There is another choice.

Trading spirituality for religion is like turning down the gift of a free V-12 Lamborghini Aventador that you inherited from your parents to start making payments on a 1971 Ford Pinto from a shady car salesperson. Just because your parents conceived you on the back seat of a Chevette, Gremlin, Corvair, Vega or Pacer doesn't mean that you have to do the same to your kids. There is another way.

Once again, we must follow the example of our African ancestors when it comes to supernatural belief; get rid of the deadly racist western religions and embrace African Spirituality. Even Carl Sagan recognized that fact: "Science is not only compatible with spirituality, it is a profound source of spirituality."

MY CHURCH. A brief synopsis for those who haven't read my previous books yet. I spent 6 1/2 years in a Catholic Seminary under the strict guidance of the Jesuit Order, which is the very best of the Catholic Church; and I was an excellent student.

During the course of my studies, I was able to access the original bible in the Latin and Greek languages. I know the full content of the complete bible.

Fast forward to April 19th, 2015, I became a twice ordained minister, with all the rights and privileges thereof, certified by the

Open Ministry and the Universal Life Church, the Monastery. Among the many duties of the ministry, acting in persona Dei capitis, I received the authorization to wear the clothes of the trade, perform baptisms, weddings and funerals, listen to confessions, collect tithes, give spiritual direction, annoint the sick, speak in tongues, forgive sins, perform exorcism, listen to problems from the followers, pre-nuptial and marriage counseling, teach doctrines and many other secret and sacred religious tasks.

The opportunity to open my own church was included in the package. In my triple role as a counselor, exorcist and spiritual leader, I jumped on the idea immediately and founded the "Church of the Tasty Griot" (Amazon.com/ books). Then, I wrote a book to present the church to the future followers and believers.

I founded my church on August 23rd, 2015, and it is a misnomer meant to be more of an outlet for free thinking, an invitation to dialogue. In other words, a common sense church. One mission of the church is to clean up the religious garbage being peddled around, teach the absolute truth of the gospels, find and destroy absurdities, fight ignorance and educate.

The church does not accept donations. We did not and will not apply for a 501 (c) (3) to receive a tax-exempt status, because money is not our God. Saving souls is not our business, either. We teach others how to be free and happy, true natural unconditional freedom.

Science and religion have misled us so far. How long are we going to allow ourselves to be deceived? What is taking Jesus and Neil deGrasse Tyson so long? Why do Christians wait for Jesus to show up at their services when he is supposed to be everywhere already?

"The Church of the Tasty Griot" seeks to promote true natural freedom, the liberating spirituality, dotted with openness and adaptation, over the doom and gloom of organized religions. Spirituality is the opposite of religion as it elevates people, while religion keeps them in submission and fear. Frightening people with sin and threatening them with eternal damnation is meant to keep people in line: you confess your sins to a clergy member, go to elaborate churches to worship, told what to pray and when to pray it. One minute you are told to stand up, bow your head and close your eyes, the next you may "sit on command" like a dog. Religion threatens and terrifies, speaks of sin and of fault. Spirituality gives you inner peace, encourages living in the present and not to feel remorse for which has already passed.

With Spirituality, one can lift the spirit and learn from errors! Religion invents, does not investigate or question. Spirituality discovers and questions everything.

Spirituality is usually associated with an inner search for enlightenment. We cannot find it in a church or by believing in a certain way. Spirituality is an individual phenomenon. It is your way of loving, accepting and relating to the world and people around you. Some people have achieved a spiritual connection through practices such as meditation, while others were struck by spirituality while walking, surfing, gardening, or even working. Typically, spirituality involves feeling a connection to a larger reality and finding a deeper understanding of one's own nature.

Spirituality is a process for discovering who you are, and why you are here. Religion is for those who are asleep, Spirituality is for those who are awake. There is no fixed creed, doctrines, code or bull (papal or otherwise), Curia, heresy, council, precepts, sin, hell, Cardinals, Bluejays, Robins and it is certainly not bound by a written idiotic text. We celebrate our similarity, common journey, share our experience and genuinely inquire about each other.

We hold very dearly the respect for and the memory of our ancestors, acknowledge the natural beings that interact with people daily, nurture the natural beliefs and practices which touch on and inform every facet of human life. Therefore, we cannot separate our spirituality from the everyday. It's a way of life that covers all aspects of life; it's not a theocracy or religious totalitarianism.

BLACK SHEEP. Organized western religion has a special name for blacks. It calls them sheep, because it still can not bring itself, doesn't have the moral fortitude to see and accept them as full- fledged human beings. A black man or woman should not be limited and forced to stay on a religious plantation to become a lamb, fish, sinner or piece of bread. A human is not and should never, ever, be called a sheep. Following a fairy to become one of his "sheep" is a slap in the face of common sense. Where do sheep end up? At the slaughterhouse. That's how slavery began, dehumanized the Africans, and turned them into commodities. Western religions are branches of the white supremacy agenda, supported by the American Eugenics movement.

MONKEY SEE. Just because a European idiot peed in the punch bowl, doesn't mean that everyone else should follow his example. Moving from one cult to another is not the answer; as explained earlier, there is no better religion, cult or sect. Religion is a pile of manure and different denominations are different angles to look at the same pile of manure. Once again, switching plantations doesn't free a slave, leaving the plantation does.

A black man doesn't need religion, he has spirituality woven in his nature. There is no spirituality in religion. I am the proud black descendant of the only men and women in the universe, to outpope the pope, outYhwh Yhwh, outElohim Elohim, outAdonai Adonai, outMuhammad Muhammad, outDarwin Darwin, outDawkins Dawkins. Let me reiterate that God's existence is far less important to me than the existence of Snow White or unicorns; what is of great importance to me is God's carry-on luggage full of hatred and human disasters.

MY PROPHECY. A drunk squatting and taking a dump on a dinner table doesn't concern me, unless I have to sit at the same table. The only reason we must keep an eye out for the religious misfits is they are infiltrating the legislature and want to impose their beliefs on the rest of the world. Christians have their own version of Sharia law, and when the American people tire of the Christian fundamentalist's encroachment in US politics, the country will fall to Islam. Mark my words.

LATEX CHOICE. Religious racism went as far as affecting the safe use of prophylactics in the black community. Western Christians reserved themselves the right to use condoms as part of their freedom to make a personal choice; a choice which is afforded to all Caucasian populated countries. We will never see groups of Christians touting the sinfulness of condoms in Central Park, Times Square, in front of Harrods, Windsor Castle or Buckingham Palace. But, think about their racist arrogance, when they go to Africa, weasel their way into the local legislature, preach against the use of condoms in a country ravaged by AIDS, and thus deprive Africans of the same choice they hold so dearly for their white counterparts. That's when my black blood starts to boil.

Is it a reflection of their belief in the sanctity of human life when they are directly, deliberately, causing the end of the same human lives they pretend to care so much about? They are genocidal murderers hiding behind religion to implement their racist agenda, while mumbling something about the preservation of life. This is what I meant when I wrote earlier: Christians are not just idiots, they are cunning and murderous idiots. Europeans have always used more than one prong of attacks when slaughtering Negroes.

It would have been a lot better, in the opinion of many, if AIDS wasn't developed in a western lab and western tourists were not used to infect Negroes in Africa. But what's done is done!

Blacks should be more careful and not so trusting next time.

But like every cloud, the silver lining in the AIDS epidemic came when the agenda backfired and a slew of the chosen people in western countries contracted the man-made disease. Suddenly, Africans could no longer be accused of having sexual intercourse with monkeys... Soon enough, after the white man came down with the disease, the western world found a cure, although it is still not freely available to all black countries.

CREDO. I passionately hate Judaism (Zionism) and Islam for starting the slavery of Africans, in 550 AD. Was it worth it to waste another human so you could have what you think is an easier life? I have no respect for Christianity and Islam for the same reason they didn't show any respect for the millions of innocent people they slaughtered. Was it worth it to burn another human alive at the stakes so you could satisfy your hallucination? I feel pity for Atheism, which only offers a gentle rebuttal mostly to the lunacies of Christianity, with a rare polite occasional poke to Islam.

One doesn't need to be a brain surgeon or a rocket scientist to understand that Judaism (really Zionism), Islam, Christianity and Atheism started together from the glorification of deliberate voluntary stupidity and racism. They came from the same racist source, and smell like a dead skunk rotting near the cesspool of a pulpwood mill, at high noon. We cannot ignore the foul smell.

OFFERINGS. Sometimes, the human sacrifices and slaughter resulted from their religious beliefs, many times it wasn't. Christians, Muslims, Zionists, and Atheists kill for the same reason: racism. These genocidal murderers are responsible for millions of deaths, with Catholicism maintaining the lead in snuffing out innocent black lives. They used and still use their belief as an excuse to butcher Negroes while hiding behind their lunacy. It wasn't religion, but racism that joined the Arab, Jew, French, British American, Spanish, Portuguese, Danish, Dutch and Italian terrorists in the slave trade. Slavery was a racist war on all non-European nations of the world; religion was only an added necessary excuse.

Slavery was the ice cream, religion was the cone, and Europeans didn't need the cone, they wanted the ice cream. They would have used a plastic cup to get the ice cream or slurped it from their hands.

If they had a better sense of morality, where were the Atheists, among them, to stop that nightmare? They couldn't have all been religious madmen? In 2017, many have still not returned their membership cards to the main office of the British Ku-Klux-Klan.

# SECRETS OF RELIGION

What most Christians don't know or don't care to know is that the bible, which is now mostly known as the King James Version, was a racist political and religious decision that has nothing to do with God and everything to do with control of the masses.

The main biblical purpose was to sideline Africa and suppress African ideas and doctrines. Everyone could benefit from a bit of research before diving into a cult, since it will eventually become very costly and degrading. Granted that many people were indoctrinated at birth, when they didn't have a say in the matter, it becomes more dire for them to backtrack and correct the familial mistake with a bit of facts. Parents are great and loving, unfortunately they can also be wrong. While I cherish and adore them, I don't follow blindly in the footsteps of my parents who taught me many priceless principles, yet told me about monsters under the bed, knowing that they are not real, possibly.

History and religion are not twins, like many are peddling; they are more like water and fire, as anyone using history is bound to discover that it silences religion.

UNDENIABLE FACTS. When it comes to religion, facts are not required, trust needs not be earned, it is readily, naively, granted to anyone with a bible. A stranger, who came out of nowhere, can settle in any local church and start babbling the following day, regardless of his murky past. Any crook can go on TV, start preaching and collecting money; there will be no shortage of poor and uneducated volunteers bringing in cash donations.

Many parishioners always willingly defend any corrupt preacher when criminal or social misdeeds are uncovered and revealed.

Another accepted religious falsehood rests because many do not understand the consequences deriving from the differences between the Hebrew and Greek bibles. They are not identical for a specific reason; with the latter being the bible of the ancient church. Today's biblical version comes from the Hebrew translation, not the Greek. How many people know that?

As decisions were being made, many books were matter-of-factly excluded, like one called apocrypha by the Catholic church and pseudepigrapha by the Protestants. Thus, the believers, who never played with a full deck, have a partial bible to brag about. They gave reasons that many of the accounts described in the books were too outlandish in nature, like the Book of Tobit and Judith in the Apocrypha, which can not be relied on and have no plausible interpretations or benefits.

Martin Luther's questioning of many doctrines and being pissed off at the Catholic church didn't help, so he started his own sect. Something that was not afforded to Arius of Africa who was told to shut up or else. Once again, the racism of the Catholic church was out in the open for all to see. But few noticed, and not many care, even now.

All these debates, coercions, dealings, arguments and dissentions happened, despite the command of the supposed holy writer and inspiration of the bible to avoid changing the smallest thing. What we can say when the biblical God commanded that not one iota, tittle or jot shall be changed, yet we have thousands of different versions which are called "translations?" From the Greek, Jewish, English, German, Lutheran, British, some 200 American versions, it appeared that they changed more than a title, jot and iota. Just like the gods and goddesses, if we must go by the Christian tenet, only one of these thousands of versions is true, and the rest is just pure abomination. Which one deserves to be called the true "word" of God? This is another fact against the bible, another secret of religion.

Thus, people, who are ardent believers, based their faith, really assumption, on a partial bible and don't have a clue that what they carry under their armpit is only part of a bigger book they were judged incapable and too immature to understand... or too dumb to comprehend. Christians are living their lives, teaching others, judging others, arguing over a partial Bible. they don't even have the full version. No amount of drugs or hard liquor could produce this level of stupidity. They are like athletes running just the first 100' of a marathon and claiming victory. At the end of the day, even after the original bible itself was decided on, in 325 AD, by the Council of Nicaea, the books of the bible covered only the fake, made up chosen fairytales stolen from African folklore, dubbed historical religious events by dimwits, starting presumably around 1 AD, when the calendar was reset* by the European religious powers.

(Note*: The reset of the calendar was another move against Alkebulan. The current coordinated universal year 2017 sits between the Hebrew calendar of 5777, Assyrian calendar of 6767, and the Egyptian calendar of 12.5 trillions years.)

THE SCHISM. So the different egos clashed over what they should and shouldn't include in the bible, under the supervision of a political figure. It's worth nothing that Flavius Valerius Aurelius, aka Roman emperor Constantine I, who converted to Christianity as a last ditch desperate act, is the same scumbag who started the first incestuous family, had ties with criminal figures and didn't hide his feelings or actions when it came to bestiality. This is one of the European creeps who presided over the creation of the bible.

Anyone with any "religious or political power," in 325 AD, had a say in the decision of editing the bible. But not Arius of Africa. It was obviously not a decision of God, but rather of over 1800 eccentric and egocentric European men dressed in robes and one crazy emperor, with the ultimate goal of excluding Africa from any debate. This is the start of the degradation of Africa and Africans by the then emerging western world.


Every bishop could bring with him 2 priests and three deacons. The Council of Nicaea, which gave birth to the bible and Jesus as the son of God, something that was against Arius' belief and teachings, was accepted of course by the Catholic church, the Eastern Orthodox, Oriental Orthodox, and the Assyrian church of the East. This is why Europeans will always have control over Blacks, because they can unite and come together, even when the object of their unity is as inane as the creation of a fairytale.

Later in 1382, many books, which were an integral part of the early Greek bible and even the King James Version of 1611, were sidelined. Most of these books were the true link between the Old and New Testament. The Puritans disapproved of them and removed them from their Geneva bible in 1600, relegating them to the dark closet of history. By 1629, many unpopular books, which were part of the Septuagint, became somewhat known as Deuterocanonical or Apocrypha, hidden or secret books. This is another dirty secret of western religion as refined by Judaism, under the control of the beanies.

TWO EXAMPLES. When it comes to the decision of the 1801+ attendees to scrap certain books, anyone can understand that the first and second book of Esdras are pure imagination. The strange part is why they were demoted and not the other outlandish books which could remain in the "approved" bible. There is not that much difference between them, none is more believable than the other. From the onset of Genesis to the last word of Revelation, the bible is just one big joke played on humanity. From a talking snake with hands and feet deceiving human beings to the psychedelic creatures described in Revelation, the bible is just one great long hallucinating acid trip. If so, then why delete certain and not other similar accounts, even if they didn't bring that much to the table? Would that be considered too much of a bad thing? Let's take a look.

- THE FIRST BOOK OF ESDRAS starts with one of the largest barbecues ever, to celebrate the Passover on the 14th day of the first month. Once again, God and the inspired monks decided that a specific year was not deemed necessary to convey. However, we absolutely love the colorful names of the participants, nothing like stale Mike, Paul, John, Luke, even Jesus or Billy Bob. Another unanswered question is how much barbecue sauce they needed after Josiah gave 30,000 lambs and kids, 3,000 calves; Hilkiah, Zechariah and Jehiel gave 2,600 sheep and 300 calves; Jeremiah, Shemaiah, Ochiel and Joram gave 5,000 sheep and 700 calves? Followed by many unanswered questions like: how long it took to cook all that meat and did they have to gather any extra oak or cherry firewood during the Sabbath? How much dry rub did they use? Who won the best barbecue of the desert?

After all that good belly bursting eating, God, somehow like clockwork, got real pissed off at his people again, (seems like déjà vu), and ordered the Chaldeans to fight the Israelites. 1 Esdras 1: 53 ... these killed their young men with the sword around their holy temple, and did not spare youth or maiden, old man or 54 child.

We can also see the same pattern developing when everything was stolen from the temple of a God whose favorite hobby is to ask his people to steal everything in sight. One may inquire how such a hands-on God, who was hanging around 24/7, in those days, allowed anyone to steal his stuff? How was it possible for mere mortal human thieves to swipe all this booty under the watchful eyes of an almighty, omnipotent and omniscient God who is everywhere at all times? Not me. Unlike the haters, I understand that someone could have distracted God at a bingo game. There is something about yelling BINGO that neutralizes all divinity. Or maybe, just maybe, God was feeding his flesh and blood to the believers at a buffet church service. But I am not complaining, because I know by now that God works in delirious ways.

Sacred dishes, royal treasures, chests of the Lord were taken from the temple and transferred to Babylon with the survivors. There were survivors? After the book said clearly, "these killed their young men with the sword around their holy temple, and did not spare youth or maiden, old man or 54 child." How can there be survivors when they didn't spare anyone? Let gloss over that fact to note that the loot included 1000 gold cups, 1000 silver cups, 29 silver censers, 30 gold bowls, 2410 silver bowls, 1000 other dishes, for a total of 5469 utensils. But rest assured, believers, when God's blood pressure and cholesterol come back to normal, they will return all that in due time. There is this grand feeling when one understands God has that everlasting see-saw relationship with his people; one minute he wants to make love to his people, the next minute he really wants to screw them.

Like in the "regular" bible, misunderstanding shows up in the story, out of nowhere. In 1 Esdras 3: 4, three young men placed a bet among themselves and the whole thing became a big deal around the kingdom. The account of the first bet was like Brad Paisley's song "Alcohol", the second was alike Toby Keith's "Angry American," and the third was a combination of Beyonce's "Single lady" adapted to any religious rant from George Carlin.

Then the trek to Jerusalem is recounted with 42360 people (over the age of 12), 7337 slaves, 245 musicians, 435 camels, 7036 horses, 245 mules, and 5525 asses. That was a lot of asses! And that didn't include the women.

But like in the popular version of the bible, whatever wrong is done can be corrected with a sacrifice. 1 Esdras 8: 65-67 counted

12 bulls, 96 rams, 72 lambs, and 12 billy goats as the perfect medication to correct God's attitude. It seems that God's fetish went from humans to the killing of animals and trees. One may wonder why did he create trees if he hates them so much? And that's from the beginning of the world with the tree of knowledge all the way to Jesus losing his mind over a fruitless fig tree. How did God find the time to even check on anything else? There are so many damn trees. Bet God could never walk thru a forest without constant shots of Hydralazine, or jab blocks.

It's time to pay attention, now. 1 Esdras 8: 83-86 is about God's continued agenda of a pure race, coupled with the theft of land (world domination) that didn't belong to the chosen ones. That notion is reinforced in 1 Esdras 8: 92-94. Later, the same God got really pissed that his people had married "foreigners" and commanded them to get rid of the women from different nations (xenophobic). A segregation clause in order to assure protection? These three actions are the qualifications for white supremacy. A God, who supposedly created humans, wants to prevent inter-tribal marriages and unions because that would pollute the genes he is trying to perfect for a superior race. And Hitler is the bad guy?

All they had to do afterward was to bribe God with a sacrifice of a few rams and he was back to his normal self. Seem like sacrifices were part of the Jewish God's medications.

- Esdras 9: 5-6 confirmed a recurring "problem" with the bible, the writer was not willing to volunteer a complete date (ninth month, on the twentieth day); again, not the year that the described event happened.

- THE SECOND BOOK OF ESDRAS, which is really the Fourth book of Esdras, is about things seen in dreams, almost another version of Revelation, but with many more apocalypses. It starts, once again, like so many passages left in the current bible, with a jealous Lord complaining about not getting any respect from his people, not being the one and only God of the Israelites. A common boring theme.

2 Esdras 1: 24 described a dejected God who finally found some trace of common sense, decided to salvage his pride, and decided to find another chosen people. To hell with the old disloyal and unfaithful heathens! So Yahweh reversed everything he did for the Israelites in 2 Esdras 2: 10-11.

2 Esdras 3: 1-3 reminded the reader that it's all a dream, in a recount of the biblical creation. 2 Esdras 7: 1-2 reaffirmed that it is a dream; 2 Esdras 11: 1 mentioned again it's just a dream; 2 Esdras 13: 1 repeated it's a dream.

2 Esdras 5: 1-13 is an apocalypse; 2 Esdras 6: 19-28 is another; 2

Esdras 7: 19-44 is another one; 2 Esdras 13: 2 is yet another apocalypse.

2 Esdras 5: 14 then I awoke, and my body shuddered violently, and my soul was troubled, so that it fainted. (no account if the writer was indulging in funny things).

2 Esdras 6: 38-57 is another of several recounts of the biblical creation.

2 Esdras 9: 38-47 and 10: 1-59 are basically where the Lord's prayer came from, a sign that there were some potent drugs around the desert.

2 Esdras 11: 2-46 is an apocalyptic acid trip which he awoke from in 2 Esdras 12: 3.

2 Esdras 13: 13 the writer awoke, yet again.

2 Esdras 14: 44-45 God inspired him to write 94 books in 40 days (common time frame in the bible) of which the first 24 would

be available to the public while the remaining 90 would be reserved for the wise men (2 Esdras 14: 45-47). (biblical math: 24+90=94)

Whoever came up with the idea of 40 days and 40 nights, or the three days deal for the resurrection, should have patented the idea, because he would be rich today.

- Esdras 15: 5-63, 16: 1-26 is the big apocalyptic finale with the curse on Egypt, Arabia, Asia, Syria, etc... (Arabia and Syria, that's understandable, but Egypt and Asia?)

BOTTOM LINE. It is no wonder that all western organized religions have a contempt for Africa. It started before Arius, never ended at any time and is still part of the pure race ideology which originated in the Catholic church. The western God is a Nordic white supremacist. From the slaughter of indigenous people around the globe, slavery from 550 AD until now, the mangling of young able African bodies, King Leopold II of Belgium in the Congo, the genocidal apartheid seen in South Africa, Greece's Golden Dawn, the current genocidal apartheid being shown in the Palestinian land bridge between Africa and Asia, all the way to the skin tone of a Band-Aid, one can see the continuous attempts made at creating many white monopoly capitals to invade or degrade Africa.

THE VATICAN. Meanwhile, the pope is dealing with the same issues that made the cult so attractive to pedophiles.

The Legion of Christ religious order, stained by revelations that its founder sexually abused seminarians and fathered several children, is facing a new credibility scandal: The rector of its diocesan seminary in Rome is leaving the priesthood after admitting he fathered two children of his own. In a letter released by the Legion on Saturday, October 7th, 2017, the Rev. Oscar Turrion said he fell in love with a woman a few years ago during a time of turmoil in the Legion, fathered a son and, a few months ago, a daughter. Turrion, a 49-year-old Spaniard, had been rector of the Pontifical Maria Matter Eclesiae International College since 2014.

The Vatican took over the Legion in 2010, after revelations that its late founder, the Rev. Marcial Maciel, sexually abused seminarians and fathered at least three children with two women. It ordered up a wholesale reform, but the scandal hurt the Legion's credibility and stained the legacy of St. John Paul II, who had been a leading Maciel supporter.

In a separate development, the Vatican said Saturday that leaders of the Australian Catholic Bishops Conference have traveled to Rome to discuss "the restoration of trust" amid a sex abuse scandal involving Australian cardinal George Pell, a top adviser to the pope.

Like Jesus, these priests love little children.

# JESUS VS YHWH

In his book "The end of faith", Sam Harris offered the following account from C.W. Dugger, about a 2002 religious clash between Hindus and Muslims: "... A pregnant woman's belly was slit open, her fetus raised skyward on the tip of sword and then tossed onto one of the fires that blazed across the city..." The author concluded that the cause of the above described behavior was not economic, racial or political, but religious in nature.

SAME STORY. A similar account eerily matches the above story, except it happened 84 years earlier, halfway across the globe. "Mary Turner was a young black 18 years old wife, who was 8 months pregnant. On May 19th, 1918, after protesting the lynching of her husband, Hazel Hayes Turner, the previous day. They tied her up and hung her upside down by her ankles in Lowndes County, Georgia (USA). They soaked her clothes with gasoline, then burned from her body. They split her belly open with a knife like those used in splitting hogs. Her baby fell to the ground and gave 2 faint cries. A member of the white mob crushed its head, while he yelled: one less nigger. Then the mob shot hundreds of bullets into Mary's body. It would be impossible for someone to find a religious, economic, or political cause for the actions of the monstrous maggots who perpetrated this murder. They were racist jackbooted Aryan thugs and Confederate terrorists.

The 2 above accounts are separated by 7790 miles. It would not be difficult to choose the most repugnant account. The conditions that preceded Mary Turner's murder have been in place since 325 AD.

SIMILAR EVIL. But of religion and racism, which is worse? Racism grows in the fertile soil of ignorance and stupidity; usually manifest in people with little education and not much common sense, people who tend to hold the belief that skin color can determine human traits. So does religion.

From a sick Eugenics notion, they made the jump to the insane ideology that a person with a specific skin color is superior to others with different skin tones. The concept of race started with the Romans, who decided that physical differences resulted from environmental factors. Then, in time, humans were divided into distinct groups when George Cuvier came up with three different races. James Cowles Prichard decided on seven, Louis Agassiz on twelve and Charles Pickering on eleven. It wasn't long before Christoph Meiners, born in Warstade, a German practitioner of scientific racism, chimed in. Soon enough, an idiot named Francis Galton, a pioneer of Eugenics, took over and transformed what became virulent racism to a new level: a powerful weapon to foster fear and hatred. They officially linked skin color to the purification of American society. Like religion, it was easy to spread to the ignorant masses.

Racism is perpetuated mostly by people teaching others at an early age, either by word or example; so does religion. Just like a good religious family takes their kids to a church, a good supremacist family takes their kids to a klan's meeting or a lynching. Children in a religious house are raised to believe they are superior to other kids who don't share their belief, they are taught that they are the chosen people of their God who is the only true one and that others, like the Muslims, are terrorists who want to kill them. Children in a white supremacist house are raised to believe they are superior to other kids who don't share their skin color. They teach them to hate other races who, they profess, exist for the sole purpose of defiling their lily white family tree. Both sides are not beyond using physical assaults and murder to fulfill the agenda of their terrorist organization.

Religion and Eugenics have joined their forces and are now moving together toward the same goal.

Sometimes it becomes very hard to differentiate and separate religion from racism, because they are the same. Is it religious or racist, when, in a perfect fundamentalist world, Muslim women may not wear the hijab or niqab in European countries, but the white police forces can parade around all day long, looking like ISIS militants?

Who or what made Nathan Belford Forrest hide his face behind a hood, his body in a robe, and his ideology behind a fake sense of patriotism?

Was it racism or religion that caused Phelim M'Quirk, a member of the Latter-Day Saints cult, to declare: "No black man who will not work according to what ability the gods have given him for working, has the smallest right to eat pumpkin, or to any fraction of land that will grow pumpkin, however plentiful such land may be, ... any work that the black man may do for himself is not work." Once again, the arrogance and stupidity of the racist orator are clear because growing pumpkins does not require labor work.

IT'S A DAMN MIRACLE. We do not find violent religious extremists only in Afghanistan, Iran, Mauritania, Saudi Arabia, Sudan, the Vatican or Yemen, we can also find them in Phoenix, Arizona USA. There is no difference in ideology between a Southern Baptist, Timothy McVeigh, Osama Bin Laden, George Bush, Henry Alfred Kissinger, Bill Clinton, Dylann Roof, Barack Hussein Obama, the Klansmen who bombed the 16th Street Baptist Church in Birmingham, Ala. or Samuel H. Bowers Jr, the imperial wizard of the Mississippi White Knights of the Ku-Klux-Klan, who, with his terrorist maggots, murdered three civil rights workers. Only the locations of their deeds were different.

On Tuesday June 13th, 2017, in Phoenix, Arizona (USA), all hell broke loose as a resolution condemning white supremacy and the growing white nationalist alt-right movement, revitalized by the Trump presidency, was initially rejected at the Southern Baptist convention annual meeting. While black evangelists objected to the cult's continued support for retrograde ideologies, racial bigotries and xenophobic biases that justified slavery and segregation, the white evangelical supremacist massas, under the cover of religion, maintained the cult's belief in the biblical curse of Ham*, in Genesis 9:18-26, when their God, through Noah, supposedly ordained descendants of Africans to be subservient to Anglos.

[*Note: For more on the biblical curse of Ham (and cheese), please read my book "2 burgers and a beer" available @Amazon.com /books]

This is a prime corroboration of my earlier statement that racism and religion grow in the fertile soil of ignorance and stupidity.

The biblical passage has absolutely no reference to dark skin, that these racist goofballs could have interpreted or even misconstrued as the sign of a curse. The decision to blame blacks could very well result from meetings when they drank lots of mushrooms and angel trumpet tea or indulged in hard drugs. But, at the end of the day, all the drugs and hard liquor in the world could not produce this level of stupidity. The Southern Baptist cult, which was founded to support slavery and segregation, just decided to continue the hallucination that the curse in question happened when their god locked all Negroes in a tanning bed in the middle of the desert.

Black pastor Thabiti Anyabwile reacted with the following tweet: "any church that can not denounce white supremacy without hesitancy and equivocation is a dead Jesus denying assembly."

I have a few better, more generous and fitting words to describe such a cult. Black religious leaders do not understand the game being played, yet they are on the field, in their brand new uniforms, looking as stupid as the pope with his dunce hat. You must have a working brain to understand what you are dealing with. You must stop being reactors to become actors. You must stop acting like the descendant of the Caucasian man and more like his ancestor. And don't expect any help from Michael, Gabriel, Raphael, Suriyel and Salathiel. They only help white supremacists.

HYPOCRITES. So far, without exception, black pastor Thabiti Anyabwile and all the other .6 (point six) idiots have been supporting, teaching and spreading the same message to negroes, as the white man. Having been denied access to their own history and because of these black wolves in sheep clothing, most blacks will live their entire lives thinking the universe was created in 4004 BCE, by a white fairy, for the benefit of the first people to exist, white Adam and Eve. No one and nothing existed before that date. The great Egyptian Dynasties, Kingdoms, heck the Pyramids and all other black accomplishments are just figments of the imagination.

In doing so, these AA batteries are accomplices to the destruction of their own glorious history, hell bent on joining the Nordic crowd, trying to pass and be able to be considered as Anglo-blaxons. They ran away from the Kool-Aid and jumped into the properly brewed Yorkshire Earl Grey Cream tea. These remote control, these so-called black religious leaders are adding fuel to the white supremacist fire that claimed civilization started with the Greeks and Romans, not the Egyptians who were black. Like their white masters, these black thieves are impervious to the true black experience.

Until 1665, many whites were repulsed at the suggestion that blacks could go to heaven, which was created by white supremacists for white supremacists. Why would I, as a black man, want to go there?

Should a Negro dream of and apply to join a club where he can only be a cook, dishwasher or tree hanging decoration? Jesus might need to hang a few more darkies to brighten up his lily white paradise decorated with white clouds, created for people dressed in white robes, next to his burning cross.

It's worth mentioning that Christians used the same cross symbol as the KKK; the Klan added gasoline and flames, the Christians added the body of a blond hair, blue eyes Nordic fairy. Both did it with the same intent.

Religion has done enough to the black race: enough black men have been slaughtered, enough black women have been raped, enough black babies have been sacrificed, enough black families have been destroyed.

ACTUAL BIBLICAL PASSAGE ABOUT HAM (hold the cheese, please!) While the bible remains the most ignorant, racist and outlandish book around, this is the actual passage where the white evangelical supremacists claimed that God used dark skin as a curse on Ham. It is part of the same religious racist libel and bashing of Africa that started after the West Asian traitors were kicked out of Africa? Here is the biblical passage:

Genesis 9: 18 And the sons of Noah, that went forth of the ark, were Shem, and Ham, and Japheth: and Ham is the father of Canaan. 19 These are the three sons of Noah: and of them was the whole earth overspread. 20 And Noah began to be an husbandman, and he planted a vineyard: 21 And he drank of the wine, and was drunken; and he was uncovered within his tent. 22 And Ham, the father of Canaan, saw the nakedness of his father, and told his two brethren without. 23 And Shem and Japheth took a garment, and laid it upon both their shoulders, and went backward, and covered the nakedness of their father; and their faces were backward, and they saw not their father's nakedness. 24 And Noah awoke from his wine, and knew what his younger son had done unto him. 25 And he said, Cursed be Canaan; a servant of servants shall he be unto his brethren. 26 And he said, Blessed be the Lord God of Shem; and Canaan shall be his servant.

Once again, this happens when a preacher, crook, pastor, thief, priest, evangelist may select a biblical passage, read that passage to you, explain that passage to you in his words, tell you how to react to that passage. Negroes are in fact accepting the inane dictate of these crooks that blacks are inferior to whites, too stupid to know their own history, too dumb to read and understand a biblical passage on their own, in their own language. And black pastors have been teaching the same crap alongside their white buddies, for centuries. All of a sudden, they are offended now. Pass the collection plate, please, it's confession time.

How many black preachers, crooks, pastors, thieves, priests, evangelists living high on the hog, have been spreading the nonsensical manure of the bible all over the poor black neighborhoods? All their politico-religious tirades or sermons designed to keep the black sheep enchained and confined in submission in the church's corral.

Black pastor Thabiti Anyabwile, and every other Negro preacher, crook, pastor, thief, priest, evangelist living high on the hog, know very well about the designer suits, the man-dresses, the expensive watches and jewelry, the flashy cars, the big mansions and churches, the phony duck walk and swag, the stupid cadence in delivering their sermons. What they failed to foresee is, at the end of the day, nothing could lighten up their skin color enough and make them true members of the white club.

At the 2017 Southern Baptist convention annual meeting, the black preacher, crook, pastor, thief, priest, evangelist found out that he was just another Negro. All the money and ass kissing in the world couldn't help erase the biblical curse that his adopted "white brother" has put on him.

COMMON SENSE. As anyone can see in the biblical passage, there is no mention, at all, of skin color as a curse. People in Africa have been black for a long time, a very long time. The biblical agenda was just altered, like everything else, to adapt the curse to fit Africa which existed millions of years before these hygiene deficient stink bums came along. We can try to explain it to the gang of white evangelical skinheads, Nazis and klansmen, but we can not understand it for them.

Here comes another prime corroboration of my earlier statement. The most profound example of the stupidity of these neo-Nazis rests in this collateral thought: what kind of a curse would dark skin be, when it processes the sun better than white skin? A black skin naturally regulates the amount of vitamin D produced by sun exposure, to replenish the body's ability to repair itself. The white skin can not do the same with the ultraviolet light; when it tries to, it ends up with melanoma, because white people are creatures of darkness. And their God saw that it was good.

But the almighty supremacist could not stop at the dark skin alone, so the Aryan God added more curses to blacks: great athletic abilities, knowledge of sciences, skills in basketball, golf, football. But the Christian God showed his Machiavellian, yet funny side, when he secretly cursed the black man with boxing skills that the white devils would only discover when they step in the ring against the cursed Negroes.

YOU ASKED FOR IT. This kind of racist theological interpretation is the kind of manure that can be expected from the descendants of a white race who came from a tree with a single straight trunk and no branches, an icon of incompetence, evil, mass murders and inbreeding. These looney birds practice their legendary deception when they pick and choose whatever can deflect attention from their own curse.

The bible does talk about curses; let's find out what skin

color that the biblical God truly thinks is a disease:

- Exodus 4: 4 And the LORD said unto Moses, Put forth thine hand, and take it by the tail. And he put forth his hand, and caught it, and it became a rod in his hand: 5 That they may believe that the Lord God of their fathers, the God of Abraham, the God of Isaac, and the God of Jacob, hath appeared unto thee. 6 And the Lord said furthermore unto him, Put now thine hand into thy bosom. And he put his hand into his bosom: and when he took it out, behold, his hand was leprous as snow. 7 And he said, Put thine hand into thy bosom again. And he put his hand into his bosom again; and plucked it out of his bosom, and, behold, it was turned again as his other flesh.

"Leprous as snow", snow is white. Moses was a black Egyptian, the Nubian incestuous child of Pharaoh Seti I and his daughter Bathia; his "other" flesh was black like the rest of his body.

Maybe one day, these white evangelical skinhead idiots will open and read their bible or get a first grader to explain it to them.

- Job 10: 9 and wilt thou bring me into dust again? 10 Hast thou not poured me out as milk, and curdled me like cheese?

Which people is more likely to tote around a milky body with cellulite, varicose veins and cottage cheese?

- Leviticus 13: 1 And the Lord spake unto Moses and Aaron, saying, 2 When a man shall have in the skin of his flesh a rising, a scab, or bright spot, and it be in the skin of his flesh like the plague of leprosy; then he shall be brought unto Aaron the priest, or unto one of his sons the priests: 3 And the priest shall look on the plague in the skin of the flesh: and when the hair in the plague is turned white, and the plague in sight be deeper than the skin of his flesh, it is a plague of leprosy: and the priest shall look on him, and pronounce him unclean. 4 If the bright spot be white in the skin of his flesh, and in sight be not deeper than the skin, and the hair thereof be not turned white; then the priest shall shut up him that hath the plague seven days: 5 And the priest shall look on him the seventh day: and, behold, if the plague in his sight be at a stay, and the plague spread not in the skin; then the priest shall shut him up seven days more: 6 And the priest shall look on him again the seventh day: and, behold, if the plague be somewhat dark, and the plague spread not in the skin, the priest shall pronounce him clean: it is but a scab: and he shall wash his clothes, and be clean.

- Leviticus 13: 38 If a man also or a woman have in the skin of their flesh bright spots, even white bright spots; 39 Then the priest shall look: and, behold, if the bright spots in the skin of their flesh be darkish white; it is a freckled spot that groweth in the skin.

- Numbers 12: 10 And the cloud departed from off the tabernacle; and, behold, Miriam became leprous, white as snow: and Aaron looked upon Miriam, and, behold, she was leprous.

- 2 Kings 5: 27 The leprosy therefore of Naaman shall cleave unto thee, and unto thy seed for ever. And he went out from his presence a leper as white as snow.

- 2 Chronicles 26: 19 Then Uzziah was wroth, and had a censer in his hand to burn incense: and while he was wroth with the priests, the leprosy even rose up in his forehead before the priests in the house of the Lord, from beside the incense altar. 20 And Azariah the chief priest, and all the priests, looked upon him, and, behold, he was leprous in his forehead, and they thrust him out from thence; yea, himself hasted also to go out, because the Lord had smitten him. 21 And Uzziah the king was a leper unto the day of his death, and dwelt in a several house, being a leper; for he was cut off from the house of the Lord: and Jotham his son was over the king's house, judging the people of the land.

So if anyone at the Southern Baptist convention annual meeting wanted to find a curse, there is one in the bible they never opened or read, and it doesn't apply to Negroes. Let's move on.

GOTCHA. A viral video captured the awkward moment a woman stood up in the middle of a church service and accused a Mississippi Pastor, Billy Walker, of sleeping with her daughter. The video which was posted by a member of the church showed the woman screaming and shouting at the Pastor. She said that Walker had been having an affair with her daughter for three years.

The incident reportedly happened on October 8th, 2017, at the Word Fellowship Baptist Church in Prentiss, Mississippi. The woman alleged that Pastor Walker reported her daughter to the police because her daughter confronted him over his affair with another mistress. "After all this time you're going to press charges against her", the woman, wearing blue top and floral skirt yells. "And it took her to catch you with another woman of the church for her to finally get mad. I'm a mother, that's my child. No mother in this church would do what I'm doing for my baby. Three years you've been messing with her. And I know about it", the woman continues. According to the lady who uploaded the clip, Pastor Walker's wife, Vivian, was in the church when the drama unfolded.

DailyMail reports that the church is yet to confirm or comment on the allegations. Shocked church members sat motionless as the mother yelled at the Pastor to leave her child alone.

ANOTHER PREACHER. A 29 year-old North Carolina woman whose newlywed husband told 911 he believed he killed her after overdosing on cold medicine was found to have been stabbed and slashed 123 times, officials said. Wannabe preacher Matthew James Phelps, 28, is charged with first-degree murder in the Sept. 1, 2017, death of his wife, Lauren Hugelmaier Phelps. "I had a dream, and then I turn on the lights and she's dead on the floor," Phelps told a 911 dispatcher. "I have blood all over me, and there's a bloody knife on the bed, and I think I did it." Phelps said he took too much cough medication. First responders found the bloodied Lauren curled in a fetal position on her bedroom floor, according to the autopsy report. A medical examiner counted 24 stab wounds and 20 cuts to her head and neck; 13 stab wounds and 11 cuts to her torso; 16 cuts and one stab wound on her right arm; 35 cuts and three stab wounds to her left arm.

LUNATIC CON-MAN. An evangelical pastor and President Donald Trump supporter says Catholicism is a cult-like pagan religion and the success of the religion is due to "the genius of Satan". In a video posted on YouTube, Dr. Robert Jeffress, a Southern Baptist pastor, says that the Roman Catholic Church is the result of the Babylonian cult system founded by the Book of Revelation.

All western organized religions copied the rites and hierarchy of the Mesopotamian, Babylonian and Chaldean civilizations. All of them. When it comes to Satan, he is not that stupid and could not have screwed up that bad to make the Catholic sect what it is.

THIEVES AND CROOKS IN SPINDALE, N.C. The AP reported that when Randy Fields' construction company faced potential ruin because of the cratering economy, he pleaded with his pastor at Word of Faith Fellowship church to reduce the amount of money he was required to tithe every week. To his shock, Fields said church founder Jane Whaley proposed a divine plan that would allow him to continue tithing at least 10 percent of his income to the secretive evangelical church while helping his company survive: He would file fraudulent unemployment claims on behalf of his employees. She called it, he said, "God's plan."

Fields and 10 other former congregants told The Associated Press that they and dozens of employees who were church members filed bogus claims at Word of Faith Fellowship leaders' direction, and said they had been interviewed at length about the false claims by investigators with the North Carolina State Bureau of Investigation and the U.S. Department of Homeland Security. The former members estimated the fraudulent claims would have drawn payments totaling in the hundreds of thousands of dollars over a six-year period.

In February, the AP cited more than three dozen former Word of Faith Fellowship members who said congregants were regularly punched and choked in an effort to beat out devils. The AP also revealed how, over the course of two decades, followers were ordered by church leaders to lie to authorities investigating reports of abuse. Furthermore, the AP outlined how Word of Faith created a pipeline of young laborers from its two Brazilian congregations who say they were brought to the U.S. and forced to work at businesses owned by church leaders for little or no pay. The price of a refusal could be beatings administered by fellow church members and public shaming by Whaley. Church members were expected to keep tithing regardless of their financial situations and Whaley kept close tabs on "who was giving what."

A member named Bryant said: "I remember after I was on unemployment for a few months and Jane said, 'You're still on unemployment, right?' And I said 'yes.' And she said, 'Thank you, Jesus! Thank you, Jesus!'"

"Every week we'd go to the unemployment office and put down that we looked for work at other companies operated by Word of Faith Fellowship leaders," Rick Cooper said. "Those companies would vouch for the Word of Faith members at the unemployment offices. What's amazing to me is that this went on for years and no red flags ever went off."

Cooper said Whaley told him Covington's business needed the money because "the devil had been attacking the company's finances" and the minister might lose his house. Cooper said he relayed the information about the illegality of the practice to Covington, who exploded. "He started screaming at me at the top of his lungs that I was wicked," Cooper said.

ONLY A HOLY MAN WOULD. Anyone can Google the horrific story of the 40 to 50 rapes of Mechelle Vinson by one piece of scum. The branch manager, Sidney L. Taylor, who repeatedly sexually assaulted her, is a married man with seven children and a deacon in his church.

MORE EVIL. Religion makes it possible for racism to thrive in all the poor neighborhoods of the US, especially the black ones, the unfortunate destitute of a racist society. Religion exploits the poorest and less educated, and is not beyond finding preys by skin color, mostly using the racist sword to manipulate people.

Racism is not beyond using the religious sword to manipulate people.

The most important question blacks should ask themselves when it comes to religion: Which book, with nothing added to and nothing removed from, was used to enslave the black nations? Then a follow-up question should be: What is the purpose of using the same book, right now, to "enlighten" the Negroes of today?

GIDDY UP. The four horses of the Apocalypse were the bogeymen created to scare the bejesus in superstitious Negroes, one of several European means to an end. There is absolutely no reason for anyone to handle Christianity, Judaism, Islam or Atheism with kids gloves. Doing so is what is revving the audacity of a few shysters to believe they can control people, hijack countries and governments. Sure they can buy or lobby many crooked legislators and government officials, but when innocent lives are threatened, decent people ought to march like peasants on Frankenstein's castle with torches, batons and pitchforks to rectify the abuses. I am not in favor of feeding Christians to the lions, only because I like lions.

SANITY. Religion and racism are assaults on civil liberties and nothing should be allowed to trample on the Constitution, the Declaration of Independence, and the natural, universal, inalienable rights of all people. Undermining national morale and encouraging resignation and fatalism, the alliance between church and government was made to drain money from the poor indefinitely. The people should be aware of wickedly induced divisions that served to keep the masses from correcting the wrong being done to them. Christianity, Islam, Judaism and Atheism are also real threats to the National Security of the US, and the security of the world. They are what they are, racist death cults, blood sects, financial Ponzi schemes and anyone who thinks otherwise is an idiot.

INVISIBLE WATER. There are 2 different teachings in the Catholic cult: one for the clergy and the other for the laity. One example is how many everyday Christians are left to falsely believe that the word "paradise" is interchangeable with "heaven". Paradise is a place of knowledge that one can reach while alive, whereas heaven can be reached only after death. Hell is definitely located "down there", whatever that means, because every heavenly tale describes good spirits looking "down" at the banished souls in the frying pan.

The only downside of hell is an omission that can be pinned directly on the Devil. He is a slacker and procrastinator; after all these years, Satan has yet to make a phone call to a professional because there is still no plumber or water in hell. Maybe it wasn't done because it would be hot boiling water; still it's a code violation. Satan has been too busy visiting God and stroking the almighty's ego; and he is not doing a good job updating his own abode.

Catholic tales always depict the souls in hell as thirsty

prisoners begging for water, in the pit. Apparently, the pope has many mysterious ways to know what's going on in hell, on a daily basis. If Satan installs a water cooler, there is a good chance that many more Christians will likely vacation at his resort.

Luke 16: 23 And in hell he lift up his eyes, being in torments, and seeth Abraham afar off, and Lazarus in his bosom. 24 And he cried and said, Father Abraham, have mercy on me, and send Lazarus, that he may dip the tip of his finger in water, and cool my tongue; for I am tormented in this flame.

SHAKIEST BELIEF. The Achille's tendon of religion is the fact that believers don't have a clue about what they believe in, don't know how to clearly explain their belief or how the heck to describe their cult. Christians are living their lives, teaching, judging, arguing over a partial bible; they don't even have the full version of instructions they need to be Christians. All they care about is that glory be given to their specific fairy. They are also impervious to the fact that the original God Ausar was replaced by Yahweh, Auset became Mary and Heru became Jesus, from the African mysteries 4,425 years earlier.

Christians should also be aware there are things that don't require a retort, just a good belly laugh: a 14 years old virgin whore getting pregnant without a man, reverence for the right side of the body, beating the left breast, an invisible fairy impregnating a material human to create another fairy who existed already, parting of a sea, a gang of Red Sea pedestrians doing the watermelon crawl at the bottom of the ocean, a chosen people walking around in circles in the desert eating manna three times a day (for breakfast, lunch and dinner) for 40 years, a flying fairy on a magic carpet, the Kaparot ceremony, a fairy walking on water and rising from the dead, a fairy riding a winged horse to heaven, the laws of reading the Megillah, Birchat Kohanim, ... and the list of silly rituals and stories goes on, and on, and on. Ad nauseum.

MOLDY BREAD. Still addicted to leaving milk and cookies for Santa, many people are apt to believe, of course, that a fairy, who never existed, fed 5000 and 4000 people respectively with 5 barley loaves and 2 fishes. After the 9000 patrons have eaten to their hearts' content, the servers at the open air seaside desert restaurant picked up 12 full baskets of leftovers. All they had to begin with were 5 loaves and 2 fishes. And they got it from their God, who wrote it in his infallible bible:

- Matthew 14:16 But Jesus said unto them, they need not depart, give ye them to eat. 17 And they say unto him, we have here but five loaves, and two fishes, 18 he said, bring them hither to me. 19 And he commanded the multitude to sit down on the grass and took the five loaves, and the two fishes, and looking up to heaven, he blessed, and brake, and gave the loaves to his disciples, and the disciples to the multitude. 20 And they did all eat, and were filled; and they took up of the fragments that remained twelve baskets full 21 and all they had eaten were about five thousand men, beside women and children*.

(*Women and children mentioned here.)

- Mark 6:30 And the apostles gathered themselves together unto Jesus, and told him all things, both what they had done, and what they had taught. 31 And he said unto them, Come ye yourselves apart into a desert place, and rest a while: for there were many coming and going, and they had no leisure so much as to eat. 32 And they departed into a desert place by ship privately. 33 And the people saw them departing, and many knew him, and ran afoot thither out of all cities, and outwent them, and came together unto him. 34 And Jesus, when he came out, saw much people, and was moved with compassion toward them, because they were as sheep not having a shepherd: and he began to teach them many things. 35 And when the day was now far spent, his disciples came unto him, and said, This is a desert place, and now the time is far passed: 36

Send them away, that they may go into the country round about, and into the villages, and buy themselves bread: for they have nothing to eat. 37 He answered and said unto them, Give ye them to eat.

And they say unto him, Shall we go and buy two hundred pennyworth of bread, and give them to eat? 38 He saith unto them, How many loaves have ye? go and see. And when they knew, they say, Five, and two fishes. 39 And he commanded them to make all sit down by companies upon the green grass. 40 And they sat down in ranks, by hundreds, and by fifties. 41 And when he had taken the five loaves and the two fishes, he looked up to heaven, and blessed, and brake the loaves, and gave them to his disciples to set before them; and the two fishes divided he among them all. 42 And they did all eat, and were filled. 43 And they took up twelve baskets full of the fragments, and of the fishes. 44 And they that did eat of the loaves were about five thousand men*.

(* No women and children mentioned here)

- and Luke 9:12 And when the day began to wear away, then came the twelve, and said unto him, Send the multitude away, that they may go into the towns and country round about, and lodge, and get victuals: for we are here in a desert place.13 But he said unto them, Give ye them to eat. And they said, We have no more but five loaves and two fishes; except we should go and buy meat for all this people. 14 For they were about five thousand men*. And he said to his disciples, Make them sit down by fifties** in a company. 15 And they did so, and made them all sit down. 16 Then he took the five loaves and the two fishes, and looking up to heaven, he blessed them, and brake, and gave to the disciples to set before the multitude. 17 And they did eat, and were all filled: and there was taken up of fragments that remained to them twelve baskets.

(* No women and children. ** table for 50 please)

Does it make any sense, in light of this story, that churches keep buying wafers and grape juice when they could easily continue the above tradition? A reasonable person should be able to handle that story with a good belly laugh.

GREATEST STORY. That's not all. The bible, which is the greatest story ever sold, contains 472 contradictions, 2178 absurdities, 1541 injustices, 1316 cruelties, 428 conflicts with science, 413 "family values", 384 insults to women, 253 sexual references, 231 false prophecies, 186 shocking language and only 25 references to homosexuality. Most can be found in "Spiritual Mess", "Sinful deception" and "Incestuous Savior" available on Amazon.com/ books.

Nothing yet from the biblical God about renouncing slavery, rape, human sacrifices or abuse of children and the uneducated.

CONFUSING LIE. Sometimes the pure contradiction of biblical passages can become entertaining, as proven by the following example. Any decent Christian should be able to answer this question from the bible: How many women were at the tomb of Jesus?

All the following answers are correct:

- Luke found at least 4 or more women in Luke 24:10 It was Mary Magdalene, and Joanna, and Mary the mother of James, and other women that were with them, which told these things unto the apostles.

- Mark couldn't find more than 3 in Mark 16:1 And when the sabbath was past, Mary Magdalene, and Mary the mother of James, and Salome, had bought sweet spices, that they might come and anoint him.

- Matthew knows of only two in Matthew 28:1 In the end of the sabbath, as it began to dawn toward the first day of the week, came Mary Magdalene and the other Mary to see the sepulchre.

- John couldn't find more than one in John 20:1 The first day of the week cometh Mary Magdalene early, when it was yet dark, unto the sepulchre, and seeth the stone taken away from the sepulchre.

- Corinthians said there was no woman at all in Corinthians 15:4 And that he was buried, and that he rose again the third day according to the scriptures: 5 And that he was seen of Cephas, then of the twelve: 6 After that, he was seen of above five hundred brethren at once; of whom the greater part remain unto this present, but some are fallen asleep. 7 After that, he was seen of James; then of all the apostles. 8 And last of all he was seen of me also, as of one born out of due time.

With all due respect and I mean it in the nicest way possible, people who believe that crap are, for lack of better words, bumbling idiots, including the pope.

CRIMINAL HYPOCRITE. It's very possible that the Roman pontiff doesn't believe the nonsense he is peddling, but he is still a bumbling idiot. What is not funny is when little children are being raped by a gang of child molesters and their leader breaks the law by defending, aiding and abetting them. The hypocrisy of the pope is apparent and in full display when one considers his church's stand on homosexuality, the promised heavenly gift of fiery doom to gays and lesbians from its homophobic god, and the silence of the same god when it comes to the homosexuality and pedophilia of his own priests.

On June 29th, 2017, cardinal George Pell, chief adviser to pope Francis, was arrested in Australia. Victoria state police charged him with countless sexual offenses and abuses involving children.

Children fathered by priests (more on that later), when not aborted, are usually killed with the blessings of the mother superior who witnessed the rape of the mothers in the form of the nuns going from the white to black veil ceremony. When the young women are dedicated as brides of the church, chosen Catholic priests will rape them to symbolize the hallucination. It has been going on for centuries with the knowledge of every pope, every mother superior, every higher up in the church. And legislators.

The silence of the same god is also loud and clear when it comes to the 7th commandment. The bible and the Tanakh (Torah, Nevi'im and Ketuvim), Leviticus 19:10-11*, Exodus 20:15**, Deuteronomy 5:19***, couldn't keep the Vatican and Judaism from stealing what they coveted. That's one of the many examples and reasons why religion is dangerous.

*Leviticus 19:10...I am the LORD your God. 11 Ye shall not steal, neither deal falsely, neither lie one to another.

**Exodus 20:15 Thou shalt not steal.

***Deuteronomy 5:19 Neither shalt thou steal.

FETAL SANCTITY. The Catholic church deplores and opposes abortion because, according to its invisible fairy and doctrines, it goes against the sanctity of life. The first question that begs an answer is, why a gang of child molesters, who made a vow to remain asexual, are so hell bent on making decisions that would place them between a woman's legs and in charge of her freedom to choose what's best for herself? The pope doesn't miss any opportunity to force his opinion on sex related matters around the world.

It is reckless, for some, to unleash a barrage of blame and damnation on El Salvador, where abortion is illegal. This supremacist stand was used to support and legitimize abortions in the US, where mostly black fetuses are aborted. Abortion has killed more black babies in the US, than the KKK, lynchings, Jim Crow, the Confederacy, police departments, firemen and the legislature put together. Something that should bring another notch to Margaret Sanger's tainted legacy.

Pregnant white women have the benefit of pregnancy care centers, with free testing, ultrasounds, resources, counseling, referrals and earn while you learn programs, or a TV show, like the breeding clan of Duggars who are a great poster model for positive Eugenics.

Religion has the same effect on the black community as abortion. The position of the Catholic church on abortion, from Tertullian to pope Leo XIII, has changed more times than the mind of a woman shopping for shoes. The only things that remained unchanged are the hypocrisy and lies of the church.

Can the Catholic church answer for the many infants born to the nuns who are "normally" raped by priests, during the rituals of consecration from white to black veil? What happened to the children at the Magdalene laundries? How many fetuses were saved during the Crusades, the Inquisition and witch hunts? The Catholic church will pretend to fight to save a fetus, but doesn't flinch when raping or killing a child. Or an abortion doctor.

There is absolutely no biblical verse where the Christian god showed the mildest concern for a fetus when he flooded the earth. There is absolutely no biblical verse where the Christian god showed the mildest concern for a fetus when he destroyed Sodom and Gomorrah with arson. There is absolutely no biblical verse where the Christian god showed the mildest concern for a fetus when he commanded his people to kill the men, women who have been with men, and children of other nations. We all know how the Christian God feels about kids, he murders them; we also know how his chosen disciples feel about kids, they sodomize them.

The hypocrisy is hard to deny and the real reason behind this sanctity of life hogwash is that abortion depletes the pool of potential future rape victims or contributors who will bring them donations. Christians love the truth, it's facts they have a problem with. Anyone who is not or can not be considered an active financial contributor of some sort is useless to religion.

That's why they bombed abortion clinics. What is the difference between an extremist Muslim blowing up a busload of infidels and a "good" Christian blowing up an abortion clinic? A true card carrying evangelical follower of Jesus-Christ has as much respect for human life as a towel head Muzzie with his finger on the detonator under his thobe.

KA- CHING. Christians don't give a rat's ass about the life of another human, fetus or embryo, infant, male, female, young, old; they just want to protect their future cash cow. When a fetus is aborted, Christians see it as a reduction in the long term plan to finance their cause. Who will pay for the bombs to kill the non-Christian women, men and children? Who will pay for the increasingly bigger mega churches bearing their names, lavish mansions, air conditioned dog houses, personal airplanes, expensive cars, flashy jewelry, shopping sprees for the mistresses, drugs and the service of hookers? How will they be able to build a nation under their god, where they can make their own laws that everyone else has to obey? They must protect future potential contributors.

YHWH is the head of the venomous snake, the source of the other three calamities so catastrophic to the human race, specially the black tribes. There is a reason why Islam and Christianity are as violent as Judaism, they are its progeny. Yahweh is the original European terrorist fairy who commanded and ordered the murders of unbelievers; Allah is just a copycat, another coming. Yahweh al-Jesus ab Allah ben Jehovah is the author of the Pentateuch and

Tanakh and he is sharing the Talmud and Midrash with his followers. When goddamn G-d encountered so many nations to smite, he was forced to split himself into 3 personalities, the father, son and a bird to diversify, to accommodate his mysterious and delirious genocidal ways. Later, he was hired and cast as Allah, in the Quran, to reprise his updated mission of supreme destroyer of infidels.

The traitors, who invented Judaism, inherited all the violence from their benefactors, the well dressed Roman thugs who paraded around in tunics, which were nothing more than mini-dresses. From its inception as the beloved creation of the British and Zionists, the western religious trinity of Judaism, Christianity and Islam, has been rife with racism. There is no difference among them, even if a subtle superficial language is used sometimes to falsely attest to the contrary. Islam murderous rampage across Africa is no different than the current Zionist oppression of Palestine, or the Roman Catholic Crusades, Inquisition and massacre of heretics.

Despite the precepts advanced in the Mikra, Judaism has its source in the raids of ancient Egyptian tombs to steal whatever could be swiped. They stole many things they couldn't understand. The religious trinity was also created to facilitate, support and tentatively rationalize the involvement of Jews in the slave trade and trafficking of Africans, which they started in 550 AD. Zionism, Christianity and Islam were and are still branches of the same business.

END DAYS. There is a vernacular saying: beware what you wished for. Judaism has failed to control its nightmarish spawn, and now the dogs are growling at and attacking their British owner.

Today, Zionists lament the Nazi death camps (more about that, later) which were not a direct inheritance from medieval

Christianity, just as castrating young black males before selling them as eunuchs was not a direct inheritance from Islam and Judaism. There are very specific reasons why both of these instances are now part of our shameful history; the main causes were racial and financial. The Nazis were trying to counter Poland's aggression and save Germany's economy, the Zionists were making money selling black human beings. In both cases, the Jews were the catalyst that enabled a slaughter, a genocide. The alleged persecution of Jews didn't come solely as a result of a religious squabble, but as an economic and financial consequence of their greed and lust for money.

And we must complete the tale of the Nazi death camps (more about that, later) by mentioning that the Allied Forces were not choir boys, after the defeat of Germany. That holier-than-thou, hush-hush feat would be repeated during the Gulf wars. The Allies knew of the conditions in Germany 3 years before they did anything to rescue anyone. During the final collapse of Nazi Germany, between 4 millions German PoWs fell into US hands. Tens of thousands would die of hunger, exposure and neglect; and millions more would still be imprisoned many months after the war has ended.

What makes the Nazi behavior toward the Jews reprehensible, and not the Jewish behavior toward the Africans they butchered? What makes the Nazi behavior toward the Jews reprehensible, and not the Jewish behavior toward the Palestinians they are slaughtering every day? What makes Hitler a criminal, and not Benzion Mileikowski, the butcher of the West Bank? What makes Hitler a criminal, and not king Leopold II of Belgium who butchered 80 millions Africans in the Congo? What makes Hitler a criminal, and not Heinz Alfred Henry Kissinger?

What makes Hitler a criminal, and not Christopher Columbus who is responsible for the slaughter of 119 millions

Native Americans? What makes Hitler a criminal, and not Bartolome de Las Casa who is responsible for the addition of 274 millions Africans to the MAAFA?

Was it because of religion or racism that the ancestors of the Jews were kicked out of Africa? After all, the ancestors of the Jews received their original knowledge directly from the Africans, and have bastardized and used that gift against Africa, ever since. Was it because of religion or racism that the Jews were kicked out of Spain in 1492? Was it because of religion or racism that the Jews were kicked out of 109 locations on the planet, by 1948?

When the Zionists kill and slaughter people, they always claim it's for a just cause; when they receive fair and equal treatment, it's because of anti-Semitism. Anyone can compare their different interactions with the Nazis and the Palestinians. When the Abes have power, they are arrogant and pitiless; but when conditions are reversed, the beanies coward in a corner with tears on their cheeks, complaining about how unfairly they have it. Lie and deception are the only virtues they possess. They have not given up on the tradition of spilling the blood of black infants, and are still sucking the lives and strength from Negroes all over the world.

(For a more detailed history of the racism of the Jews, please refer to Papa time, available at Amazon. com/books)

# ALLAH VS JESUS

Let's not kid ourselves. While Judaism is hitchhiking a ride on the British coattails toward a new world order of white supremacy, the agenda remains the same for Christians and Muslims to reach a unified world with the forcefully imposed worship of their individual fairy. Christians hide their actions behind sophisticated propaganda and double talk, Muslims are more open about their goal. The reason Christianity seemed to be a more docile and subdued cult than Islam, is because it works in mysterious and delirious ways like its fairy.

People are more apt to freely volunteer stories about Islamic violence and suicide bombers. The broadcast of the London's attacks echoed for many days, with grief and the promise of retaliation attached, yet when a country in the Middle East is bombed, there is joy and great pleasure from Londoners who rejoice in awe of the destructive power of their weapons. Money is the only difference between detonating an explosive package in a crowded market or bus, and dropping one from an airplane. Both are terrorist acts. The same goes for a group of towel head Muzzies flying planes into buildings, Zionists murdering sailors on the USS Liberty and a gang of racist killers disembarking from the Santa Maria, the Nina, the Pinta, or the Mayflower.

Muslims are exploding toward total world conversion, Christians are gambling for the Apocalypse and a chance at the Rapture lottery. Both are locked into a deadly battle to win the ultimate prize: an imaginary ultra rich underage virgin.

CRAZY MUZZIES. The main reason Islam is expanding by leaps and bounds, while Christianity and Judaism are in recession, remains the same: Muslims will splatter themselves all over the place for Allah, while Jews will postpone any worship of G-d Yhwh at the sound of a penny and Catholics are too distraught ignoring and covering the sins of their priests. Other happy Christian sects are too busy collecting money. Muslims will actually stop their normal everyday lives, several times, get a piece of cardboard, face East (unless they ask me for directions), get down on both knees and bow many times to the air in front of them. In public, they will genuinely treat their fellow Muslims with respect, way more respect than can be found among members of other Christian cults. They will also kill their brothers who wander too far from the precepts of the Quran.

Now, that's a staunch believer!

Islam fooled even Muhammad Ali, the greatest, when he said that the cult abolished all divisive classes of distinction. Ali was already a world renown celebrity. Of course, Islam wouldn't prejudice against him. Since that fateful day, the champ was used to promote Islam. But anyone who visits Mecca can testify to not only the divisions but the racism pervasive in Islam. Did Ali ignore the fact that the Muslims practiced slave-raiding and slave-trading in Africa? To this day, in 2017, they have not stopped their human trafficking business.

LUNATIC PARTNERS. Islam is Judaism's concubine that rules the harem when Christianity is out shopping for Negroes to kill. The affair started in 550 AD when they united in the profitable business of slavery. When Christianity found out, she asked not for a divorce, but demanded a cut in the action.

Islam is a catch-the-runt net created by Europeans because they knew that a great many Negroes were stupid enough to get trapped in it. If they didn't believe that Moses led a gang of Red Sea pedestrians out of Egypt, if they couldn't stomach Jesus living with 12 men, then Islam came along with the promise of plentiful pussy in the afterlife, if they would only believe that Muhammad flew on a winged horse to heaven. Oh! and there is the small clause about killing infidels around the world. The same memo was forwarded by Judaism to Christianity.

BIG MO, LITTLE JOYSTICK. Polygamy and the carte blanche to chase after any woman they desired are quite possibly the main attractions to Islam for many Negroes. Allah approved not only of Muhammad's rape of a little girl, but also his sexual conquests: Sawda, Ramla, Hafsa, Zaynab bint Khuzayma, Hind, Juway, Safiyah, Maymunah, Mariyah, Mulayka, Fatima, Asma, Al-Jariya, Amra, Tukana, and any other victims or slaves from raids and war. Among Muhammad's other wives were the rich Hadrat Khadijah who hired 2 African tutors to educate the illiterate camel boy, Zaynab bint Jahsh who was the divorced wife of his own adopted son, Rayhana who was a Zionist widow he grabbed after killing her husband, and the most memorable Aisha bint Abi Bakr, a 6-year-old little girl, still playing with her dolls, who was sexually abused at 9-year-old by the carpet flying pedophile molester.

Like Zionists and Christians, people hooked on Islam have a serious virginal complex. They developed the cult to compensate for the size of their small appendage. They are afraid of a relationship with a real mature woman and hide behind the weak hope of making up for their shortcomings by selecting a virgin who will be "tighter" and less experienced. Virgins, specially little 6 years old kids, make them feel adequate. The solid proof is found when one understands why the towel heads killed any Negro who looked at the women in their harem. There are many Magnolia trees in Zanzibar.

PAUL OF TARSUS. When it comes to Christianity, one needs chest waders to navigate through the fecal cult. As written in my previous books, being a Christian only allows someone to do and say things that would put a normal person in a straight jacket. One simple question that usually stumps believers: How can you call yourself a Christian, when you don't have a clue about the contents of the only book that can tell you how to become one?

Another question to Christians is, if I lie to you every time we talk, would it get to a point, one day, when you would believe me? Read your bible, that's what your god has been doing to you, for 2000 years.

It takes a special breed of people to accept many life altering and influencing doctrines at face value. Without question. A Christian readily believes whatever a religious leader tells him and will even follow any given advice. Despite the fact that many church leaders are drug dealers who are advising people on ways to live a clean life, adulterers who are counseling married people, thieves who are giving financial advices to indebted people and deciding how much tax free money should be given to them. And Catholic priests who are in a class on their own.

It's extremely hard for anyone doted with common sense to gloss over religious absurdities like: Deuteronomy 28:57, Leviticus 26:29, 2 Kings 6:29, Hosea 13:16, Jeremiah 13:14, Psalm 137:9. But many either don't pay attention or are incapable of understanding their own vernacular language.

It's very hard for anyone doted with reason to forget inspiring religious statements like: "You are called by the Lord to be a success, to enjoy wealth, to enjoy health, and to enjoy a life of victory." It was addressed to people who don't have much and who are looking to a higher power for help. John Hagee said: "poverty is a curse". Paul Crouch, Kenneth Copeland and Creflo Dollar claimed to be gods, themselves. Suzanne Hartern Hinn, Benny's wife, told churchgoers: "if your engine is not revving up, you know what you need? A holy Ghost enema right up your rear end, because... God won't tolerate it". In 2008, Todd Bentley reported that God told him to kick a woman in the face to heal her. Kenneth Copeland declared: "I am a billionaire because it's the assignment that the Lord gave me." At a church service, Leroy Thompson screamed: "Money, come to me now." Mike Murdock was more to the point when he advised his followers to get rid of their debts by charging a $1000 donation to their credit cards. Pat Robertson told a husband to leave his wife who has Alzheimer's.

And who can forget the married, charismatic and flamboyant Jimmy Swaggart, preaching against adultery and promiscuity from the pulpit? Coming from the backwoods of Ferriday, Louisiana, uncle Jimmy flew in on the wings of Pentecostal Christianity, to become a successful businessman. Fired up like a July 4th barbecue grill, the Holy Spirit inspired pastor could rant incessantly, weep, thrust the bible high in the air, strut the stage this way and that way, whip followers into a devotional frenzy. With an income of 150 million dollars a year, 3 spacious homes, a personal jet, a luxurious retreat in California, Jimmy Swaggart didn't waste any time defending his God and faith when Jim Bakker, a rival from the PTL network, couldn't get a hard-on to sex up Jessica Hahn, his hot church secretary. A smiting Swaggart described Jim Bakker as a cancer on the body of Christ. Marvin Gorman was next on the to-do-list of Jimmy Swaggart's sinners who needed to be chastised and put out of the business of his Savior. He was a beacon of the faith when the Lord spoke to him and said: "Jimmy, my beloved son in whom I am well pleased, there are a few prostitutes who need to share in my mercy. Go help them." Caught the third time around with a prostitute, Jimmy Swaggart declared: "The Lord told me it's flat none of your business".

The tolerance of Christians is also legendary. Christianity may be the only religion, cult, sect, where one member can seal the hellish fate of another member just because of a difference of opinion, long before death or the Rapture. Any Christian will hand a one-way ticket to hell to another Christian who doesn't see things his or her way, despite the precept in Matthew 22:13- 14 and Luke 13:23-24. All biblical teachings find their importance in the individual Christian willingness to accept or ignore them. Every single Christian is a cafeteria believer who walks to the religious buffet table to pick and choose what s/he likes.

Take for example the practice of witchcraft which is forbidden by religious edict. Hundreds of thousands of innocent people were tortured, burnt alive, hanged and many lives were lost as a result of that edict, yet millions of believers, from all over the world, flock to stores in New Orleans, every year, to purchase hexes and good luck charms deemed to influence human affairs, in a supernatural way. Christians can also momentarily discard their religious belief to wear their lucky underwear before a ball game; the rabbit's foot is getting obsolete, but you can bet on a "God bless you" if you sneeze.

At your leisure, whenever you have some time to waste, please try to make some sense out of the following biblical verses: Ezekiel 23:20, Deuteronomy 21:18-21; 23:1; 25:11-12; 28:30-31, 35; Exodus 23:19; Ephesians 5:4; 6:5; Leviticus 9:10; 15:19-20; 20:15; 21:17-23; 25:44-46; Numbers 31:17-18; 2 Kings 2:23-25; Matthew 21:18-22; Luke 3:11. If you do, please drop me a line.

VBS IN SESSION. Despite the fact that Christians are always intolerant, most times they can be a joy to have around, because they can pull off many great comedy routines. Real fun is sipping a rum and coke while listening to a Christian explain the doctrine of the holy Trinity, the greatest religious mind-twister of all times. Christians who have tried, ended up more confused than before they started, and before long, the look on their faces will tell the entire exhausting drama.

You can quickly wipe the smile off a Christian's face by concluding that the "unity in the Trinity" also meant that Jesus sexed up his own mom when the Holy Spirit got some.

Another way to have fun with Christians, you can be the hero of the day, is to help them understand the precept of John 3:16

: "The biblical God sacrificed himself to himself, to appease himself so that mankind might be saved from his hate through his love."

Noah's flood is another good subject of conversation to have with Christians who will be more than happy to repeat the nonsense that their God made it rain for 40 days and 40 nights. After the regurgitation of the biblical absurdity, then the simplest questions will make them stutter. How could 22' of flood water cover Mount Everest which stands at 29,029'? How did Noah fit all those animals in such a small place? What effect did all that rain have on the polar ice caps?

NOAH. Speaking of the 595 years old man who built a boat in the middle of the desert after a voice in his head told him to do so. Here is the original biblical story of Noah that most followers don't even know about, because they were judged stupid and unable to understand it. It can be found in the old bible. "The entrance of Noah into the Ark took place on the day of the eve of the Sabbath (Friday), on the seventeenth day of the blessed month of Iyar (May). On the Friday, in the third hour of the morning, the beasts and the cattle went into the lowermost storey; and at midday all the feathered fowl and all the reptiles went into the middle storey; and at sunset Noah and his sons went into the Ark, on the east side of the third storey, and his wife and the wives of his sons went to the west side. And the body of Adam was deposited in the middle of the Ark, wherein also all the mysteries of the Church were deposited. Thus women in church shall be on the west side, and men on the east side, so that the men may not see the faces of the women, and the women may not see the faces of the men. Thus also was it in the Ark; the women were on the west side, and the men on the east side, and the body of our father Adam was placed between them like a raised stand or throne. And as quietness reigneth in the Church between men and women, so also peace reigned in the Ark between the wild beasts, and the feathered fowl, and the creeping things or reptiles. And as kings, and judges, and rich men, and poor men, and governors, and sick men, and beggars, live in concord, that is to say, in a general bond of peace, so also was it in the Ark. For lions, and panthers, and savage beasts of prey lived in peace and harmony with the cattle; and the beasts that were fierce and strong lived in peace with those that were timid and weak; and the lion with the ox, and the wolf with the lamb, and the lion's whelp with the calf, and the serpent with the dove, and the hawk with the sparrow."

And the baloney with the hogwash. Many lunatics, who have been deserted by common sense, are still trying to explain how all these animals could fit in the Ark, and how Noah could have taken care of them. There is no better way to spend a few hours than to listen to these religious experts. The comedy clubs don't come close to delivering this degree of laughter and delightful entertainment.

DELUSION. On the other side of the annoying spectrum, many wandering believers, peddling an "Awake" flyer, can look at anyone and vomit that the bible is the word of their god who wrote it himself with his own fingers on tablets of stone at the top of Mount Sinai; that Jesus is the human son of god and only the people who placed their faith in him will be saved and go to heaven. On the day of the rapture, Christians will flap their arms like buzzards, fly to meet Jesus in the air, on cloud nine, the one that feels like Charmin. No comedian ever thought of these jokes.

SOMETHING ABOUT MARY. Another great conversation to have with a believer is the case of the virgin. Jesus is not enough for Catholics, that's why they worship the virgin Mary, too hot for earth, too sexy for heaven. The house of Yahweh was a pretty quiet and restrained place, with God just wandering around looking for ways to multiply his screw-ups and kill little children. All that changed when Mary had a little lamb and his name was Jesus. Her earthly body was forced into heaven by the Munificentissimus

Deus, and she turned God into a peeping Tom. No one knows what happened to Joseph, one of Mary's many lovers. (More about Mary later.)

The two main obsessions of western organized religion are virgins and people flying into heaven with their material bodies. With the help of NASA or Google, there are apparently a few more celestial bodies who should be visible, yet no one can see them: Jesus, Mary, Enoch, Elijah, Hercules, Apollonius of Tyana, Yudhishthira, Sant Tukaram, Chaitanya Mahaprabhu, Swami Ramalinga, Mira Alfassa, Meera Bai, Serach, Eliezer, Hiram, Ebed-Melech, Jaabez, Bithiah, Peshotanu, Francis Bacon. No word if the last flyer had any egg with him.

My reaction is always the same, be nice and laugh at the jokers.

WWJD. What was Jesus doing? A Christian is free to practice his/her hallucination until it becomes harmful to others. My concern, once again, is not what a Christian believes in, more compelling to me is rather he is driving a car or influencing the next law of the land.

Suppose he is flying down the highway at a conservative 80mph, next to another car with a sane family and baby on board, and that lunatic believes that he hears the trumpets of the Rapture... then what? If he is in a voting booth and hears the Holy Spirit coaching him to vote for David Lane, Pat Robertson or any other holy screwball,... then what? Which situation is the greater danger to society?

PARENTAL GLITCH. Reality doesn't seem to be of any value for a Christian. Many believers sit quietly in a church, and listen intently to an orator's opinion that Jesus loves children; which sounds great in a speech and looks good on paper. But at this point, what is the reality for the kids? In 2000 years, Jesus hasn't got around to show much love for sick children; he failed them in the New Testament and is still failing them by the millions when they need him the most. And about his love for children, considering he lived with 12 men, is it the same love as his representatives in the Catholic priesthood who also live with men? They love children too, a lot.

Today's kids are being literally screwed on a daily basis, indoctrinated and brainwashed to follow thoughtlessly in their parents' muddy tracks, on the way to the religious land of fairies. "Telling children there is a pot of gold at the end of the rainbow is a parental privilege, packing their lunch to take them on a trip to retrieve that gold is where the insanity begins." (My journey into reality)

If prayers worked, I would be on my knees, hands clasped, eyes closed, begging the Christian god to come get the good tolerant and perfect specimens he "left behind", until the fairy obliges.

Jesus needs to step up to the plate, keep his word and rapture his followers. So what, if they crucify him again, it will only be a few hours before he is back in heaven again, unemployed and collecting dust. And Jesus wasn't that great of an item anyway, otherwise the father would have used him to correct Adam and Eve's little snack problem. Why didn't the biblical God used Jesus instead of the flood or the arson in Sodom and Gomorrah? If the biblical Christian god is real, truly just and fair, all his followers will be flushed down the heavenly toilet at their death.

CATHOLIC BREAK. 'Twas the day before Easter Sunday and all through the church, creatures were stirring, specially the altar boys with their backs to a wall, trying to keep the temptation away from the priests. The inner sanctum was decorated with gold, white lilies filled the ornate vases, the altar was spotless, the ironed vestments were laid in immaculate order, and Father Murphy was in the confessional booth, doing his best to process the sinners and scrub away their sins.

At about 10am, the eggs he consumed earlier in the morning, came down the pike and he needed to use the bathroom. Since all the other priests were busy in this very lucrative season, he called out to deacon Joseph who happened to be walking by: "Joe, I need to go relieve myself, can you take over the confessional booth?" "But father Murphy, replied deacon Joseph, I am not a priest, and I don't know a thing about this side of confession." "It's easy, just listen to the sins, and pick a penance from the posted list. That's it! There is nobody else but you, I have to go, or I am gonna soil myself" said father Murphy, before he briskly walked in the direction of the toilets.

Deacon Joseph begrudgingly sat in the center of the booth, and a man was already waiting on the right side. "Father, forgive me for I have sinned, said the man. I stole money from my wife." Joseph looked at the list and found the penance for stealing money from the wife. In a toned down commiserating voice, deacon Joe said: "My son, you will do 4 Hail Mary and you are forgiven."

The next sinner, on the left side, couldn't wait for his absolution and, as soon as Joe leaned forward, mumbled "Father, forgive me for I have sinned. I killed my neighbor's cat yesterday." Joseph looked at the list again and found the penance for killing a neighbor's cat: "You will do 6 Our father and 7 Hail Mary, then you will be forgiven. Go and sin no more." He smiled and thought that Father Murphy was right, this confessional gig is a piece of cake.

Minutes later, a beautiful, sexy, gorgeous woman with big boobs entered the right side of the confessional booth. Joe became immediately entranced by her beautiful bedroom eyes, the moist pouty lips and thought how lucky he was to be so close to, he guessed, a 38-24-36 goddess. She slowly parted the slit of her red mini-dress to free her long toned legs, gently kneeled down, took a short resigned breath and said in a sultry voice: "Father, forgive me for I have sinned"... She hesitated for a few guilty seconds, and finally decided to let go of her transgression, "I had anal sex last night." Deacon Joseph blushed, gulped down the extra saliva in his mouth, licked his lips to retrieve the seeping drool and finally got a firm hold of himself. He consulted the list,... lo and behold, there was no penance for anal sex. He must have overlooked in all this excitement, so he peeled his eyes off the beautiful vision waiting for salvation, and slowly scanned the list again,... to no avail. The dreamy nymph gave him a sensually seductive-looking glance, then bowed her head as she waited for a penance... With a sense of urgency, Joe peered through the opening of the curtains to see if father Murphy was on his way back. No such luck. The priest was probably still yelling the name of his savior and cursing, as he excommunicated the digested eggs from his bowels.

There was no other priest around to be seen... Deacon Joseph was stuck... The nubile maiden was waiting for a penance...

The baffled deacon finally noticed little Johnny, the altar boy. He called out to him and asked "Johnny, have you seen father Murphy or any other priest?" "Well, about 10 minutes ago, I saw father Murphy running like a bat out of hell, and the other priests are busy with confession" answered Johnny. Joseph was still stuck... and the woman was still waiting for a penance...

Thinking it was worth the gamble, deacon Joseph risked it all: "Johnny, do you know what father Murphy gives for anal sex?"

The large grin on the boy's face signaled to deacon Joe that he had hit pay dirt. "Sure, replied an excited little Johnny, 2 candy bars and a soda."

JESUS' TWIN. There is a You tube video of Christian poster boy Jimmy Carter, bragging that the US wasn't involved in a war under his administration. But the old toothy president failed to utter one word, or brag about his support of NSSM 200 and NSSM 201, parts of a global population control agenda hatched by Henry Kissinger thru food genocide, on April 24th, 1974. It also included securing control over mineral and fuel resources in Africa, maintaining political destabilization in poor black countries for continued exploitation. The high point of this white supremacist policy was that a black woman having a baby anywhere in Africa became a threat to the national security of the US. Even Sharia law is not that extreme. This was and still is basically a Jesus approved, new and improved systematic agenda of continued assisted genocide for Negroes. With a program like this, who needs a war?

When a war was desired, Britain used Germany's legal and natural right to fight off Poland's aggression, as an excuse to start World War II and reach the primary intended goal of eliminating Germany's economic superiority. Still, many will continue to blame everything on Hitler's hatred of the Zionists, just as many will still cling to the Nazi holocaust hoax to avoid talking about the MAAFA, which remains the only real and true holocaust.

JEHOVAH WITNESSES. While visiting my grandson, son and his wife, I answered a knock on the door, on 05-26-2017, to find 2 religious manure peddling women, one black and one Caucasian. Here they were, two lost "sheep" at my door, looking for a ram to add to the herd. They politely inquired if I had any time to talk and were distributing several booklets titled "Awake". They identified themselves as Christians, my favorite people in the whole world to talk to. Well, let me put it this way, I always make time to talk to Christians. As a matter of fact, I would reschedule any urgent lifesaving operation just to talk to self-proclaimed Christians.

The fun started early enough because they didn't have a clue, of course, like most Christians, about what is in the bible. When the conversation was gently guided toward Exodus, they took the bait. They looked at each other when I asked: which exodus? They didn't know there were 2. Then, their free fall continued.

The game was on, when the entry of the "Israelites" into Egypt came to the forefront. Anyone with a pulse knows that there were no Jew, no Israelite and no Hebrew in Egypt during the time of the biblical Joseph; anyone with a heartbeat also knows that the starving West Asians who entered Egypt were never enslaved by the Egyptians. These Jehovah's witnesses didn't know. They were dumbfounded by the information they received, yet, were not beyond protesting my statement that their bible was wrong as demonstrated with my dated facts and empirical evidence. They couldn't counter my true historical facts, yet, wouldn't admit that their biblical god, if he existed, was an almighty idiot. They mildly objected to their sect being described as a plantation where fools are enslaved to raise money for mansion dwelling masters.

There were many good-natured moments in a game where they thought they could outsmart me. For example, they asked me with a smile to disprove the existence of their God. I responded with a cute grin that I would not able, either, to disprove the existence of Santa, the Tooth Fairy, the Easter Bunny, Elmer Fudd, leprechauns or the pot of gold at the end of the rainbow. They continued that billions of people believe in Jesus and the bible. I glossed over the obvious: billions also believe in Santa, the Tooth Fairy, the Easter Bunny, Elmer Fudd, leprechauns or the pot of gold at the end of the rainbow. I replied: "If billions of people believe in a foolish thing, it is still a foolish thing. Just because you think a voice in your head exists doesn't make it so."

In kind, I asked them to provide specific dates for the biblical (historical is the word they used) events they were talking about. They couldn't. Their God would have to take a back seat to true historical facts, because he failed to even use common sense in his biblical confession. Like I said before, History is more powerful than the Christian God.

I explained to them, in very simple terms, that because they could see many things didn't equate to a God creating them. A blue sky, beautiful trees, animals running around, humans pretending to know everything, were just that, a blue sky, beautiful trees, animals running around, humans pretending to know everything, not some brilliant proofs or evidence that a fairy made anything. And the bible is proof of nothing, absolute nothing, just like another book is not proof that three little pigs built houses of straw, sticks and bricks.

Defending their Jehovah, they were as impenetrable as rocks. My words spoke to them, they accepted my information bit by bit, sentence by sentence, fact by fact, they knew I was right.

They acquiesced, but in the depths of their eyes, I knew they would refuse to believe in the end and did not possess the slightest hint of common sense necessary to understand and accept any reasonable fact or argument. Their ears, and eyes, and minds were shut closed.

How may I advance such nicety? The eyes are the windows of the soul, and I could tell by the darkness that someone forgot to pay the electric bill. During our conversation, both women were furiously busy with their tablets, trying to keep up with the biblical verses I was unloading on them from memory. Not one was really listening to what I was saying. I could see their wheel turning, but I knew the hamster was long dead. Every statement I made to them was backed up by empirical evidences from history and compared against a specific biblical passage or precept, even most of my personal arguments and opinions came with biblical verses to illustrate how stupid organized religion was. They were bogged down in time by a book they inherited from a gang of goat herders from 2000 years ago. They were trapped like fishes by the receding low tide. Hope was the next house they visit, maybe they will be lucky enough to find an easy Christian there. They will never have a chance to read "the 3 little pigs", and that is a shameful literary sin.

When one of them touted the virtues and way of life of Hinduism, my immediate question to her was "if you know that Hinduism is better, why do you continue in the cult you are in?" I also had to correct her wrong information that Hinduism was the world's oldest religion; because African spirituality is the only true first religion.

After many attempts at sharing a bit of reason with them, I came to the sad conclusion that no one can fix stupid. They had no fact, no empirical evidence, brought nothing to the table, yet the conversation became an argument they had to win at all costs.

They were more interested in defending their cult than finding the truth. As they departed, overloaded with new information that, if used properly, could help them reach sanity, rather than pointing out any factual or logical error from my statements, one of them resorted to the old Christian cop-out. I could hear her mumble something to the effect that I used to be a Catholic. What a comeback! The last act of a desperate and foolish woman, in denial, who would not accept common sense if it was gifted to her.

That is one telltale sign of the flawed indoctrination of her cult. She was indoctrinated, brainwashed, radicalized, fighting her own mind, her own reality, her own reason, her own sanity, her own common sense to validate and defend what some wolf in sheep clothing had told her. One would think that the leaders of the cult would genuinely want to educate their "flock", have good associates capable of peddling their biblical manure. Apparently, they will opt to dumb down any temp worker or volunteer who can afford to waste a day. God dammit!

A CLOWN NAMED CHARLIE. The Jehovah's witness cult belief is based on the biblical teachings of former Presbyterian, turned Congregational church member, turned Second Adventist Charles Taze Russell who decided that Jesus was elected to run heaven after his triumphant earthly return in 1874, while Satan and the demons were cast back on earth in 1914. Previously, in 1879, the Watchtower was first published after Charles began to doubt not only the religious creeds and doctrines he believed to be harmful errors, but also God and the bible itself.

That, of course, was seen as heresy even by the rest of the lunatic farm. We all remember that heresy led many innocent people to a fiery death at the stakes, as many were barbecued for their denial of imposed religious dogma.

Prior to 1931, between 1917 and 1928, the name of this cult and their doctrines changed many times. Jehovah's Witnesses were also known as Millennial Dawn, Bible student movement, People's Pulpit Association, the Brooklyn Tabernacle, and the International Bible Students Association. A big departure from other sects is that the book of Revelation seems to be the main focus of the cult, while the bible itself is off limits to the followers who are not allowed to read it, have private or personal biblical thoughts. In 1936, the cult rejected the idea that Jesus died on the cross.

Charles Taze Russell believed the Great Pyramids of Giza were built by the Hebrews and not the Egyptians, between 2580 and 2560 BCE, in the 4th Dynasty (we will give him that 33 to 111 years discrepancy). There is a slight inconvenient problem with his belief: there were no Jew, no Israelite and no Hebrew before 1280 BCE when the traitors were expelled from Egypt by king Tutmosis I, in the second exodus. The first exodus, which is wrongly described as the famous waltz through the Red Sea, happened in 1450 BCE, under the Egyptian king Seti.

Charles Taze Russell died in 1916 and was buried in a

pyramid shaped tomb. So, in the end, he sought refuge in African spirituality.

It is not strange that when the grim reaper tapped them on the shoulder, these so called religious leaders always abandoned their belief. Chased by a mob, Joseph Smith, of Moron faith, I mean Mormon, was shot while trying to escape from a second- floor window. In the end, the Mormon founder and theocratic king yelled out a few Masonic SOS words to express his distress.

THE BLOOD OF JESUS. When it comes to the fairy in charge of the salvation of their souls, Christians fully support the New Testament and the worship of Jesus, but don't seem to be too fond anymore of the previous messed up God of the Old Testament. From his biblical confession, the antiquated vinegarish fairy Christian God defined himself as a cunning, thieving, unremorseful criminal bully, with a temper always flaring like a pack of hemorrhoids, a bad attitude toward babies, children, women, men and trees, who smites the weak and runs from the strong. That became too much even for his followers, as a gentler god would be like using honey to catch more flies. Along came a new savior to replace the retiring old fart. This passing of the torch has been a religious tradition since Osiris and later, when Zeus passed the torch on Mount Olympus.

Unlike his old father who spends all his money, and keeps begging for more, Jesus saves. But with a new savior comes a new rule, a new covenant: now, a soul can only be saved by the blood of Jesus, meaning that every one who came to this planet, or elsewhere, before the death of Jesus, is SOL. Without his blood, no one, not even his father, can get into heaven. Jesus has the only key and he is not sharing unless someone bathes in his blood or drinks it.

God the father is fast becoming a mirage, along with his cousin Satan. These two buddies must be somewhere, banging their heads on a celestial wall, crying, wondering when everything started to go so wrong for them.

ISLAND BLOOD. In the Caribbean, the Catholic priests knew that many people were up to no good when they visited the church; they were not true believers and suckers. There was a long period of time, when the faithful customers, after taking part in the Sacrament of Communion, were required to show their empty mouths to the officiating priests. The reason was that many followers were taking the wafers home and stabbing them with knives to see if they could draw the blood of Jesus,... to use in Vaudou ceremonies. The priests kept threatening the flock and repeating the warning that anyone who did so would go straight to hell.

HELL YES. Judging by their past and current lies, Catholics have the wrong idea of hell. At the Catholic Seminary where I spent many years, there was a joke that the priests tried in vain to quell with sticks and rulers.

So it goes that a priest died and was sent to hell. Satan welcomed and led him to his office, to process his registration. As they walked past a vast amphitheater with dancing poles adorning many bars full of joyful patrons, the priest confessed: "Hey, I heard it's infernal in here, weeping and gnashing of teeth, torment, people suffering the worst abominations, souls burning on brimstone and hot coals in a lake of fire, and..." The devil interrupted him and said: "Look around you, do you see anyone suffering? Everywhere, you will see there are only smiling people enjoying themselves. This was another lie of your church to control you." The priest smiled as the horned one continued: "Do you like to smoke weed?" The priest, shocked at the simplicity of the question, answered "as a matter of fact, I have enjoyed a few puffs after mass with the nuns". "Great, said the hoofed one, you are gonna love Mondays. We get the best ganja, and we smoke until our lungs explode". The priest flinched. The devil reassured him: "But you should not worry, because you are already dead". The priest relaxed as they continued to walk toward the rectory. The devil winked at a Southern Baptist resident and asked the priest: "Do you like to drink?" Sheepishly, the priest admitted to his weakness. "Great, said the pointy tailed one, you are gonna love Wednesdays. We get the best booze, and we drink until our livers raise the white flag. But you should not worry, because you are already dead". The smoking fairy used his pitchfork to open the door to his office as he asked the priest: "Do you like women?" The priest blushed and looked around one more time, because he hasn't seen too many women since he entered the kingdom of Sheol. By now, Satan was reading the record of his life, and, with a devilish smile, informed him: "Well, you are not gonna like Sundays anymore."

IOTA AND TITTLE. Every so often, changes are made to the biblical texts to conform to copyright laws, despite the internal godly warning to avoid changing one iota, jot or tittle. It is deemed necessary to render several questionable passages even more confusing, while the 7427 outlandish absurdities and contradictions are allowed to remain in the greatest story ever sold. One of my contentions is, after so many revisions and re- versions, does anyone still know the absolute true and real content of the bible?

So many passages have been removed from the original version that not many people know about the sexually charged drama that played among the members of the first family? So, to contribute somewhat to the salvation of a believer, as my good deed for the month, here it is from the original bible:

STORY OF THE FIRST FAMILY. So Adam and Eve went down from that holy mountain of Eden to the slopes which were below it, and there Adam knew Eve his wife, thirty years after they went expelled from the garden of Eden. And Eve conceived and brought forth Cain and Lebhudha (Luluwa), his twin sister, with him; and Eve conceived again and she brought forth Habhil (Abel) and Kelimath (Aklia), his twin sister, with him. And when the children grew up, Adam said unto Eve, "Let Cain take to wife Kelimath, who was brought forth with Abel, and let Abel take to wife Lebhudha, who was brought forth with Cain." And Cain said unto Eve his mother, "I will take to wife my twin sister Lebhudha, and let Abel take to wife his twin sister Kelimath"; now Lebhudha was beautiful. When Adam heard these words, which were exceedingly displeasing unto him, he said, "It will be a transgression of the commandment for thee to take to wife thy sister, who was born with thee. Nevertheless, take ye to yourselves fruits of trees, and the young of sheep, and get ye up to the top of this holy mountain. Then go ye into the Cave of Treasures, and offer ye up your offerings, and make your prayers, and then ye shall consort with your wives." And it came to pass that when Adam, the first priest, and Cain and Abel, his sons, were going up to the top of the mountain, Satan entered into Cain and persuaded him to kill Abel, his brother, because of Lebhudha; and because his offering was rejected and was not accepted before God, whilst the offering of Abel was accepted. Cain's jealousy of his brother Abel was increased. And when they came down to the plain, Cain rose up against his brother Abel, and he killed him with a blow from a stone of flint. Then straightway Cain received the doom of death, instead of curses, and he became a fugitive and a wanderer all the days of his life. And God drove him forth into exile in a certain part of the forest of Nodh, and Cain took to wife his twin sister and made the place of his abode there.

Now let's analyze the events presented here. Adam and Eve* waited 30 years and 5 1/2 hours to have sex? No wonder they heard a talking snake. Adam's reasoning "It will be a transgression of the commandment for thee to take to wife thy sister, who was born with thee" is flawed: Aklia was also Cain's sister, but Adam was on the first power trip and wanted Cain to marry her instead of his twin Luluwa who was black. Why would Cain have to settle for an obviously uglier woman when the bible said that Luluwa was better looking than Eve? Then Cain killing Abel over such a minor detail is the worst reaction to a parental decision in the history of the world. This is the kind of tale that can be expected from Yiddiots with half a hat on their head; the African sun fried most of their brains.

(Note*: Want to know a lot more about the first couple, plese read "The lost books of the Tasty Griot" @Amazon.com/books)

ADAM AND EVE TIMELINE. This is the religious beginning of human life, according to the bible.

- Born in the evening of the 6th day of biblical creation.

- Kicked out of the garden of Eden, evicted, 5 1/2 hours after they were invented (born).

- First meal eaten at 83 days after creation.

- First day at work, 84 days after expulsion from the biblical garden of Eden.

- First sexual encounter at 30 years and 5 1/2 hours after their biblical creation.

- First wrestling fight between Cain at fifteen and half years old against his brother Abel at twelve and half years old.

- First murder: Cain at seventeen and half years old defeated Abel at fifteen and half years old (1 year discrepancy.)

This timeline has been removed from the popular bible, and everyone can see why. If a serious and intelligent editor took a correcting pen to the bible, it would not be long before it became the shortest book in the world. Something that would be amazingly beneficial to the world, because this new bible would only have the covers and no page within.

# THEISM

All organized religions are about control and thrive on the lack of education of their followers. Millions gather to prove that misery loves company. Atheists are the ones with the droopy faces on the sidelines, too serious to laugh at the religious jokers. We all know that Christians don't play with a full deck! Christians are the ones holding no card at all, screaming BINGO at the religious poker table. Atheists can't take or appreciate a good joke.

Who is to say that believers are not playing a joke on everybody? Who is to say they really and truly believe in their cloud dwelling fairy? Who can be sure that Christians truly believe in a God riding the waves of nothingness before the biblical creation? Who is to say Christians truly believe that Satan can possess a person for the sole purpose of using him/her as an interpreter, a human megaphone to convey his messages? How can a sermon be credible when the orator doesn't have a clue what he is talking about? For all we know, Christians may go to church to socialize because they are lonely, don't have many friends or hobbies. Maybe Christians have too much time on their hands and don't need to spend anymore family time. Or it could be because they don't want to spend a Sunday, bored to death, listening to their family members.

Remember your uncle Joe, who would not just shut the heck up? Church may be the perfect place for an informal catwalk to show off their good "Sunday" clothes. Or, Christians may be in transition, a group of mild-mannered sadomasochists who like when someone puts them down as sinners and promises the devil will spank them in hell. They may give their last dollar to the presiding crook because they expect to, and have a firm belief they will win the lottery on their way home. Maybe the thief keeps the donation as a user fee for his building. There are a lot of valid reasons no one can really know for sure if Christians are really that stupid.

ATHEISM. Looking at the origin of the word, we find that "Atheism" came from the Greek A (Ana)= without and Theos= god. The word Theos eventually gave way to "belief in a god or gods" which later translated into cult, sect or religion. Somehow, theology (Theos-logos) became the study of religion instead of gods. Augustine redefined Theo-logia of Hippo as reasoning or discussion concerning a deity.

COMMON SENSE. For a group of people claiming to be without a deity, it is remarkably odd and somewhat laughable that atheists devote so much of their time and have so much reasoning, so many discussions about deities. There are a few complaints made, that the word atheism is ill chosen to describe them... It is not. Merriam-Webster defines religion as a cause, principle or system of beliefs held to with ardor and faith. We describe faith as a firm belief in something for which there is no proof; something that is believed, especially with strong conviction. These definitions clearly identify atheism as a religion.

I know and expect some wise guy to raise his hand and advance: "it's like calling bald a hair color, or abstinence a sex position". Yeah! For somebody who doesn't know what bald is or a sex position. Duh!

Today's atheism is a cult with many facets; it encompasses 1) secularism which is the belief in separation of church and state and that all beliefs are equal, 2) agnosticism which is the belief that it's impossible to know if there is a god, 3) humanism which is the idea that human reason drives us, not higher powers, and 4) atheism itself which is the belief that maybe there is no god.

Atheism is the new toy, the new game for children who never grew up. A new version of "I know you are, but what am I?" Christians talk to their imaginary friend, while atheists lament they don't have an imaginary friend to talk to. Atheists seem almost jealous that Christians have an imaginary friend they can talk to at all hours of the day or night. All that is required is a donation and a mute, invisible God will lend an ear to whatever problem the Christian person is experiencing. As stated before, religion provides instant perceived gratification and will spit out an answer faster than Porky Pig can say "that's all folks."

With all the requests believers make of him, God has become an insomniac whom they can talk to. He is a good listener who never talks back and cannot be blamed for not doing something because he is always half asleep. And God doesn't get a break. Imagine people were praying during the "3 days" when Jesus was relaxing in the tomb. When he rose from the dead, the angels handed him the prayer transcripts right before he sleepwalked out of the tomb.

Atheists are the fools locked outside of churches to protect the fools inside. Both sides are alike a group of thieves who stole a car, and not one of them knows how to drive.

THE HITCH. The greatest loudmouth to champion Atheism was the late Christopher Hitchens. Many loved the Hitch, he was a man of principles, opinionated but fair, he knew what to say and in what manner. He never, ever, uttered a bad word to denigrate blacks or Africa. He kept racism out of his lectures. Hitch was the worst nightmare of a religious idiot; he didn't take shit from any of them and he didn't give a shit, because he wasn't in the shit business. He gave religion back the hell it created and, along the way, almost got mother Teresa pregnant. He is solely responsible for the newly found public interest in atheism. He was very entertaining and is missed.

After Hitchens' death, Atheism seemed to have changed into a mild rejection of Catholic doctrines and dogmas, with a limited amount of cautious and polite condemnation of Islam. Right now, the most vocal and omnipresent Atheists are Kenyan born British Richard Dawkins, Californian Sam Harris, vlogger AronRa (aka L. Aron Nelson), and internet personality Matt Dillahunty.

SAME HYPOCRISY. Atheism perceives Islam as a violent cult (which it is), and it should also Christianity which uses the western militaries to bomb the same Muslims. Many Atheist lectures portray Islam in all its murderous deeds, yet classify Christianity only as a mere delusion, without mentioning the ongoing crimes. Atheists will say nothing concrete about the inherent deadly propensity of Christianity to butcher unbelievers, or simply non-members of their cults, the same as done by Islam. One of the recurring condemnations of Islam rests in the 109 verses of the Quran ordering the death of infidels; Christianity has the same order to kill people who don't worship the Christian God. Anyone found working on the Sabbath and even an old man gathering sticks on a Saturday. It is hypocritical to slam Islam and not Christianity when both cults are doing the same thing.

Meanwhile, Atheism says little about Judaism because discretion, reservation, caution, prudence are recommended to "avoid a rush to judgment." We know atheists for an almost reverence of Judaism which may fly under their critical radar, most of the times. While past murderous Islamic sponsored acts in London and Paris warrant non-stop reviews, debates, coverage and condemnation in the western news, not one word will be heard about Judaism's influence in Israel dropping 100 tons of white phosphorus bombs on the Palestinian children getting out of school in downtown Gaza. No Atheist remembers the bombing of the Mubaret Phillistine care home for Orphans and Handicapped in Beit Lahiya district, in 2014, and the murder of Suha and Ola Wishah, two physically disabled women. No Atheist remembers the Gaza massacre, Operation Cast Lead, from December 27th, 2008 to January 18th, 2009, with 1417 Palestinians murdered, 5303 wounded and 50800 displaced. Atheists can find no fault with

Zionism. Even if they did, the label of anti-Semitism would have been used to summarily dismiss the factual accounts or force them to retract any criticism of the butchers of the West Bank.

Past, present and future barbaric acts perpetrated by Muslims are the main course in most atheist lectures, while they used a load of quotes from biblical absurdities to foolishly mask the many past, present and possible future murders perpetrated by Christians. People consider it a virtue for Zionism to handle past, present, and future slaughters with silence. The hypocrisy becomes even more explicit when the Zionist past is relegated to perpetual darkness, perpetual blackout, perpetual lies.

It's worth mentioning again: Records kept by the Germans prove they exterminated between 1.5 and 2 million Soviets and Russians, some of Jewish persuasion. The victims, according to one survivor of four different concentration camps, were of some thirty nationalities. So why is it just a Jewish fiesta?

No one seems to remember the Bolshevik Jews murdered 66 million humans in Russia, and butchered another 10 millions in Holodomor. 80 million Blacks were butchered in the Congo by King Leopold II of Belgium. And Hitler is the bad guy? If you want to see a true holocaust victim, look at any black man, woman or child, because the MAAFA, the black holocaust, wasn't made in Hollywood.

Above and beyond the daily slaughter of Palestinians, there are many things that can and should be mentioned when atheists lecture about the causes of pain and suffering in the world, alongside the Muslim and Christian criminal records. Things like Lusitania to bring the US into the war; Kristallnacht; Bromberg massacre; the King David massacre of July 22nd, 1946; Operation Susannah/ Lavon Affair in 1954; JFK assassination on November 22nd, 1963 and RFK in June 1968; USS Liberty on June 6th, 1967; Black September 5th, 1972; Entebbe; 1982 Abu Nidal; Pan Am flight

73; Beirut Marine barracks October 23rd, 1983; Achille Lauro 1985; English policewoman shot in 1984; Alia airliner 1985; Lockerbie December 1988; AMIA 1992; Luxor Egypt 1992; Khobar Towers 1986; Karin-A 2000; two airports attacks in 1985; LaBelle disco 1986; OKC Murrah building 1993; TWA flight 840; World Trade Center 1993; Port Arthur massacre 1996; Birmingham 1998; Egyptair 990 (MSR990); USS Cole; September 11th, 2001 (the most brazen of all Israeli attacks); flight 587 2001; Bali bombing; Kenya missile strike 2002; Madrid train 2002; Manila 2003; CIA bomb in Gaza 2003; Mossad bombing of 2 airliners over Russia 2004; countless assassinations of diplomats and scientists around the world; etc... One may wonder why atheists have such a hard time finding a cause for human pain and suffering from the Zionist files.

Another atheist fault rests in the undercurrent of bias in detailing their view. For example, all acts of "terrorism" are assigned to Islam, because many atheists are in denial and refuse to understand that dropping white phosphorus bombs on school children, or butchering a wedding party with a drone strike are also terrorist acts.

FINK BAR CONFESSION. Who can forget or ignore: "If we get caught they will just replace us with persons of the same cloth. So it does not matter what you do, America is a golden calf and we will suck it dry, chop it up, and sell it off piece by piece until there is nothing left but the world's biggest welfare state that we will create and control. Why? Because it is the will of God and America is big enough to take the hit so we can do it again and again and again. This is what we do to countries that we hate. We destroy them very slowly and make them suffer for refusing to be our slaves." (The Fink's bar diatribe of 1990 from Benzion Mileikowski, the butcher of the West Bank, aka Benjamin Netanyahu.)

One can never be too careful, because the Polish devil Mileikowski still owns the flaming sword. Maybe Atheists are afraid to anger the chosen people of the sky fairy Yahweh who flooded the earth, rained fire on infants and babies in their cribs in Sodom and Gomorrah, slaughtered millions of children on an almost daily basis in the Old Testament and stole land that didn't belong to them. Palestine is just the continuation of that "promise" from their British god to keep getting free land, where they can eat their manna. But first, they must smite the rightful owners, like they did in the Americas and Africa. Atheism has failed frequently to declare that Judaism, Christianity and Islam are three terrorist organizations, three dangerous and deadly cults. In its primary mission, atheism has failed the world.

MAN UP. There is more to fighting religion than standing in fuzzy pink bunny slippers, sipping tea; there is more to fighting religion than being nice to people who worship murderers, genocidal creeps and maniacs. Atheism has failed the world for not coming out more forcefully and defending the children of future generations from the immediate harm of all western religions. If more whites than negroes were being butchered, atheism would have taken a better, quicker, stronger stand against western religions. But like any other western institution, atheism will sacrifice a few of their own, as long as, in the end, they can waste millions more negroes.

SAME OLD REALITY. Atheism is seen as an opponent of established organized western religions, when it is really an extension of, an addition to them. Atheism is the new, improved and adapted other side of the religious coin. They work in concert for the greater good of white supremacy, by bashing black nations and people. It's a tango, a bump and grind, no, a dance macabre where atheists limit themselves to refuting any mostly Catholic nonsense, despite the believers' modus operandi to stick to their idiocy. Once in a while, Islam cuts in to enjoy the smoky atmosphere and partner in the bloodbath.

Richard Dawkins and Sam Harris are partying like it's 1776. Imagine that: Britain and its American military extension are at the forefront of atheism. Is it a way to get ahead of the curve and assure control over the ever-growing number of people who are escaping the religious corrals? When the world is finally purged of Islam, Judaism and Christianity, atheism will no longer stand; it will fall on its face, because they have removed its crutches at the same time.

For now, atheism is a financial farm under construction. Atheist sites are now begging for donations to fund their cause, just the same as other churches and religions. Will they also apply for a 501 (c) (3) and receive a tax-exempt status? It's nothing more than another desperate move to control the uneducated masses, by corralling as many idiots as possible in front of the pseudo-spiritual slaughterhouse. Atheism is the new holding pen for people who escaped the lameness and stupidity of other religions. There, like in the religious cults, the new adepts will be "baptized" by chosen leaders, holding them upside down until the cash falls out of their pockets.

The new coming out of the closet atheism is only a move to join the religious club as the new member of the fraternity. The divergences are only smokescreens. No one really knows what atheists want. In so far, they complain (b*tch is a better word) about the ignorant Christian beliefs in genocidal fairies and hallucinations they inherited from a gang of goat herders from 2000 years ago; yet, like a dog chasing its own tail, they promote the right of the same screwballs to believe in what they want.

Asinus asinum fricat.

MORE TRUTHS. In my book Papa time (Amazon.com/books), I described how western religions were created to control the masses, especially the ones with dark skin, thru ignorant ramblings and threats. Atheism is to Christianity,

Islam and Zionism what the new Testament is to the Old Testament. A lousy sequel. It is the same pile of manure, and atheism is just the newest angle to look at the cesspool. That's why they sound like people who constantly shout into the wind how they would spend the lottery jackpot to end human suffering, but never bothered to buy a ticket. None of them can find a reality kiosk.

The world doesn't need another "elitist club" to know how to dismiss the Torah, the Quran or the over 7427 idiocies of the bible; what the world needs is a serious organization to put an immediate end to human genocides, fight and keep the religious idiots from taking over the world governments. It is frightening to imagine these new evangelical Abraham armed with nuclear weapons and the rest of the world looking more and more like Isaac.

RED FLAGS. To spread a message of supposed reason, atheism employs carefully selected speeches, with craftily selected words, to project an image where the UK and US are described as the best that humanity has to offer, the supreme Aryan inspired model for earth and the rest of the universe, while Africa is riddled with AIDS and every other imaginable diseases. They used a very similar approach to establish slavery and organized religion. The onslaught on Arius is still ongoing.

They portray Africa as hell on earth, while the UK seems like a perfect garden of Eden for Atheists, with snakes like Leon Brittan, Cyril Smith and Jimmy Sevile, a truly heavenly paradise where 261 high profile British people shared the forgivable and benign sin which came in the form of 113,000 cases of child abuses in public institutions, just in the year 2014. Children of all faiths could not find a better place to be, between 1997 and 2013, than the wonderful Northern English city of Rotherham.

A few atheists relish a revolting, disgusting and offensive

sense of pleasure in attempting to screw or denigrate black countries when choosing examples to back or illustrate their assertions. Scientists, like Atheist pope Clinton Richard Dawkins, should know the source of most diseases affecting Africa, yet never confessed to the truth. These Atheist brain farts provided another proof, the evidence that, like religion, atheism is confined between the geopolitical borders of the orator's respective country and that makes it a lot like an extension of the religious agenda. Hopefully, atheism will not become the new tool for the continued destruction of Africa.

SAM HARRIS, In "Letter to a Christian Nation", the author had much fun reciprocating the "love" he received from his many Christian readers. However, the author deliberately muddled the tone of the book to give a free pass to his beloved Zionism. The opening salvo was about the hateful communication received from Christians as a backlash to his previous book "The end of faith". Setting Muslims aside for a moment, he singled out the Christian perpetrators in a divide-and-conquer strategy, as he wrote that such hatred drew considerable support from the bible. Maybe the hatred of Palestinians, by his people, drew considerable support from the Mikra.

In a subsequent paragraph, Mr. Harris exposed his obsession with the biblical virgin birth while he ignored the obvious. Come on, Sam! You have the original bible, you should know that the virgin Mary was nothing but a whore. Get over the virginity fixation, there is something about Mary more fun to explore; something that Christians would love to hide if they ever thought of it. "If Jesus was one with the father since before the beginning of time, is one with his father now and will always be one with his father for eternity, then Jesus was with his daddy when he nailed the virgin Mary. In other words, Jesus sexed up his own mom in order to be born. The encounter described in Matthew 1:18-25* and also Luke 2:1-20**, not only illustrates a lusty sexual orgy between the father, son, holy spirit and Mary, but, since the "virgin" was married to Joseph at the time, she committed an adulterous act" (Incestuous Savior @ Amazon. com/books). A bastard savior, born of incest and adultery, elevated to the status of a god is way more fun than if a 14-year-old whore was a virgin. Baby Aishah Bint Abi Bakr was a 6-year-old virgin and few people are that baffled by or fixated on her virginity.

(*Matthew 1:18 Now the birth of Jesus Christ was on this wise: When as his mother Mary was espoused to Joseph, before they came together, she was found with child of the Holy Ghost. 19 Then Joseph her husband, being a just man, and not willing to make her a public example, was minded to put her away privily. 20 But while he thought on these things, behold, the angel of the Lord appeared unto him in a dream, saying, Joseph, thou son of David, fear not to take unto thee Mary thy wife: for that which is conceived in her is of the Holy Ghost. 21 And she shall bring forth a son, and thou shalt call his name JESUS: for he shall save his people from their sins. 22 Now all this was done, that it might be fulfilled which was spoken of the Lord by the prophet, saying, 23 Behold, a virgin shall be with child, and shall bring forth a son, and they shall call his name Emmanuel, which being interpreted is, God with us. 24 Then Joseph, being raised from sleep, did as the angel of the Lord had bidden him, and took unto him his wife: 25 And knew her not till she had brought forth her firstborn son: and he called his name Jesus.)

(**Luke 2:1 And it came to pass in those days, that there went out a decree from Caesar Augustus, that all the world should be taxed. 2 (And this taxing was first made when Cyrenius was governor of Syria.) 3 And all went to be taxed, every one into his own city. 4 And Joseph also went up from Galilee, out of the city of Nazareth, into Judaea, unto the city of David, which is called Bethlehem; (because he was of the house and lineage of David:) 5 To be taxed with Mary his espoused wife, being great with child. 6

And so it was, that, while they were there, the days were accomplished that she should be delivered. 7 And she brought forth her firstborn son, and wrapped him in swaddling clothes, and laid him in a manger; because there was no room for them in the inn. 8 And there were in the same country shepherds abiding in the field, keeping watch over their flock by night. 9 And, lo, the angel of the Lord came upon them, and the glory of the Lord shone round about them: and they were sore afraid. 10 And the angel said unto them, Fear not: for, behold, I bring you good tidings of great joy, which shall be to all people. 11 For unto you is born this day in the city of David a Saviour, which is Christ the Lord. 12 And this shall be a sign unto you; Ye shall find the babe wrapped in swaddling clothes, lying in a manger. 13 And suddenly there was with the angel a multitude of the heavenly host praising God, and saying, 14 Glory to God in the highest, and on earth peace, good will toward men. 15 And it came to pass, as the angels were gone away from them into heaven, the shepherds said one to another, Let us now go even unto Bethlehem, and see this thing which is come to pass, which the Lord hath made known unto us. 16 And they came with haste, and found Mary, and Joseph, and the babe lying in a manger. 17 And when they had seen it, they made known abroad the saying which was told them concerning this child. 18 And all they that heard it wondered at those things which were told them by the shepherds. 19 But Mary kept all these things, and pondered them in her heart. 20 And the shepherds returned, glorifying and praising God for all the things that they had heard and seen, as it was told unto them.

Another paragraph of the book explored an obvious comparison between Christianity and Islam, but again excluded Judaism, which clearly belongs in the mix. In a part of the book, Harris somewhat deplored the biblical nod to slavery, yet failed to condemn the "Kosher Nostra" for starting it. Once again, slavery was a war on all non-European nations of the world; religion was used to boost the racism that gave birth to slavery. Sam could have extended the book with one more short sentence to mention the present religion-based apartheid and genocidal slavery imposed on the Palestinians by his cult. We deem the biblical take on slavery immoral, yet not one word about the enslavement and daily murder of Palestinians in their own country, by his darling Zionism.

Then the succinct exploration of the Ten Commandments happened, with the utter failure to note that they were actually stolen from the Egyptian positive assertions, and altered to reflect and conform to the tenets of the religious agenda of white supremacy. Just another way to ignore any accomplishment of the black people, and keep supporting the inane hallucination that the civilized world started with the Romans, who were no more than well-dressed thugs in minis.

They made a quick mention of the Nazi holocaust, yet they didn't say a word about the MAAFA. It is laughable when Judaism parades a Red Sea pedestrian as a bona fide holocaust victim, when every single black man, woman and child is a real and true holocaust victim. Does he remember the widespread cannibalism created by his people in Ukraine?

Should someone remind him of the names: Genrikh Yagoda, Yigal Amir and Yezhov?

BENZION MILEIKOWSKI. What would be Sam's opinion on the news that Israeli political leaders lashed out at Polish born Prime Minister Benjamin Netanyahu's eldest son for posting an "anti- Semitic" caricature aimed at his father's critics? Former Ku Klux Klan leader David Duke and others shared the post. Avi Gabbay told Army Radio the post "crossed every line imaginable," saying it was a "very sad" day for Israel and the Jewish people when the prime minister's son posts a cartoon that the leader of the Ku Klux Klan agrees with. Many wondered whether Yair Netanyahu, who enjoys a life of privilege at taxpayers' expense, state-funded driver and bodyguard while living at the prime minister's official residence, absorbed such ideology at home.

The Mileikowski (Netanyahu) family is also facing a slew of corruption allegations. They have questioned the prime minister about his ties to executives in the media, international business and Hollywood. It has engulfed his associates in a probe relating to a possible conflict of interest involving a $2 billion purchase of German submarines. Israel's attorney general has said he intends to indict the prime minister's wife, Sara, for fraud over her bloated household expenses.

BOTTOM LINE. Europeans write most European books, for Europeans, with the intended goal of bending all the rules that would keep them from bragging about achievements that never occurred and they never even thought of. When people manipulate the truth, atheism becomes as believable as Judaism, Christianity, and Islam. Just another angle to look at the same pile of manure.

# NYANKOPON VS YAHWEH & ALLAH

The stereotypes abound in many lectures and documentaries peppered with suggestive interjections, where Africa is whitely portrayed as the land of diseases and hunger, hordes of cannibals cooking human flesh in cauldrons, amazing dancers nonetheless naked savages, a third or fourth world continent with uncivilized, lazy and stupid negroes who need help to do everything. Half way across the globe, drunk shirtless white supremacists, praying to Jesus for rain, talk about Native Americans as nothing more than savage rain dancers adorned with feathery accoutrements. Once again, it requires very little effort to hate a man whom you have wronged.

Allowing and tolerating western emissaries in their midst became a curse for Africans who, to satisfy human and political ties, accepted many cunning advices from people who hated and still hate Africa.

Was there a credible exigent circumstance for the white man in Africa? What gave the white man the presumption that he has a natural right to enter a black country, dominate the people, take their land, and compel them in some way to labor for his benefit?

The black man's wants and needs are few and simple: to take care of himself and his own. One of the western world order demands on the black man is that, besides his family, he has to produce more to satisfy the starving European, who doesn't want or know how to grow crops. So the system is forcing the black man to become a hired servant of the white man. In doing so, Eurabians, in their determined haste to get rich, are still so blind to the wellbeing of others that they don't shy away from adopting methods that are barely distinguishable from slavery. Booker Washington said: "There is all the difference in the world between working and being worked."

Someone said "The white men, at one time, robbed Africa of Africans, now they rob Africans of Africa". That's when they were not introducing diseases like sleeping sickness, influenza, syphilis, tuberculosis that would be blamed later on the lack of hygiene of blacks. How quickly or selectively the Aryans forgot who taught them about soap and water. One day, Eurabians will learn that the same way they erased the accomplishments of others, the same way their fake memories will be erased.

TIMELINE. 32 trillions years ago, Africa became the home of the first humans. They were black. Around 24000 BCE, it is said that Caspian type white men invaded the continent from the North and displaced the Negroes of the Nile Valley. They kicked out the invaders and life returned to normal, with a greatly flourishing commerce in Uganda, Tanzania and Ethiopia, which went 3000 years without a major war. Then a great famine caused a migration from Western Asia to Africa. Information about the black country was first obtained by the starving members of the Ibarus people who have been the guests of Egypt, from 1680 BCE until their second expulsion in 1280 BCE, for treason.

Mark Twain said: "If you pick up a starving dog and make him prosperous, he will not bite you". The above quote remains the principal difference between a dog and Zionist. The Abes didn't even wait to finish the free meal given to them by Africa, that they had already turned against their benefactors. Supported by their Rothschild god, the Zionists accumulated immense wealth with money laundering, financing terrorism all over the world.

That's one of the many reasons they were expelled from every single country in the world and why Hitler paid them back in kind.

There were no Israelite, Jew or Hebrew before 1280 BCE, in history. In 70 BCE, after the Romans destroyed the last Hebrew temple, many of self-proclaimed Jews- Israelites- Hebrews moved back to West Africa and stayed until 770 AD. An important event happened in 325 AD, with the council of Nicaea that gave a tremendous boost to Judaism and its extensions. Then, the Western Roman empire collapsed in 476 AD, took down Christianity with it and created a vacuum for Islam to rise.

The rape of Africa started in 550 AD, when Jews and Arab Muslims went into business together. Judaism and Arabism are the two racist movements at the very beginning of the enslavement and destruction of Africa. They started it, profited from it and are still at it today in 2017. On their way to steal, pillage, loot and burn foreign lands, the thieves switched the principal export of Africa, from crops to black men, women and children.

Within 10 years of Muhammad's death, in 640 AD, his followers invaded Egypt. It made the ease of the Islamic invasion of Africa possible because the Muslims were of the same skin color as the Africans. The lure of Islam remained in the false belief that Muslims give negroes a better level of equality than the white man who suffered many setbacks, because every black murdered by a Jew was a reset of race relation and a fostering of mistrust, coupled with the opening of old wounds. 20 years later, Islam had reached the Atlantic ocean, with Ukba Ben Nafa. By 708 AD, Islamic forces had completely invaded and taken control of North Africa. Egypt had become a white man's country. Islam has colonized Africa by means of violent conquest, pacific propaganda, commercial influence and inter marriage; in the end, Islam has destroyed Africa.

Europa saw the dark ages, along with the consolidation and extension of slavery in all its cruelty and racism. Arab Muslims went to a level of cold-blooded barbarism and violent savageries against negroes that only the French could duplicate and even surpass after 1517.

In 1415 Portugal joined the club, by capturing Ceuta.

FAKE HISTORY. A perfect example of the ignorance and down right cunning stupidity of white Americans can be observed on Columbus day, with the exhibition of the European utopia, honoring a dead white supremacist who was NOT a navigator, nor an explorer, but just a genocidal murderer who hitched a ride aboard the ships of the black Pinzon brothers. (More about that later.)

PARTNERSHIP. The year 1776 was a historical date that saw the birth of a nation, as America became the extended military arm of Britain in the slavery and world domination business. They lay the foundation for the secret society called Illuminati and the American Eugenics movement. It was the beginning of the new world order as we know it, when desperate, armed and corrupt idiots joined forces with very rich idiots to take over control of the world. They usurped the political power from the various governments and instituted their own rules. Nothing was beyond the stupidity of these unusually enlightened and lit morons, who distinguished themselves with everything from ignorant legislations, statements, Roc sign, deadly schemes, all-seeing eye, Free Masonry, primitive symbols, compass and squares, serpents, the sun, even a Monarch butterfly was netted. From eternal flame, pentagram, inverted pentagram, goat head, order of the Eastern Star, 666, monster drink, skull, obelisk, to the Google Chrome logo, nothing was too outlandish for these geniuses to show their newly found power... not even the grave of Jehovah's witness founder Charles Taze Russell in the shape of a pyramid. They flexed their destructive power on all and bragged about becoming the new masters of the world.

"Who knows himself a braggart, let him fear this, for it will come to pass that every braggart shall be found an ass." (William Shakespeare.)

With that, corruption in the Anglo-American states attained the status of structural calamity. Like a stage 4 cancer, it spread at all levels, and in every nook and cranny of the world with many secondary cancers. From 1517 to 1791 slavery became a successful white international enterprise, as the depopulation and destabilization of Africa continued with all able-bodied Africans marked and condemned to certain death by the European world.

The American Civil War (1861-1865) was a bigger version of the Hatfield-McCoy feud, fought between 2 inbred factions over the right to marry their sisters and cousins.

PEPE LE PEW. The French were so stupid in the way they implemented slavery and abused negroes they destroyed their own venture. Africa was the goose that laid the golden eggs. The feeble-minded French killed it, plucked it, cut it up and cooked it. Now they are reeling with indigestion, and the idiots are still blaming the goose.

Payback knocked on the French front door with a pretty nasty butt whooping from Haiti between August 14th, 1791 and November 18th, 1803. By January 1st, 1804, France was knocked back in a permanent stupor as they could see its soldiers in their true colors, as French poodles which were trained to heel. Fortunately, all the pimps and Johns "de la putain francaise" were also present, to experience and share in what happens when abused black men get pissed off. When we are good, we are very good; when we are bad, we are even better.

Beaten and demoralized, France still launched a new venture in 1830, and sacrificed 150,000 men to impose colonial ruling on Africa. By 1854, France conquered Senegal, on the way to stealing the largest share of land in North Africa. And that's not their crowning achievement.

The French, no strangers to imbecility, armed and trained the Muslims to invade Africa. The Muzzies also received support from the British government, which did so as a "means of preserving order." Lo-and-behold, today, France and Britain are now facing the consequences of their ignorant actions, as their city streets echo the long cry: Allah-u Akbar. Ash hadu al-la-ilaha ill-Allah.

BLUE NOSES. On December 4th, 1857 missionary David Livingstone made his famous speech, when he announced in Britain: "Africa is now open, do not let it be shut again. I go back to Africa to try to make an open path for commerce and Christianity. Carry the work which I have begun." They shared this lethal approach with a dying British empire in dire need of raw materials to support a fledging and dying economy. In 1870, Cecil Rhodes started making money from the sale of African diamonds. But it wasn't until 1874 that Henry M. Stanley started the pillage of and scramble for Africa. Britain, which had no previous intention of African conquest, joined the frenzy, and invaded Sierra Leone, Gambia and the Port of Lagos. Following in the footsteps of the Muslim rapists, Britain sodomized Africa with God, gun, and greed. In 1876, Africa suffered more European invasions from Spain (Fernando Po) and Italy.

1876 was another atrocious and dire year for the country of Africa, just like 550 AD and 1517. Never in the planet's history has a country suffered so much and lost so many of her children to pure, unadulterated hatred and racism. No other nation in the world had to deal with the disgraceful fate that was heaped on Africa, which was plundered, pillaged, looted, invaded, bombed, enslaved, colonized, with everything stolen from the national resources to the bones of the dead.

HOAX-LOCAUST. Whenever the word "holocaust" is

mentioned, people immediately think of the well publicized Hollywood event during which the Nazi regime allegedly killed 1.5 to 2 millions people, some of Jewish persuasion. The Holocaust was more than a Jewish event. We should always remember Salomon Morel and Abraham Gancwajch when talking about the holocaust.

The Nazi regime found its ideal in the US. Emulating the leaders and the "master race" agenda of the American Eugenics Movement, the Nazis deliberately killed all people who were deemed undesirable to the Nazi vision of an Aryan world (Negative Eugenics). Records kept by the Germans prove they exterminated: blacks (especially Afro-German Mischlinge aka Rhineland bastards), minorities not considered Aryan, leftists, communists, Russians, Czechs, Greeks, Gypsies, Belgians, Dutch, Italians, homosexuals, Aktion T4, Jehovah's Witnesses, Serbs, mentally and physically handicapped, Poles, resistance fighters, Russians POWs and civilians, Socialists, Spanish Republicans, trade unionists, Ukrainians, clergy, Yugoslavians, prisoners of war of many nations, Boy and Girl Scouts, Buddhists, Muslims, Freemasons, communists, deportees, political prisoners, and still others whose identity may never be known. The victims, according to one survivor of four different concentration camps, were of some thirty nationalities. So why is it just a Jewish fiesta?

Karen Silverstrim, MA candidate at the University of Central Arkansas, wrote: "The prisoners were divided into six penal categories and given patches on their clothing for identification purposes. They assigned ordinary criminals green; political prisoners wore red; asocials (slackers, prostitutes, procurers, etc. wore black); homosexuals wore pink; conscientious objectors wore purple, and the Jewish people wore yellow. Many non-Jewish victims also died in concentration camps by gassing, lethal experiments, relocations, starvation, street executions, overwork, or beatings. A greater number perished because of the aggressive tactics of the Nazis in rounding up their victims and in street assassinations."

Just the same as the American Eugenics movement*, the Nazis promoted xenophobia and racism against all non-Aryan groups. Black sub-Saharan or North African residents of Germany and their offspring of German mothers were also victims of Nazi racial policy. In Mein Kampf, Hitler described the children of marriages to African occupation troops as a contamination of the white race "by Negro blood on the Rhine in the heart of Europe" who were "bastardising the European continent at its core". According to Hitler, "Jews brought negroes into the Rhineland, with the ultimate idea of bastardizing the white race which they hate and thus lowering its cultural and political level so that the Jew might dominate". Hitler's racist conviction toward blacks was borrowed and lifted directly from the annals of the American Eugenics Movement*. During the last elections in Israel, Benzion Mileikowski, the butcher of the West Bank, echoed the exact same penchant that Africans were polluting the Jewish blood line, contaminating the lily white Zionist society. And Hitler is the bad guy?

(Note*: For more info on the American Eugenics Movement, please read "Deadly faith" available at Amazon.com/books.)

THE MAAFA. But no one dares talk about two of the worst examples of genocide and ethnic cleansing in history, which took place in Africa. The first started in 550 AD with the slave trade and is ongoing; the other happened in the Congo state. While slavery is well documented and kept in the dark closet of history, an equally repulsive event is on the shelf right next to slavery.

In 1878, Henry Stanley met Dr Livingstone in the Congo. What were they doing there? They were spies working for the benevolent King Leopold II of Belgium. In 1885, the genocide started as the ruthless King Leopold II of Belgium allied with Arab slave trader Tippu Tip, to decimate the Congo. In his quest to get gold, ivory, diamonds and rubber that didn't belong to him, just like any other Eurabian would, he butchered millions of Congolese people, depopulated entire villages, and used the "battue" technique in massive hunts to slaughter ivory bearing elephants to the point of extinction. As Catholic as John J. Dilulio Jr, the Belgian king, in a blood-soaked tyranny, subjected the peaceful negroes to the most vile and inhuman treatment that his Nordic greed and barbaric nature could muster. They forced blacks to meet quotas on his plantations, just like most western businesses of today, and they subjected the ones who failed to whippings and mutilations. If they deemed an underproductive worker important to the business, his wife and children would have their hands cut off instead of him. Belgium's present economic success still reeks of the blood of these Africans.

King Leopold II of Belgium founded the International African Association as a "philanthropic" organization* to spread missionary work and western culture in the Congo. In the end, the Congo became a killing ground for the deranged and racist King Leopold II of Belgium, who slaughtered 30 millions of negroes for financial gain and his own pleasure. They lined negroes up and shot, just so King Leopold II of Belgium could see how many of them his bullets could go through. They executed them just like negroes are today, in the streets of the US.

King Leopold II of Belgium is a "hush" word, never mentioned in any debate or lecture on crimes against humanity, so the western legacy can maintain the audacity and hypocrisy to trash Hitler, Pol Pot, Mao, Stalin, and Mussolini.

(Note* Isn't it strange that they still use this practice today?)

EXTRA EXTRA. Everywhere else in the world, the Europeans were on a rampage as Britain slaughtered the Aborigines of Australia; the US massacred the Native American and Philipino nations, France butchered the North Congolese,

Spain wiped out the North and Central Native Americans, Portugal decimated the Angolans and Amazonians, Germany wiped out South West Africa. It is very telling that everything of a nefarious nature in the world was and is still being done by the white European.

The western agenda is a garish, money grubbing, vulgar system which discriminates against Negroes and ignores the poor. It requires very little effort to hate a man whom you have wronged.

In South America, the Spanish and capitalists destroyed the codices, temples and archeological, ceramic works, stone sculptures from the very impressive Mayan civilization.

In 1876, 1/10 of North Africa was under European control; in 1879, the Baptist faith invaded the Congo and by 1926, 90% of Africa was under European control.

AMERICAN PRIDE. The US remains the only country which can challenge the French when it comes to the savageries displayed against blacks, with hundreds of thousands, if not millions, of graphic recorded testimonies to the demented tendencies of the American white supremacist. Everyone knows about Mary Turner in Lowndes County, in Georgia. Here is the story of another black girl in the US.

CELIA Around 1820, Robert Newsom and his family left Virginia and headed west, finally settling on land along the Middle River in southern Callaway County, Missouri. By 1850 (according to the census), Newsom owned 800 acres of land and livestock, that included horses, milk cows, beef cattle, hogs, sheep, and two oxen. Like most Callaway County farmers, Newsom also owned slaves.

Celia was a slave, probably born around 1836 in Missouri. She was bought, during the summer of 1850, from a slave owner in neighboring Audrain County, by widower Robert Newsom, at age

14 to help his daughters do chores. Shortly after returning with Celia to his farm, Newsom raped her. For female slaves, rape was an "ever present threat" and, far too often, a reality.

We know Mr. Newsom took sexual liberties with Celia from almost the moment of sale. She had two children by Newsom, both of whom became the property of Mr. Newsom. Once back at his farm, Newsom put Celia in a cabin in a grove of fruit trees approximately 150 feet from his own home. While there, Celia began a relationship with a slave named George, unknown to the master. When Celia became pregnant, George said he would quit seeing her if she continued with Newsom. Celia tried having Newsom's daughters help her, saying she was not feeling well because of the pregnancy, however there is no record that would show they did. Celia then pleaded with the master herself, to no avail.

On the evening of June 23, 1855, the massa "visited" Celia. For the now nineteen-year-old slave, five years of being repeatedly raped by her middle-aged owner was enough. She killed him with blows to the head. She then burned his corpse in her fireplace, ground the smaller bones into pieces with a rock and hid the larger ones under the hearth and under the floor.

Initially, Celia denies involvement, but later confesses, which led to her demise. She also delivered her baby, stillborn, while in custody. The murder trial of the slave Celia, coming when the controversy over the issue of slavery reached new heights, raised fundamental questions about the rights of slaves to fight back against the worst of slavery's abuses.

The decision: After concluding arguments, Celia's attorney requested many instructions that would have allowed Celia to be acquitted if the jury found from evidence that she had killed Newsom to protect herself from his advances. After all, Missouri Statute of 1845, section 29, made it a crime for a man to "take any woman unlawfully against her will and by force..." The prosecution objected to these instructions and the judge refused to let the jury consider the statute because a "negro woman was not a woman." They sentenced Celia to death by hanging on November 16. They denied her a stay of execution.

A "negro woman was not a woman!" Nothing has changed.

PREMEDITATION. Like the New Testament, the new world order support everything that was done in the old world order. The white people knew that kidnapping was against natural laws, yet they still did it. They knew stealing was against natural laws, yet they still did it. They knew cannibalism was against natural laws, yet they still did it. They knew murder was against natural laws, yet they still did it. They knew rape was against natural laws, yet they still did it. They knew robbery was against natural laws, yet they still did it. They knew assault was against natural laws, yet they still did it. They knew drug dealing was against natural laws, yet they still did it. They knew burglary was against natural laws, yet they still did it. They knew racism was against natural laws, yet they still did it. They knew slavery was against natural laws, yet they still did it. They knew castrating black kids was against natural laws, yet they still did it. They knew lynching was against natural laws, yet they still did it. They knew arson was against natural laws, yet they still did it. They knew pillage was against natural laws, yet they still did it. They knew raiding other occupied lands was against natural laws, yet they still did it. They knew invading other people's land was against natural laws, yet they still did it. They knew genocide was against natural laws, yet they still did it. They knew grave robbery was against natural laws, yet they still did it. They knew infecting blacks with diseases was against natural laws, yet they still did it. They knew looting was against natural laws, yet they still did it. They knew using black babies as gator bait was against natural laws, yet they still did it. They knew corruption was against natural laws, yet they still did it. They did it and are still doing it.

They learned and did all that, by going against anything black, when the correct message was included in the loot they stole from Egypt, along with the bones of dead Negroes.

History will not absolve the white race, it will forget it.

VATICAN. Religion was used to mask the greed and thieving nature of the leaders of the Catholic cult. 99% of the assets of the Catholic church were stolen from black people and countries, and the remaining 1% was gained through hellish threats and trickery. The Vatican is a place where thieves go to prey.

To this day in 2017, near the porta di S. Anna, in via di porta angelica (Rione of Borgo), the Sedes Sacrorum (the Holy scrotum) has over 76 miles of stolen black artifacts and documents which are not available to or accessible by blacks. No Negro in the world may view the mementos of his history, no Negro in the world may look at or research his past, no Negro in the world may learn about his true traditions and customs, no Negro in the world may access the writing of his dead parents, no Negro in the world is allowed to bring flowers to the graves of his ancestors, because a pedophile laden cult is standing in the way. Negroes can forget about their black inheritance, because a gang of white supremacist child molesters have forbidden the presence of any dark-skin near the familial inheritance. The holy pedophiles rampaged through the black villages and swiped everything, from rituals they still don't understand, gold sarcophagi to the bones of dead Negroes. And the western world provides punishment for grave robbers?

It is primarily because of greed and racism, not religion, that the Catholic church kept sending white missionaries to Africa, especially the Niger, in 1894; knowing they would die within 2 years of their deployment, at most. Even the idiotic arrogance of Sierra Leone's bishop, John Bowen, couldn't save him from his fate.

John Newton, author of "How sweet the name of Jesus sounds," actively engaged in the slave trade in Guinea and elsewhere in Africa. The bible still condones slavery, today, in 2017.

Christianity found many arguments for slavery, through outlandish papal bulls, to just plain bull. History has painstakingly documented the intense involvement of papal buzzards in the destruction of anything black. On this entire planet, every inch of ground reeks of the blood, sweat and tears that the Catholic church yanked out of the bodies of black men, women and children.

REALITY IGNORED. They systematically did the degradation of Africa despite different views. Sir Gordon Guggisberg believed the European has not and will never have an actual home in West Africa. Edwin W. Smith, in the Golden stool, asked, "Can Europeans live in tropical Africa, in the neighborhood of black people of a much lower standard of civilization?"

The same Edwin W. Smith used a very colorful language to describe Africa, post-invasion: "Here you may see half-naked savages from the Equitorial forest mingling with more civilized Africans who ape* the Europeans in their dress." But try as he may, he couldn't escape reality. When he wrote "mentally, morally, and physically, many of the blacks are far superior to many of the degenerate whites." Professor Gregory predicted: "the ultimate supremacy of the negro over most of the African continent appears inevitable." For Europeans, Africa remained a continent, but for Africans, it will always remain Alkebulan, our pride, our country, our home, our motherland.

(Note*: Once again, a white supremacist used a selective and suggestive word to describe blacks, regardless of the fact that there is not one single ape with wooly nappy hair, thick lips and round butt.)

WAR HELP. Britain and the Allies won the war against

Germany, only because of the help they received from Africa. The Africans' labor in the mines of Katanga supplied the western powers with hundreds of thousands of tons of copper, while they reduced the Germans to melting pots and pans from their kitchens to get the metal needed for ammunitions. Manganese from the Gold Coast Colony contributed to the efficiency of the airplanes used in and after the war.

WORLD DOMINATION. What the demented hallucinating new word order freaks can not understand is: how likely is the utopia of world domination when the United British States of America will have to defeat Russia, China, Japan, India, Pakistan and other military powers to get there? It doesn't look like any of these countries will lay down and accept to be dominated by the US. Like the Roman empire, Britain will eventually be forced to accept its collective ignorance and realize that it cut its own nose to spike its face. The vast American land was stolen because Britain didn't have enough space to produce the raw materials, and they needed crops to feed the growing British populace within its borders. No import of food would lead to starvation. The effort to steal America was a waste of resources and lives. It would have made better sense to let the British empire follow in the footsteps of the Romans.

And what a waste! To steal a beautiful land, and butcher the legal residents, only to turn a paradise into a giant shopping mall.

Blacks should not be required to die in order for the confederate Aryan skinheads to live their lily white chosen lifestyle. People will die at any time of the day or night. What's repulsive is the senseless taking of black lives. The time has come for eurabians to rectify the parasitic colonial relationship they have with African people, by returning or paying for all the stolen resources they have benefited from for thousands of years, at the expense of African people.

What has Africa benefited from? Nothing. After all the European conquest, invasions, colonialism and now imperialism, there is still a need for simple, basic drinking water in Africa. One can inhale the poverty imposed on Africans. If managed properly by the African people, Alkebulan would have remained the richest country in the world. There is still time.

KISKEYA. In the Caribbean, there is a little black county which is suffering the same fate as the Motherland. Even as the western world tries to hide its shameful history and genocidal agenda, there are many things that a European can never understand about Ayiti.

- How to spell or correctly use a Kreyol word.

- In less than 20 years, they slaughtered 19 millions of Bohio's Tainos so Christians could steal their gold while carrying a bible that commands: Thou shalt not steal, and thou shalt not kill.

The January 1804 spring clean-up by Jean-Jacques Dessalines was not a senseless extermination of the whites on the island. It was just payback in kind, an expression of his distaste and repugnance for the atrocities perpetrated on his people.

Dessalines showed an amazingly compassionate restraint in executing the white terrorists, which lasted only 3 months, between early February 1804 until April 22nd, 1804 compared to 274 years and counting of white supremacists killing his people.

Every single day, since 550 AD, Negroes have been abused, kidnapped, uprooted from Ethiopia (Africa), with families split and sold on different markets, treated like animals, murdered, branded, raped, beaten, humiliated, tortured. Slaves could not talk, answer questions or even look at their racist white masters. Punishments included but were not limited to: burned alive, stuffed with gunpowder and lit, ground in machines, buried to their necks next to ant mounds, nailed to boards, devoured by specially trained dogs, babies were buried so their heads would be kicked off like footballs, etc...

One could hardly expect the slaves of Haiti to embrace and kiss the racist French maggots after the war of Independence. Two thousands years of humiliation, abuse and deprivation cannot be expected to find a voice in a whisper.

Today, every murdered black is like a cold beer added to the tab, that white supremacists will have to pay before leaving the bar. Just when you thought you were the alpha male, the black bartender will come to collect his money. No excuse will be accepted and you will pay for the products that you consumed, or go to jail for obtaining food and lodging with the intent to defraud.

- Jean-Jacques Dessalines was not a pitiless barbarian like the slave owners, he was just a great humanitarian who followed the Christian God's command in Exodus 21:23 And if any mischief follow, then thou shalt give life for life, 24 Eye for eye, tooth for tooth, hand for hand, foot for foot, 25 Burning for burning, wound for wound, stripe for stripe.

Why was the above biblical precept good enough for white terrorists and not black freedom fighters?

- Yes, you can take it to the bank. On November 18th, 1803, Haiti beat the daylights out of all the combined western powers of the time. And they had it coming.

- Yes, the slaves of Haiti turned Napoleon's lily white utopia of world domination into a black reality.

- Yes, the slaves of Haiti put a stop to Thomas Jefferson's ideology of annihilation of the black government.

- The spark for the Haitian revolution didn't originate at the

French revolution, but on the coasts of Africa with the kidnapping of Negroes since 550 AD. Haitian slaves never gave up their dream of freedom or their love for Alkebulan, the Motherland.

- All the tumult and conflicts in Haiti, from January 1st, 1804 to the present time, are the collateral consequences, the continued repercussions and after shocks of slavery. This is the creation of the western world with its 128 divisions of skin shade and ancestry.

- Dark skinned Haitians don't hate light skinned ones; like democrats and the Tea Party, they just have a difference of opinions. But it's a black thing better left alone, because whites could not understand it.

- Your look so fake, insincere, empty and phony when patronizing the many accomplishments of Francois Dominique Toussaint Breda L'Ouverture, Jean-Jacques Dessalines and Martin Luther King Jr. It is just plain pathetic. At the end of the day, you admired them so much that you froze Toussaint to death in a jail cell in France. You pumped Dessalines and Martin Luther King Jr full of bullets.

You hated us and have never been our friends.

PRESENTLY - The US is a country where scams, Ponzi and pyramid schemes are as common as a car driven down the streets, and the only solution so far remains to blame it all on black Nigeria.

- Europeans decry the infighting between the African tribes as savage encounters, as they continue to supply weapons to both sides of the created conflicts. Yet, westerners regard their bombing of the same Africans as a beautiful expression of their technology, and a great humanitarian gesture.

- The kidnapping of young Nigerian girls by the group known to the western world as Boko-Haram will never be blamed on Britain, which created the conditions for the Islamic group to form.

- Police forced Muslim women in Austria to remove their facial coverings, on a Sunday in 2017, as an anti-burqa law came into effect. A woman wearing a niqab facial veil, which only leaves the eyes uncovered, was seen being told to remove her veil by two police officers in Zell am See, a city south of Salzburg.

The so-called "burqa ban" prohibits facial coverings, including niqabs and burqas, and also places restrictions on surgical masks, ski masks and clown make-up worn in public. However, police officers may dress like ISIS militants.

White women wearing a burqa are called nuns, black women wearing a burqa are called terrorists. No word yet, if they will ask the nuns to strip.

- If Britain, US and France can claim places in Africa, there is no reason Russia can not claim Mount Everest.

- European countries remain the safest places in the world for war criminals, guilty of crimes against humanity, to live in. They are out of the reach of justice and can live without fear of being indicted, arrested, or jailed. Heck, hardened criminals run most of these nations and keep adding to their impressive genocidal records.

- Africa is still on the auction block with the old slave traders becoming the new negro killers. In an obscene and racist scheme of world depopulation, the American Eugenics Movement is slaughtering Africans who live in a country bigger than Europe, India, China and the US put together; with fewer people by size than India. Yet, many idiots continue to promote the idea that Africa has an overpopulation problem.

- The slaughter of indigenous people is ongoing as the New

York Times reported at least 10 members of an uncontacted tribe in Brazil's Amazon Basin were allegedly killed last August 2017 by illegal gold miners, according to Survival International. The organization, which advocates for indigenous rights, said the massacre included women and children and may have wiped out one-fifth of the tribe. Members of the tribe were gathering eggs along a river in the Javari Valley, in the country's remote west, when they came across the miners. The miners later boasted about the slaughter at a bar in the nearest town and even showed off a hand-carved paddle they claimed to have stolen as a trophy. Leila Silvia Burger Sotto-Maior, Funai's coordinator for uncontacted and recently contacted tribes, told the Times "They even bragged about cutting up the bodies and throwing them in the river." At least two other tribes in the region have seen their land invaded and are now surrounded by ranchers and others, Survival International reported. "The invaders are landowners, hunters, miners. Many indigenous are being killed in isolation, but we don't know the exact dates or number of deaths."

HEINZ ALFRED is the worse terrorist scum to ever soiled humanity. "Control oil and you control the world, control food and you control people" will forever remain the most bastardly demonic genocidal concept ever devised by a human maggot (my excuse to the natural maggots). The quote, which became the motto for the American Eugenics movement, came from the sewer rat, a German born Rothschild Zionist named Henry Heinz Alfred Kissinger who is responsible for many war crimes, crimes against humanity, and more deaths than Genghis Temujin Khan, Hitler, Stalin, Mao, Pol Pot, Franco and Mussolini combined.

Henry Heinz Kissinger's idiotic concept of world domination thru the control of the food supply is flawed and is bound to fail soon. The GMO agenda, from the American Eugenics Movement, was implemented to kill more negroes, using companies that can produce enough engineered food, medicine and "diplomacy". People who can not even spell agriculture and know absolutely nothing about producing crops are deciding behind a desk, while they have sidelined real farmers. It is up to par with every other western idea and schemes. The momentous efforts of the agri-business system of assisted genocides are very telling of the lack of intelligence and foresight of the self-chosen decision makers for humanity. Once again, when greed is coupled with stupidity, the only offspring possible is utter failure.

There is a better way than the moronic monopoly of concentrating crops destined for the world in the US only. Why not share the bounty with Africa and the rest of the world, instead of that selfish "all for me and none for you" attitude?

Fairness enriches both; him that gives, and him that takes.

The main injustice of the American Eugenics Movement is that it wants to eliminate people based on the lives that its own policies have negatively affected and altered (please see Deadly faith @Amazon.com/books). Their goal, instead, should be to remove the people responsible for these policies that have failed humanity and disrupted the lives of so many.

(For a more detailed account of the struggle facing the black people and nations, please see "2 burgers and a beer" @Amazon.com/books.)

# AVE CAESAR

"Man's capacity for justice makes democracy possible, but man's inclination to injustice makes democracy necessary," (Reinhold Niebuhr)

Since time immemorial, humans have always respected the rights of the individual. Along with rights came responsibility which dictates certain behaviors as acceptable to a society and the ones that were prohibited. From there, the rule of law was born. It was a matter of time before the rules were changed and redefined to remove all the rights from an individual and sell them to distinct groups. In due time, after many legal maneuvers, an opportunity arose to transfer the consequences of prohibited actions, from the individual who could be indicted, to a corporation or government which became immune to prosecution. Thus, democracy, which originally meant "rule of the people", was sabotaged and became the new fake front used by a few shysters to cover their deeds. Murders and genocides became "legal" many times defined by the groups, and could therefore be recklessly conducted on behalf of the "selected and specific groups" with no fear of reprisal or prosecution.

In a real democracy, the people exercises its power by electing representatives from among themselves to form a governing body to protect the safety and well being of said people. With great power comes great responsibility. A legal constitution regulated all actions of the government, federal and accepted civil laws. We expect all citizens to benefit equally from agencies and programs created by the government they elected.

THE RED VECTOR. When the law favors the rich and powerful, then uses its illegal power to permeate different countries, a dysfunctional world ensues where people are abused and live in fear of their government or a central imperial master.

The real threat to the national security of a country is not terrorism, but an abusive greedy government riddled with corruption.

The American dream has turned into greed, inequality and racism.

Greed creates more corruption, corruption creates more greed; it's a vicious and destructive cycle. Many have succumbed to greed; it is getting harder and harder to find an honest politician, because what money can not buy, money can usually rent. When a greedy government, influenced by money from lobbyists, shows a conscious disregard for the welfare of the people and becomes willfully blind to their grievances, justice can no longer prevail or even exist. The citizenry gets screwed.

Justice is the finding of the truth. The truth can not be selective. When the road to justice is polluted, certain people rise above the law? History has seen many such tyrants and genocidal lunatics at all levels of a dysfunctional society.

There are cases after cases of madmen and women slaughtering innocent people at the altar of their delusional utopia.

There are cases after cases of people like Rush Limbaugh, pastor Zachery Tims, and other drug dealers and users, who may sell and use hard drugs when the average negro gets thrown in jail for 10, 20 years for minor possession of marijuana over 20 grams?

There are cases after cases of so-called important people who may avoid paying taxes. The Panama papers involved 300,000 corporations with 15,600 shell companies involved in illegal activities, money laundering, tax evasion, fraud, evading international sanctions. Many members of the US government and their lobbyists are on the list of the culprits. What has been done to correct and rectify the crimes? Nothing. Nobody went to jail. Any black citizen would have been subjected to wage garnishment and or jail time. Why are the rich Aryans allowed to avoid paying taxes, with offshore accounts like the Panama papers, while they throw Ms Lauryn Noelle Hill and Wesley Trent Snipes in jail?

They ignored justice in so many other ways, especially with an added dose of racism. Why does an unarmed Negro deserve the death penalty for ignoring a police officer's order to move to the sidewalk when the blue cowards backed down from the armed white people at the Cliven Bundy ranch, without firing a shot?

Cops can see invisible guns in any unarmed Negro's hand, yet are blind to armed white supremacists walking down a street in Charlottesville. (More about that later)

THE PRECEPT. There is no other instance in any business, anywhere in the world, beside American politics, where an employee, once hired, decides on the wages and benefits s/he wants, hijacks the company, makes the rules, keeps the owner out of the business, and if the owner dares question the work being done, s/he is dragged into a court by the employee or sent to jail. There will be no meeting about it, because the employee also rules that the employer, the people, should not have a say in what s/he does. To further supplement a largely undeserved income, the employee also decides that it is acceptable to take bribes and sell the already paid for services to the highest bidder, foreign or domestic. Talk about a criminal scheme and enterprise.

People don't run for public office to help anyone but themselves, and they run because the position allows them to use the office for personal gain. The real lure of a position in Congress is the rewarding side business that comes with it. From lucrative "speaking engagement", paid speeches, well-paid lobbyist positions and outright bribes, while the country and Constitution are out of sight, on the back burner. "So much money floating around, so little time to collect it" is the patriotic motto of the US Congress.

The US Congress is the only body in the entire world, which can challenge and defeat a cesspool when it comes to contents. One day, I started watching a video of Congress in session. After about 15 minutes, I realized that watching paint dry, grass grow, or molasses running uphill in the winter would be a better use of my time. The tremendously diligent and proficient work, they were doing, could only be put in perspective by looking at many of our honorable leaders who were busy picking their noses and eating the boogers, when not falling asleep in their chairs, listening to their own BS.

Not a day goes by without an incident from lawmakers who think they are above the laws they enact.

CASE. In March 2016, they arrested Kyle Tasker, a politician, and sentenced him (May 10th) to 3-10 years in prison, after he pleaded guilty to charges of drug possession and trying to lure a 14-year-old girl into a sexual encounter.

AFTER CASE. Scott Rothstein is an example of how a crooked lawyer, of Ponzi scheme fame, can enjoy the American dream with the complicity of law enforcement, mayor, governor, prosecutor, etc...

AFTER CASE. Michael T. Flynn, National Security Advisor, was forced to resign on February 13, 2017 over conversations he had with Russian envoys about sanctions during the transition, possibly violating the Logan Act.

AFTER CASE. Jeff Sessions, Attorney General, lied under oath to the Senate Judiciary Committee on January 10, 2017, stating that he "did not have communications with the Russians." On March 1, 2017, he has amended his statement to the opposite. They have not charged him with perjury, which is a felony.

Attorney General Jeff Sessions is facing calls from

lawmakers to once again appear before the Senate Judiciary Committee and answer questions on his participation in Russia's alleged interference in the US presidential election.

AFTER CASE. The Paradise papers exposed that Commerce Secretary Wilbur Ross failed to disclose ties to Vladimir Putin's son-in-law during the confirmation hearing for his Cabinet post.

AFTER CASE. A U.S. senator called for a criminal investigation of executives from credit bureau Equifax Inc. for stock sales after a massive data breach this summer and said their actions were comparable to insider trading. Senator Heidi Heitkamp is either a hypocrite or an idiot, Congress does the exact same thing.

Thinkprogress.org reported on 10/24/2017. "In the dead of night, Republicans vote to give lawsuit immunity to banks. Tuesday night, as many Americans were preparing to go to bed, an evenly divided Senate voted to give broad lawsuit immunity to credit card companies, auto lenders, credit reporting companies like Equifax, and many other financial firms. Vice President Mike Pence (R) broke the 50- 50 tie in the Senate, and the House approved the lawsuit immunity measure. We expect President Trump to sign it. The resolution passed by the Senate overrides a rule created by the Consumer Financial Protection Bureau (CFPB), which prevents many financial firms from engaging in two abusive practices."

AFTER CASE. It's 10/21/2017, and we are finally at the high point of the Mueller investigation into the Russian meddling in the last US elections. After many titillating months of innuendos, the Networks have announced that a first indictment and arrest will come on Monday 10/23/2017. Like the coverage of the hurricanes, they rounded up all the idiots available to talk about it. Speculations abound from former and retired political analysts who have no ties to the investigations in progress. The saying "no comment on any ongoing investigation" went out of the window, as morons lined up in front of the cameras to predict what the masses can not wait to hear two days later.

They don't know, have absolutely no idea who the suspect is and what the charges will be, yet are willing to talk for 2 damn days, fill the airwaves for two solid days with "no valid information."

AFTER CASE. Paul Manafort, who joined the Trump's presidential campaign in 2016, has been indicted along with Rick Gates and George Papadopoulos. On October 30th, 2017, Paul Manafort and Rick Gates surrendered to the FBI on 12 felony charges of conspiracy against the US, money laundering, failing to register as foreign agents and making false statements for actions that took place.

Arrested after he arrived at Dulles International airport, on July 27th, 2017, George Papadopoulos pleaded guilty to lying and started singing like a happy canary. The plea agreement shows he is cooperating with the investigating team of Robert Swan "Bob" Mueller III, the Special Counsel for Russia investigation.

Paul Manafort, who has been indicted and arrested on treason charges for the Russian collusion in the last US election, is requesting a bail hearing and he wants to use his Trump Tower condo as collateral for his bail. The judge replied he needs to know more about Manafort's finances before he will consider the request. And Manafort is more of a flight risk than a common pigeon in the park.

Rumor has it that next to be indicted will be Michael Thomas Flynn, Trumps's former National Security adviser, followed by Trump's son-in-law Jared Corey Kushner, the current senior adviser.

This is a perfect example of American democracy at work

and the level of respect reserved for the rule of law. Anyone who still has any doubt about the American justice system can just imagine Paul Manafort as black and poor. Would a negro be allowed to post bail after an indictment on treason charges? If you are white and rich in America, you are above the law and justice; you may do as you please. Shoot people, urge a foreign country to hack into the computers of a US political candidate, even collude with a foreign nation that you keep accusing of being unfriendly and you were in a senseless war against from 1947 to 1991, to tamper with US election.

AFTER CASE. Dr. William Bradford resigned from the US Department of Energy Office of Indian Energy amid reports he had made racial slurs directed at Barack Obama. Bradford had claimed that some comments resulted from identity theft and not his.

AFTER CASE. Roy Moore has no intention of quitting his 2017 race for U.S. Senate in Alabama despite a swirling scandal involving accusations. He assaulted a 14-year-old and pursued teenage girls when he was in his 30s. Moore's senior campaign adviser Brett Doster said: "No. Nothing is getting him out. He's not going anywhere."

A former prosecutor who worked in Alabama with GOP Senate nominee Roy Moore in the early 1980s told CNN on Saturday that it was common knowledge that Moore dated teenagers, and people thought it was weird. "It was common knowledge that Roy dated high school girls. Everyone we knew thought it was weird", former Etowah County deputy district attorney Teresa Jones told CNN national correspondent Alexander Marquardt. "We wondered why someone his age would hang out at high school football games and the mall. But you really wouldn't say anything to someone like that."

Jones worked as deputy district attorney for Etowah County, Ala., from 1982 to 1985. Moore worked in the same office as deputy district attorney from 1977 to 1982.

AFTER CASE. In the wake of heated protests in St. Louis following the acquittal of the cop who murdered Anthony Lamar Smith, a self-described Christian lawmaker from Pennsylvania endorsed running over protesters who block roads. While sharing a news story about the St. Louis protests, Pennsylvania Rep. Aaron Bernstine (R) tweeted that "if anyone EVER tries to stop my car on a highway with negative intentions… I will not stop under any conditions."

In subsequent tweets, Bernstine called protesters "thugs and snowflakes" and vowed he "won't be assaulted in the name of free speech." Aaron is one of the esteemed leaders running the country, and he swore to defend the Constitution.

AFTER CASE. On 06-15-2017, rep. Eric Schleien, a family value proponent, was charged with one count of sexual assault and 2 counts of simple assault on a 16-year-old girl.

AFTER CASE. They convicted senator Ted Stevens of seven corruption charges in a trial that threatened to end the 40-year career of Alaska's political patriarch in disgrace. Despite being a convicted felon, he is not required to drop out of the race or resign from the Senate. If he wins re-election, he can continue to hold his seat because there is no rule barring felons from serving in Congress.

AFTER CASE. On 11/02/2017, the Court of Criminal appeals of Texas has upheld the death sentence imposed upon a former Justice of the Peace, Eric Williams, who was convicted of capital murder in connection to the deaths of 2 prosecutors and one of their wives. He was planning on killing 2 more.

AFTER CASE. Seattle Mayor Ed Murray announced his resignation after a fifth man, one of his cousins, came forward and accused him of sexual abuse. Four men had previously accused Murray of sexually abusing them. One, Delvonn Heckard, sued the mayor in April, saying Murray had paid him for sex when Heckard was a teen. Jeff Simpson is another man who accused Murray, who had been Simpson's foster parent in Oregon. This year, Oregon's Department of Human Services discovered old files that included a child-welfare investigator's conclusion that Murray sexually abused Simpson in the early 1980s.

Murray grew up in working-class neighborhoods in and around Seattle as one of seven children in an Irish Catholic family and became one of the state's most prominent political figures.

AFTER CASE. David Porter of the Associated Press reported on Wednesday, Sept. 6, 2017: NEWARK, N.J. U.S. Sen. Bob Menendez "sold his office for a lifestyle he couldn't afford" by accepting luxury trips and other favors from a wealthy doctor seeking political influence, a government prosecutor told jurors Wednesday during opening statements of the Democrat's corruption trial.

Menendez's attorney responded that gifts from Florida ophthalmologist Salomon Melgen, Menendez's longtime friend, didn't equate to a bribery agreement. Menendez's meetings with government officials, though they could have aided Melgen's business interests, were "what members of Congress do" and were meant to influence future policy, attorney Abbe Lowell said.

Menendez and Melgen were indicted in 2015 and face multiple fraud and bribery charges in a case that could threaten Menendez's political career and potentially alter the makeup of a deeply divided U.S. Senate if he's convicted.

During the government's opening statement, Justice Department attorney Peter Koski described Menendez pressuring government officials to help Melgen with securing visas for his foreign girlfriends and intervening in a lucrative port security contract in the Dominican Republic and a multimillion- dollar Medicare dispute.

Individually and through his company, Melgen also contributed hundreds of thousands of dollars to Menendez's legal defense fund and entities that supported his 2012 re-election, Koski said.

Many of Menendez's meetings and interactions with the officials occurred in proximity to Melgen's donations or trips by Menendez he paid for, Koski claimed. "He went to bat when Dr. Melgen asked, and Dr. Melgen asked frequently," said Koski, who discounted defense lawyers' contentions that the trips were innocent gifts between friends. "There's no friendship exception to bribery. There's no friendship exception to breaking the law."

Among the gifts prosecutors say Melgen gave Menendez were flights on Melgen's private jet, vacations at Melgen's private villa in the Dominican Republic frequented by celebrities like Beyonce and Jay Z, and a three-night stay at a luxury Paris hotel valued at nearly $5,000.

AFTER CASE. If anyone is rich enough and not yet connected to a powerful source, s/he can exercise the option of pay-for-play, just like the Clintons were peddling and getting rich off.

America's government is a "pay to play" system, and that is basically a government run by corruption and bribery. Justice is for sale to the highest bidder, foreign or domestic. Hillary lost the last election for no other reason than that her corruption was off the chart, out of control. They brought her to heel.

Frankly, the Clinton's email dossier, Trump's collusion with the Russians, it's all part of the scheme to keep the American taxpayers from pulling their pants back up. Barely 1/10 of 1% of Americans know the meaning of the word "dossier".

THE MORON CASE. Secretary of State Rex Tillerson said he has never considered leaving his position and affirmed his commitment to President Trump's agenda in a statement. An NBC report said that after the speech, Tillerson called Trump a "moron". When asked specifically if he had called the president a moron, Tillerson did not deny it, saying, "I'm not going to deal with petty stuff like that."

After Tillerson's statement, CNN said it had confirmed through its own sources the "moron" remark, and MSNBC reporter Stephanie Rule elaborated that the exact phrase Tillerson used was "fuc*ing moron."

Tillerson also said that he never wanted the job as secretary of state and didn't seek the post. "My wife told me I'm supposed to do this", said the former ExxonMobil CEO when asked why he had accepted the position as America's top diplomat.

FROM THE TOP DOWN. On 10/08/2017, Jeremy Berke wrote that president Donald Trump told Secretary of State Rex Tillerson that American businesses were being unfairly penalized by federal laws prohibiting the bribing of foreign officials. In 2012, Trump told CNBC that The Foreign Corrupt Practices Act, which bars US companies from using bribes for a competitive advantage, is a "horrible, horrible law" that stifles American businesses working abroad. It puts us at a "huge, huge disadvantage."

Trump's position took aback Tillerson, who had initially called the meeting with Trump to introduce the president to a prospective deputy. "Tillerson told Trump that America didn't need to pay bribes, that we could bring the world up to our own standards," a source with knowledge of the meeting told The New Yorker. (America only pays bribes when it's convenient and to boomerang money back to American politicians.)

Tillerson then relayed an anecdote to Trump from his time as the CEO of Exxon Mobil, when he met with a senior Yemeni official to discuss a deal. During the meeting, Yemen's oil minister reportedly handed him a business card, with the account number to a Swiss bank account written on the back. "5 million dollars", the Yemeni official reportedly told him. "I don't do that, Exxon doesn't do that", Tillerson responded. Tillerson told the Yemenis that they'd have to play the deal by the book if they wanted Exxon's business. A month later, they agreed.

Abolishing federal laws barring foreign bribes has been a pet issue for Trump, whose family real estate company has been involved in deals around the globe. In February 2017, the Trump's administration killed a rule that forces energy companies listed on the US stock exchanges to disclose their payments to foreign officials. Congress got rid of the rule.

THE REASON FOR THE SEASONED. There can be no change in Congress, because the old farts trained the new members through a meticulous initiation process. The principal theme is "to play by the established rules if you want any of your pork projects to even be looked at or considered."

We have moved from people-loving Pharaohs who ruled from divine power and intercession to money-loving leaders who use bribe, force, threat, and intimidation. Much like going from Spirituality, to the ogre of the Old Testament. Ethics and the rule of law can always take a back seat to a free vacation in Colorado.

LEGISLATORS. Members of Congress make and amend the laws, which means they decide what is legal and when. Why is it so hard, then, to discern the intricacies of the seriously legalized institutional corruption in the US Congress, in the form of bribery, extortion, cronyism, nepotism, parochialism, patronage, influence peddling, graft, and embezzlement? Why is it so hard to prosecute anyone in Congress? Sometimes, government officials deliberately use ambiguous language that makes it difficult to distinguish between legal and illegal actions.

The greed of many members of Congress placed them on the payroll of lobbyists who have interests that conflict with the primary purpose of the institution. Most of the lobbyists are former members of Congress themselves or their close pals.

An example of the influence of lobbyists over Congress is the vitamin industry, which is still unregulated. Companies are totally free to put anything they desire in supplements they label vitamins. Anything from inert and useless compounds to harmful and deadly ones. Free from any kind of regulation, something that was secured by bribes from very generous lobbyists, the vitamin industry, in total disregard for public safety, is dumping billion of dollars worth of countless toxic products on the market for the gullible masses to ingest. All that is needed is a disclaimer in small print that warns: "the Food and Drug Administration" has not evaluated these statements."

Another example is the tolerated legal corruption of lobbyists affecting political campaigns with contributions from wealthy donors and big corporations, to get tax cuts, subsidies, enact special laws and have unlimited access to legislators. Companies, corporations are writing or influencing the laws of the land.

Meanwhile, Congress people are more interested in publicizing their feats when they should attend to the need of the people. How can Congress side with the people they are supposed to represent when they take their orders from lobbyists? Most people are living from paycheck to paycheck; for many, hope is just a daily horizon.

SHUFFLE BOARD. Too many cooks in the kitchen spoil the broth, too many crooks in government ruin the world. They processed every foreign aid in a way to boomerang money back to the original senders. One may wonder if a war is not a created opportunity to divert money. Creating chaos and shuffling funds around, guarantee that no one can trace and find any sizeable sum of missing money. This only means the Feds and their member banks are transacting money outside the law. It's basically money laundering, which is supposed to be a criminal activity.

No one has any idea how much money they diverted during the Gulf war in Iraq. Some estimate about 8.7 billions from the loot sent for reconstruction, during 2 shipments of respectively 19, then 26 billions of taxpayers' dollars. The Pentagon lost 2.3 trillions of taxpayers' money around September 10th of 2001, and it can not account for another 6.5 trillions worth of Army general fund transaction and data. We have spent 500 billions dollars in Iraq and the country still doesn't have electricity.

No one has any idea how much money they diverted to Afghanistan, even when the trail of the money is still fresh. Someone can find out where that money went. Nobody asked or answered a question. Nobody cared, except the people who got rich. The Karzai's clan and many American politicians are still smiling and spending, living high on the sweat of American taxpayers.

Corruption is evident when congress has a carte blanche to spend, back by the stupidity of taxpayers willing to pay for it. Congress doesn't abide by any set or approved budget, doesn't refrain from dipping in other budgets or mis-appropriating funds altogether.

FOOLISH SPENDER. The average American citizen is a direct reflection of his government. He blows money he doesn't have on shit he doesn't need. Then, when totally broke, he borrows from the big vault in his mind, if he wants more crap. Never mind, it gets to a point where he is just making the minimum payment that doesn't even cover the interest charges.

One can count on the goofy smile that is usually offered when an idiot claims: "I can't be broke, I still have checks." The entire world is in awe of how much time we spend shopping, eating and blowing away money we don't have. People have come to see a credit card as an integral part of their saving accounts. They inherited it from the same British system to borrow money they don't have to wage wars they couldn't afford. But this time, we are smarter, because we have figured out a way to pay a credit debt with another credit card.

It's going to take many authentic geniuses to balance the books after this generation rides into the sunset.

LEGALIZED CORRUPTION. The Supreme Court of the land ruled that corporate money is considered "free speech", which legalizes corruption. It becomes legal for corporations to put up an insane amount of money to buy favors and produce ads smearing officials who don't bow to them. When offering something of value to a government official, intending to influence what that official does, is not considered bribery, but "free speech" by the Supreme Court which is not immune to bribes itself, corruption becomes the true law of the land. Justice becomes a luxury only corporate interest can afford by pouring huge amounts of money into the bank account of candidates and judges. And we all know very well that corporations don't hand out cash to senators and judges to show their patriotism.

This new expression of free speech was verified during the candidacy of Barack Hussein Obama for president, when the NRA and AAA went all out with smear campaign ads and lies that Obama planned a ban on weapon and ammunition. They deluged voters with a barrage of ads claiming that Obama would ban handguns on his first day in office, if elected. Obama was elected, re-elected, and never proposed a ban on handguns.

UNETHICAL MOVES. Today, members of Congress may do something that their constituents can not legally do: use inside information to trade on commodities they are supposed to regulate, from trading funds, IPOs, health care stocks (even during the health care reform debates), etc... Congress has, over the years, granted lots of favors to Wall Street, and there has never been an investigation of violation of congressional rules or ethics.

When they exit Congress, former members get very lucrative lobbying jobs from the corporations they helped along the way. Forty-three percent of the 198 members, who have left Congress since 1998 and were eligible to lobby, have become registered lobbyists. They get to lobby their friends still in Congress.

YES, ANOTHER WAY. On September 28th, 2017, President Trump accepted Health and Human Services Secretary Tom Price's resignation, the White House said, ending days of presidential criticism over Price's use of private airplanes. Price "offered his resignation earlier today, and the President accepted," White House press secretary Sarah Sanders said in a brief statement. In his resignation letter, Price told Trump he regrets how "recent events have created a distraction" from the president's agenda*, including unsuccessful efforts to repeal and replace President Barack Obama's health care law. The announcement came less than two hours after Trump called Price a "very fine man," but once again expressed his irritation about how Price racked up roughly $1 million in flight costs on private and military aircraft since taking office in February. Politico first revealed that Price billed taxpayers for the more costly flights, instead of flying commercial airlines, which would be cheaper.

(Note*: this is a common excuse for a free get out of jail card. Another example of white privilege in the US.)

On Thursday, Price said he would repay the government about$52,000 of the over 1 million for his domestic travel on chartered planes. He apologized for taking the flights.

In February 2017, USA TODAY reported on two separate stock transactions by Price involving companies that would have benefited from the Patient Access to Durable Medical Equipment Act he introduced in May 2016. A week after he introduced the bill, Price purchased up to $15,000 worth of shares in Blackstone, which owns the privately held home medical equipment company Apria. Price bought and sold health care company stocks often enough as a member of Congress to warrant probes by both federal securities regulators and the House ethics committee. Between 2012 and February, Price traded shares worth more than $300,000 in about 40 health-related companies, according to a Wall Street Journal analysis. Price was on the House Ways and Means Committee's subcommittee on health, working on measures that could affect his investments.

Price is the latest high-ranking official to leave the Trump administration, joining a list that includes White House Chief of Staff Reince Priebus, senior strategist Steve Bannon, press secretary Sean Spicer, and National Security Adviser Michael Flynn. The president also dismissed FBI Director James Comey.

HEALTHCARE. Members of Congress have access to the best healthcare coverage in the world, for free. They pay nothing because the taxpayers are stupid enough to pick the tab.

Meanwhile, the average citizen is up the creek without a paddle when it comes to healthcare coverage.

WASHINGTON (AP) Millions of people who buy individual health insurance policies and get no financial help from the Affordable Care Act are bracing for another year of double-digit premium increases, and their frustration is boiling over. Some are expecting premiums for 2018 to rival a mortgage payment.

What they pay is tied to the price of coverage on the health insurance markets created by the Obama-era law, but these consumers get no protection from the law's tax credits, which cushion against rising premiums. Instead, they pay full freight and bear the brunt of market problems such as high costs and diminished competition.

On Capitol Hill, there's a chance that upcoming bipartisan hearings by Sens. Lamar Alexander, R-Tenn., and Patty Murray, D-Wash., can produce legislation offering some relief. But it depends on Republicans and Democrats working together despite a seven-year health care battle that has left raw feelings on both sides. The most exposed consumers are middle- class people who don't qualify for the law's income-based subsidies. They include early retirees, skilled tradespeople, musicians, self-employed professionals, business owners, and people whose small employer doesn't provide health insurance.

A policy, with a deductible of $6,000, costs $740 a month in premiums, and it's expected to be around $1,000 monthly, a 35 percent increase.

DIRE PROGNOSTIC. While the faith-based economy is in a tailspin, with hundreds of thousands losing their homes, millions out of work, 16 millions American children going to bed hungry every night, constituents struggling to keep a roof over their heads and food on the table, retired seniors denied a measly cost-of-living adjustment, our representatives in Congress gave themselves an automatic pay raise, every single year. Countless of insane benefits, perks and entitlements are not enough to get them to do any legislative work or keep them from siphoning money off lobbyists. Fundraising or campaigning for their next election are way more important than attending to the people's business, the job we hired them for. It is absolutely useless to think that reforms can solve the current corruption problem in Congress, not when the public is so aloof. 545 millionaires get to have fun and run the country into the ground

What makes it even more corrupt, above everything else, is that the bribes offering, money spending companies write the laws. Remember the bail-out when the banks received 700 billions dollars to redress their greed and irresponsibility, while the American taxpayer got the shaft? Remember the bail-out when the US automakers received another 700 billions dollars allowed by EESA, while the American taxpayer got the shaft? And it's all the same, down to when citizens are issued traffic tickets to enhance revenue, when raising taxes would be unpopular.

Every administration comes in with its own cabinet made up of cronies who are supposed to "take care" of a clique. All positions, at all levels of decision making, are filled to repay big donors who contributed enormous sums to the campaign of the winner. This is happening in a country where it is said to be illegal to buy a vote, yet as soon as the inaugural ceremonies are over, clowns jumped on the political trapezes to collect bribes, fill back orders and cash pledges received on the campaign trail.

ALL FOR ME. Corruption governed even the awarding of any government contracts, like all specially labeled pork projects. Those involved deemed multi layered corruption, with no accountability or oversight, so successful that they expanded the program to pollute the entire world. Here is a glaring example:

WASHINGTON (AP) Matthew Daly reported that members of Congress from both parties, on Tuesday 10/24/2017, called for an investigation into a $300 million contract awarded to a small company based in Interior Secretary Ryan Zinke's hometown of Whitefish, Montana. The Puerto Rico Electric Power Authority awarded the contract to Whitefish Energy Holdings to help crews restore transmission and distribution lines damaged or destroyed during Hurricane Maria. The "two-year-old company had just two full-time employees" when the storm hit last month, but says it is contracting with hundreds of workers for the Puerto Rico project.

RING AROUND CORRUPTION. When they exposed a corrupt act in public, all it takes is for one hand-picked fall guy to step forward and say: I take full responsibility for... (fill in the blanks). That's it. No indictment, no trial, no probation, no jail time. This process assures that the system can freely move on to the next scheme.

When corruption is rampant at all levels, the scales of justice are no longer on the level. When justice is kept behind closed doors, with armed guards in front of them, the people prevented from and/or denied access to justice. When people are abused, desperate, and out of options, they take the easiest road to a reprieve, including killing themselves or others. That's why we find so many instances of violence in the American society. Not a week goes by without someone, somewhere, flying off the handle and sending innocent victims 6' underground.

Others contribute another way to an already decaying society. It may be hard for many to believe that drug dealers don't wake up one day to become the stellar and beloved pillars of the community they operate in, out of pure luck; they work their way up inside a corrupt system with the help and protection of the elected "defenders" of said community.

Every day, news in the US are very telling of a society in decay, of corruption going amuck, of racism becoming more and more virulent. That's why most Americans are hoping for a third World War to end it all, out of hopelessness, the last act of a desperate people.

TRICKLE DOWN CORRUPTION. The most potent effect of corruption is the dumbing down of the people living in fear of the elected rulers. Anything is used to foster the hatred that can distract the populace. The old national pastime, called racism, has been reinforced for Americans to trash each other, yet the supremacist bullies can't even notice how much they too are being screwed.

Natural rights which come with birth are being sold, every day, in offices by clerks of the government. One has to go to a government agency and purchase his natural right to hunt, fish, and exist. Many Americans just take the chance to hunt and fish without a license and hope they don't get caught. So we have a populace which is not allowed to freely feed itself. And that's not all.

PERSONAL EXPERIENCE. The last time I went to the Department of Motor Vehicles in 2016, to renew my license, I was asked if I wanted to be an organ donor. My answer was a resounding no. I told the lady that I wanted to go out with all the parts I came in with. In total disregard for my wish, she forced me to be an organ donor, overriding my personal decision not to be an organ donor. When I came back home, I instructed my son to sue the pants off them, if they removed anything from my carcass, after I die.

RACIST INBRED. Another pastime is to viciously trash and denigrate people receiving government help. In the US, there are countless of idiots ready to bash the unemployed at a moment's notice. And Americans are so stupid that the morons just assume that Negroes are. Americans will argue vehemently that there is not one white person on welfare or public assistance. Once again, blacks are perceived as welfare recipients, but not the plantation owners who sat on the porch indulging in moonshine and opium, while the Negroes did all the work during slavery.

The unemployed are not responsible for job creation; 545 leaders are. It is because of the poor performance of the elected officials that one stops being a working father, mother, brother, sister, to become a burden on the also struggling employed members of the community which resent their misfortunes.

SIGNS AFTER SIGNS. The daily desperation of the people can be seen in the many comments posted online about any subject.

The racism, bile, malice, bitterness, antipathy, hostility, meanness, venom, animosity and anger are frightening expressions of the dysfunctional mentality of the mostly white keyboard warriors. Their nasty disposition is also directed at the country as a whole; I have never seen so many unpatriotic illegal immigrants wishing and hoping for the utter failure of a stolen country they pretend to love. That is the tragedy of our American society.

# NYANKOPON VS YAHWEH & ALLAH

The stereotypes abound in many lectures and documentaries peppered with suggestive interjections, where Africa is whitely portrayed as the land of diseases and hunger, hordes of cannibals cooking human flesh in cauldrons, amazing dancers nonetheless naked savages, a third or fourth world continent with uncivilized, lazy and stupid negroes who need help to do everything. Half way across the globe, drunk shirtless white supremacists, praying to Jesus for rain, talk about Native Americans as nothing more than savage rain dancers adorned with feathery accoutrements. Once again, it requires very little effort to hate a man whom you have wronged.

Allowing and tolerating western emissaries in their midst became a curse for Africans who, to satisfy human and political ties, accepted many cunning advices from people who hated and still hate Africa.

Was there a credible exigent circumstance for the white man in Africa? What gave the white man the presumption that he has a natural right to enter a black country, dominate the people, take their land, and compel them in some way to labor for his benefit?

The black man's wants and needs are few and simple: to take care of himself and his own. One of the western world order demands on the black man is that, besides his family, he has to produce more to satisfy the starving European, who doesn't want or know how to grow crops. So the system is forcing the black man to become a hired servant of the white man. In doing so, Eurabians, in their determined haste to get rich, are still so blind to the wellbeing of others that they don't shy away from adopting methods that are barely distinguishable from slavery. Booker Washington said: "There is all the difference in the world between working and being worked."

Someone said "The white men, at one time, robbed Africa of Africans, now they rob Africans of Africa". That's when they were not introducing diseases like sleeping sickness, influenza, syphilis, tuberculosis that would be blamed later on the lack of hygiene of blacks. How quickly or selectively the Aryans forgot who taught them about soap and water. One day, Eurabians will learn that the same way they erased the accomplishments of others, the same way their fake memories will be erased.

TIMELINE. 32 trillions years ago, Africa became the home of the first humans. They were black. Around 24000 BCE, it is said that Caspian type white men invaded the continent from the North and displaced the Negroes of the Nile Valley. They kicked out the invaders and life returned to normal, with a greatly flourishing commerce in Uganda, Tanzania and Ethiopia, which went 3000 years without a major war. Then a great famine caused a migration from Western Asia to Africa. Information about the black country was first obtained by the starving members of the Ibarus people who have been the guests of Egypt, from 1680 BCE until their second expulsion in 1280 BCE, for treason.

Mark Twain said: "If you pick up a starving dog and make him prosperous, he will not bite you". The above quote remains the principal difference between a dog and Zionist. The Abes didn't even wait to finish the free meal given to them by Africa, that they had already turned against their benefactors. Supported by their Rothschild god, the Zionists accumulated immense wealth with money laundering, financing terrorism all over the world.

That's one of the many reasons they were expelled from every single country in the world and why Hitler paid them back in kind.

There were no Israelite, Jew or Hebrew before 1280 BCE, in history. In 70 BCE, after the Romans destroyed the last Hebrew temple, many of self-proclaimed Jews- Israelites- Hebrews moved back to West Africa and stayed until 770 AD. An important event happened in 325 AD, with the council of Nicaea that gave a tremendous boost to Judaism and its extensions. Then, the Western Roman empire collapsed in 476 AD, took down Christianity with it and created a vacuum for Islam to rise.

The rape of Africa started in 550 AD, when Jews and Arab Muslims went into business together. Judaism and Arabism are the two racist movements at the very beginning of the enslavement and destruction of Africa. They started it, profited from it and are still at it today in 2017. On their way to steal, pillage, loot and burn foreign lands, the thieves switched the principal export of Africa, from crops to black men, women and children.

Within 10 years of Muhammad's death, in 640 AD, his followers invaded Egypt. It made the ease of the Islamic invasion of Africa possible because the Muslims were of the same skin color as the Africans. The lure of Islam remained in the false belief that Muslims give negroes a better level of equality than the white man who suffered many setbacks, because every black murdered by a Jew was a reset of race relation and a fostering of mistrust, coupled with the opening of old wounds. 20 years later, Islam had reached the Atlantic ocean, with Ukba Ben Nafa. By 708 AD, Islamic forces had completely invaded and taken control of North Africa. Egypt had become a white man's country. Islam has colonized Africa by means of violent conquest, pacific propaganda, commercial influence and inter marriage; in the end, Islam has destroyed Africa.

Europa saw the dark ages, along with the consolidation and extension of slavery in all its cruelty and racism. Arab Muslims went to a level of cold-blooded barbarism and violent savageries against negroes that only the French could duplicate and even surpass after 1517.

In 1415 Portugal joined the club, by capturing Ceuta.

FAKE HISTORY. A perfect example of the ignorance and down right cunning stupidity of white Americans can be observed on Columbus day, with the exhibition of the European utopia, honoring a dead white supremacist who was NOT a navigator, nor an explorer, but just a genocidal murderer who hitched a ride aboard the ships of the black Pinzon brothers. (More about that later)

PARTNERSHIP. The year 1776 was a historical date that saw the birth of a nation, as America became the extended military arm of Britain in the slavery and world domination business. They lay the foundation for the secret society called Illuminati and the American Eugenics movement. It was the beginning of the new world order as we know it, when desperate, armed and corrupt idiots joined forces with very rich idiots to take over control of the world. They usurped the political power from the various governments and instituted their own rules. Nothing was beyond the stupidity of these unusually enlightened and lit morons, who distinguished themselves with everything from ignorant legislations, statements, Roc sign, deadly schemes, all-seeing eye, Free Masonry, primitive symbols, compass and squares, serpents, the sun, even a Monarch butterfly was netted. From eternal flame, pentagram, inverted pentagram, goat head, order of the Eastern Star, 666, monster drink, skull, obelisk, to the Google Chrome logo, nothing was too outlandish for these geniuses to show their newly found power... not even the grave of Jehovah's witness founder Charles Taze Russell in the shape of a pyramid. They flexed their destructive power on all and bragged about becoming the new masters of the world.

"Who knows himself a braggart, let him fear this, for it will come to pass that every braggart shall be found an ass." (William Shakespeare.)

With that, corruption in the Anglo-American states attained the status of structural calamity. Like a stage 4 cancer, it spread at all levels, and in every nook and cranny of the world with many secondary cancers. From 1517 to 1791 slavery became a successful white international enterprise, as the depopulation and destabilization of Africa continued with all able-bodied Africans marked and condemned to certain death by the European world.

The American Civil War (1861-1865) was a bigger version of the Hatfield-McCoy feud, fought between 2 inbred factions over the right to marry their sisters and cousins.

PEPE LE PEW. The French were so stupid in the way they implemented slavery and abused negroes they destroyed their own venture. Africa was the goose that laid the golden eggs. The feeble-minded French killed it, plucked it, cut it up and cooked it. Now they are reeling with indigestion, and the idiots are still blaming the goose.

Payback knocked on the French front door with a pretty nasty butt whooping from Haiti between August 14th, 1791 and November 18th, 1803. By January 1st, 1804, France was knocked back in a permanent stupor as they could see its soldiers in their true colors, as French poodles which were trained to heel. Fortunately, all the pimps and Johns "de la putain francaise" were also present, to experience and share in what happens when abused black men get pissed off. When we are good, we are very good; when we are bad, we are even better.

Beaten and demoralized, France still launched a new venture in 1830, and sacrificed 150,000 men to impose colonial ruling on Africa. By 1854, France conquered Senegal, on the way to stealing the largest share of land in North Africa. And that's not their crowning achievement.

The French, no strangers to imbecility, armed and trained the Muslims to invade Africa. The Muzzies also received support from the British government, which did so as a "means of preserving order." Lo-and-behold, today, France and Britain are now facing the consequences of their ignorant actions, as their city streets echo the long cry: Allah-u Akbar. Ash hadu al-la-ilaha ill-Allah.

BLUE NOSES. On December 4th, 1857 missionary David Livingstone made his famous speech, when he announced in Britain: "Africa is now open, do not let it be shut again. I go back to Africa to try to make an open path for commerce and Christianity. Carry the work which I have begun." They shared this lethal approach with a dying British empire in dire need of raw materials to support a fledging and dying economy. In 1870, Cecil Rhodes started making money from the sale of African diamonds. But it wasn't until 1874 that Henry M. Stanley started the pillage of and scramble for Africa. Britain, which had no previous intention of African conquest, joined the frenzy, and invaded Sierra Leone, Gambia and the Port of Lagos. Following in the footsteps of the Muslim rapists, Britain sodomized Africa with God, gun, and greed. In 1876, Africa suffered more European invasions from Spain (Fernando Po) and Italy.

1876 was another atrocious and dire year for the country of Africa, just like 550 AD and 1517. Never in the planet's history has a country suffered so much and lost so many of her children to pure, unadulterated hatred and racism. No other nation in the world had to deal with the disgraceful fate that was heaped on Africa, which was plundered, pillaged, looted, invaded, bombed, enslaved, colonized, with everything stolen from the national resources to the bones of the dead.

HOAX-LOCAUST. Whenever the word "holocaust" is

mentioned, people immediately think of the well publicized Hollywood event during which the Nazi regime allegedly killed 1.5 to 2 millions people, some of Jewish persuasion. The Holocaust was more than a Jewish event. We should always remember Salomon Morel and Abraham Gancwajch when talking about the holocaust.

The Nazi regime found its ideal in the US. Emulating the leaders and the "master race" agenda of the American Eugenics Movement, the Nazis deliberately killed all people who were deemed undesirable to the Nazi vision of an Aryan world (Negative Eugenics). Records kept by the Germans prove they exterminated: blacks (especially Afro-German Mischlinge aka Rhineland bastards), minorities not considered Aryan, leftists, communists, Russians, Czechs, Greeks, Gypsies, Belgians, Dutch, Italians, homosexuals, Aktion T4, Jehovah's Witnesses, Serbs, mentally and physically handicapped, Poles, resistance fighters, Russians POWs and civilians, Socialists, Spanish Republicans, trade unionists, Ukrainians, clergy, Yugoslavians, prisoners of war of many nations, Boy and Girl Scouts, Buddhists, Muslims, Freemasons, communists, deportees, political prisoners, and still others whose identity may never be known. The victims, according to one survivor of four different concentration camps, were of some thirty nationalities. So why is it just a Jewish fiesta?

Karen Silverstrim, MA candidate at the University of Central Arkansas, wrote: "The prisoners were divided into six penal categories and given patches on their clothing for identification purposes. They assigned ordinary criminals green; political prisoners wore red; asocials (slackers, prostitutes, procurers, etc. wore black); homosexuals wore pink; conscientious objectors wore purple, and the Jewish people wore yellow. Many non-Jewish victims also died in concentration camps by gassing, lethal experiments, relocations, starvation, street executions, overwork, or beatings. A greater number perished because of the aggressive tactics of the Nazis in rounding up their victims and in street assassinations."

Just the same as the American Eugenics movement*, the Nazis promoted xenophobia and racism against all non-Aryan groups. Black sub-Saharan or North African residents of Germany and their offspring of German mothers were also victims of Nazi racial policy. In Mein Kampf, Hitler described the children of marriages to African occupation troops as a contamination of the white race "by Negro blood on the Rhine in the heart of Europe" who were "bastardising the European continent at its core". According to Hitler, "Jews brought negroes into the Rhineland, with the ultimate idea of bastardizing the white race which they hate and thus lowering its cultural and political level so that the Jew might dominate". Hitler's racist conviction toward blacks was borrowed and lifted directly from the annals of the American Eugenics Movement*. During the last elections in Israel, Benzion Mileikowski, the butcher of the West Bank, echoed the exact same penchant that Africans were polluting the Jewish blood line, contaminating the lily white Zionist society. And Hitler is the bad guy?

(Note*: For more info on the American Eugenics Movement, please read "Deadly faith" available at Amazon.com/books)

THE MAAFA. But no one dares talk about two of the worst examples of genocide and ethnic cleansing in history, which took place in Africa. The first started in 550 AD with the slave trade and is ongoing; the other happened in the Congo state. While slavery is well documented and kept in the dark closet of history, an equally repulsive event is on the shelf right next to slavery.

In 1878, Henry Stanley met Dr Livingstone in the Congo. What were they doing there? They were spies working for the benevolent King Leopold II of Belgium. In 1885, the genocide started as the ruthless King Leopold II of Belgium allied with Arab slave trader Tippu Tip, to decimate the Congo. In his quest to get gold, ivory, diamonds and rubber that didn't belong to him, just like any other Eurabian would, he butchered millions of Congolese people, depopulated entire villages, and used the "battue" technique in massive hunts to slaughter ivory bearing elephants to the point of extinction. As Catholic as John J. Dilulio Jr, the Belgian king, in a blood-soaked tyranny, subjected the peaceful negroes to the most vile and inhuman treatment that his Nordic greed and barbaric nature could muster. They forced blacks to meet quotas on his plantations, just like most western businesses of today, and they subjected the ones who failed to whippings and mutilations. If they deemed an underproductive worker important to the business, his wife and children would have their hands cut off instead of him. Belgium's present economic success still reeks of the blood of these Africans.

King Leopold II of Belgium founded the International African Association as a "philanthropic" organization* to spread missionary work and western culture in the Congo. In the end, the Congo became a killing ground for the deranged and racist King Leopold II of Belgium, who slaughtered 30 millions of negroes for financial gain and his own pleasure. They lined negroes up and shot, just so King Leopold II of Belgium could see how many of them his bullets could go through. They executed them just like negroes are today, in the streets of the US.

King Leopold II of Belgium is a "hush" word, never mentioned in any debate or lecture on crimes against humanity, so the western legacy can maintain the audacity and hypocrisy to trash Hitler, Pol Pot, Mao, Stalin, and Mussolini.

(Note* Isn't it strange that they still use this practice today?)

EXTRA EXTRA. Everywhere else in the world, the Europeans were on a rampage as Britain slaughtered the Aborigines of Australia; the US massacred the Native American and Philipino nations, France butchered the North Congolese,

Spain wiped out the North and Central Native Americans, Portugal decimated the Angolans and Amazonians, Germany wiped out South West Africa. It is very telling that everything of a nefarious nature in the world was and is still being done by the white European.

The western agenda is a garish, money grubbing, vulgar system which discriminates against Negroes and ignores the poor. It requires very little effort to hate a man whom you have wronged.

In South America, the Spanish and capitalists destroyed the codices, temples and archeological, ceramic works, stone sculptures from the very impressive Mayan civilization.

In 1876, 1/10 of North Africa was under European control; in 1879, the Baptist faith invaded the Congo and by 1926, 90% of Africa was under European control.

AMERICAN PRIDE. The US remains the only country which can challenge the French when it comes to the savageries displayed against blacks, with hundreds of thousands, if not millions, of graphic recorded testimonies to the demented tendencies of the American white supremacist. Everyone knows about Mary Turner in Lowndes County, in Georgia. Here is the story of another black girl in the US.

CELIA Around 1820, Robert Newsom and his family left Virginia and headed west, finally settling on land along the Middle River in southern Callaway County, Missouri. By 1850 (according to the census), Newsom owned 800 acres of land and livestock, that included horses, milk cows, beef cattle, hogs, sheep, and two oxen. Like most Callaway County farmers, Newsom also owned slaves.

Celia was a slave, probably born around 1836 in Missouri. She was bought, during the summer of 1850, from a slave owner in neighboring Audrain County, by widower Robert Newsom, at age

14 to help his daughters do chores. Shortly after returning with Celia to his farm, Newsom raped her. For female slaves, rape was an "ever present threat" and, far too often, a reality.

We know Mr. Newsom took sexual liberties with Celia from almost the moment of sale. She had two children by Newsom, both of whom became the property of Mr. Newsom. Once back at his farm, Newsom put Celia in a cabin in a grove of fruit trees approximately 150 feet from his own home. While there, Celia began a relationship with a slave named George, unknown to the master. When Celia became pregnant, George said he would quit seeing her if she continued with Newsom. Celia tried having Newsom's daughters help her, saying she was not feeling well because of the pregnancy, however there is no record that would show they did. Celia then pleaded with the master herself, to no avail.

On the evening of June 23, 1855, the massa "visited" Celia. For the now nineteen-year-old slave, five years of being repeatedly raped by her middle-aged owner was enough. She killed him with blows to the head. She then burned his corpse in her fireplace, ground the smaller bones into pieces with a rock and hid the larger ones under the hearth and under the floor.

Initially, Celia denies involvement, but later confesses, which led to her demise. She also delivered her baby, stillborn, while in custody. The murder trial of the slave Celia, coming when the controversy over the issue of slavery reached new heights, raised fundamental questions about the rights of slaves to fight back against the worst of slavery's abuses.

The decision: After concluding arguments, Celia's attorney requested many instructions that would have allowed Celia to be acquitted if the jury found from evidence that she had killed Newsom to protect herself from his advances. After all, Missouri Statute of 1845, section 29, made it a crime for a man to "take any woman unlawfully against her will and by force..." The prosecution objected to these instructions and the judge refused to let the jury consider the statute because a "negro woman was not a woman." They sentenced Celia to death by hanging on November 16. They denied her a stay of execution.

A "negro woman was not a woman!" Nothing has changed.

PREMEDITATION. Like the New Testament, the new world order support everything that was done in the old world order. The white people knew that kidnapping was against natural laws, yet they still did it. They knew stealing was against natural laws, yet they still did it. They knew cannibalism was against natural laws, yet they still did it. They knew murder was against natural laws, yet they still did it. They knew rape was against natural laws, yet they still did it. They knew robbery was against natural laws, yet they still did it. They knew assault was against natural laws, yet they still did it. They knew drug dealing was against natural laws, yet they still did it. They knew burglary was against natural laws, yet they still did it. They knew racism was against natural laws, yet they still did it. They knew slavery was against natural laws, yet they still did it. They knew castrating black kids was against natural laws, yet they still did it. They knew lynching was against natural laws, yet they still did it. They knew arson was against natural laws, yet they still did it. They knew pillage was against natural laws, yet they still did it. They knew raiding other occupied lands was against natural laws, yet they still did it. They knew invading other people's land was against natural laws, yet they still did it. They knew genocide was against natural laws, yet they still did it. They knew grave robbery was against natural laws, yet they still did it. They knew infecting blacks with diseases was against natural laws, yet they still did it. They knew looting was against natural laws, yet they still did it. They knew using black babies as gator bait was against natural laws, yet they still did it. They knew corruption was against natural laws, yet they still did it. They did it and are still doing it.

They learned and did all that, by going against anything black, when the correct message was included in the loot they stole from Egypt, along with the bones of dead Negroes.

History will not absolve the white race, it will forget it.

VATICAN. Religion was used to mask the greed and thieving nature of the leaders of the Catholic cult. 99% of the assets of the Catholic church were stolen from black people and countries, and the remaining 1% was gained through hellish threats and trickery. The Vatican is a place where thieves go to prey.

To this day in 2017, near the porta di S. Anna, in via di porta angelica (Rione of Borgo), the Sedes Sacrorum (the Holy scrotum) has over 76 miles of stolen black artifacts and documents which are not available to or accessible by blacks. No Negro in the world may view the mementos of his history, no Negro in the world may look at or research his past, no Negro in the world may learn about his true traditions and customs, no Negro in the world may access the writing of his dead parents, no Negro in the world is allowed to bring flowers to the graves of his ancestors, because a pedophile laden cult is standing in the way. Negroes can forget about their black inheritance, because a gang of white supremacist child molesters have forbidden the presence of any dark-skin near the familial inheritance. The holy pedophiles rampaged through the black villages and swiped everything, from rituals they still don't understand, gold sarcophagi to the bones of dead Negroes. And the western world provides punishment for grave robbers?

It is primarily because of greed and racism, not religion, that the Catholic church kept sending white missionaries to Africa, especially the Niger, in 1894; knowing they would die within 2 years of their deployment, at most. Even the idiotic arrogance of Sierra Leone's bishop, John Bowen, couldn't save him from his fate.

John Newton, author of "How sweet the name of Jesus sounds," actively engaged in the slave trade in Guinea and elsewhere in Africa. The bible still condones slavery, today, in 2017.

Christianity found many arguments for slavery, through outlandish papal bulls, to just plain bull. History has painstakingly documented the intense involvement of papal buzzards in the destruction of anything black. On this entire planet, every inch of ground reeks of the blood, sweat and tears that the Catholic church yanked out of the bodies of black men, women and children.

REALITY IGNORED. They systematically did the degradation of Africa despite different views. Sir Gordon Guggisberg believed the European has not and will never have an actual home in West Africa. Edwin W. Smith, in the Golden stool, asked, "Can Europeans live in tropical Africa, in the neighborhood of black people of a much lower standard of civilization?"

The same Edwin W. Smith used a very colorful language to describe Africa, post-invasion: "Here you may see half-naked savages from the Equitorial forest mingling with more civilized Africans who ape* the Europeans in their dress." But try as he may, he couldn't escape reality. When he wrote "mentally, morally, and physically, many of the blacks are far superior to many of the degenerate whites." Professor Gregory predicted: "the ultimate supremacy of the negro over most of the African continent appears inevitable." For Europeans, Africa remained a continent, but for Africans, it will always remain Alkebulan, our pride, our country, our home, our motherland.

(Note*: Once again, a white supremacist used a selective and suggestive word to describe blacks, regardless of the fact that there is not one single ape with wooly nappy hair, thick lips and round butt.)

WAR HELP. Britain and the Allies won the war against

Germany, only because of the help they received from Africa. The Africans' labor in the mines of Katanga supplied the western powers with hundreds of thousands of tons of copper, while they reduced the Germans to melting pots and pans from their kitchens to get the metal needed for ammunitions. Manganese from the Gold Coast Colony contributed to the efficiency of the airplanes used in and after the war.

WORLD DOMINATION. What the demented hallucinating new word order freaks can not understand is: how likely is the utopia of world domination when the United British States of America will have to defeat Russia, China, Japan, India, Pakistan and other military powers to get there? It doesn't look like any of these countries will lay down and accept to be dominated by the US. Like the Roman empire, Britain will eventually be forced to accept its collective ignorance and realize that it cut its own nose to spike its face. The vast American land was stolen because Britain didn't have enough space to produce the raw materials, and they needed crops to feed the growing British populace within its borders. No import of food would lead to starvation. The effort to steal America was a waste of resources and lives. It would have made better sense to let the British empire follow in the footsteps of the Romans.

And what a waste! To steal a beautiful land, and butcher the legal residents, only to turn a paradise into a giant shopping mall.

Blacks should not be required to die in order for the confederate Aryan skinheads to live their lily white chosen lifestyle. People will die at any time of the day or night. What's repulsive is the senseless taking of black lives. The time has come for eurabians to rectify the parasitic colonial relationship they have with African people, by returning or paying for all the stolen resources they have benefited from for thousands of years, at the expense of African people.

What has Africa benefited from? Nothing. After all the European conquest, invasions, colonialism and now imperialism, there is still a need for simple, basic drinking water in Africa. One can inhale the poverty imposed on Africans. If managed properly by the African people, Alkebulan would have remained the richest country in the world. There is still time.

KISKEYA. In the Caribbean, there is a little black county which is suffering the same fate as the Motherland. Even as the western world tries to hide its shameful history and genocidal agenda, there are many things that a European can never understand about Ayiti.

- How to spell or correctly use a Kreyol word.

- In less than 20 years, they slaughtered 19 millions of Bohio's Tainos so Christians could steal their gold while carrying a bible that commands: Thou shalt not steal, and thou shalt not kill.

The January 1804 spring clean-up by Jean-Jacques Dessalines was not a senseless extermination of the whites on the island. It was just payback in kind, an expression of his distaste and repugnance for the atrocities perpetrated on his people.

Dessalines showed an amazingly compassionate restraint in executing the white terrorists, which lasted only 3 months, between early February 1804 until April 22nd, 1804 compared to 274 years and counting of white supremacists killing his people.

Every single day, since 550 AD, Negroes have been abused, kidnapped, uprooted from Ethiopia (Africa), with families split and sold on different markets, treated like animals, murdered, branded, raped, beaten, humiliated, tortured. Slaves could not talk, answer questions or even look at their racist white masters. Punishments included but were not limited to: burned alive, stuffed with gunpowder and lit, ground in machines, buried to their necks next to ant mounds, nailed to boards, devoured by specially trained dogs, babies were buried so their heads would be kicked off like footballs, etc...

One could hardly expect the slaves of Haiti to embrace and kiss the racist French maggots after the war of Independence. Two thousands years of humiliation, abuse and deprivation cannot be expected to find a voice in a whisper.

Today, every murdered black is like a cold beer added to the tab, that white supremacists will have to pay before leaving the bar. Just when you thought you were the alpha male, the black bartender will come to collect his money. No excuse will be accepted and you will pay for the products that you consumed, or go to jail for obtaining food and lodging with the intent to defraud.

- Jean-Jacques Dessalines was not a pitiless barbarian like the slave owners, he was just a great humanitarian who followed the Christian God's command in Exodus 21:23 And if any mischief follow, then thou shalt give life for life, 24 Eye for eye, tooth for tooth, hand for hand, foot for foot, 25 Burning for burning, wound for wound, stripe for stripe.

Why was the above biblical precept good enough for white terrorists and not black freedom fighters?

- Yes, you can take it to the bank. On November 18th, 1803, Haiti beat the daylights out of all the combined western powers of the time. And they had it coming.

- Yes, the slaves of Haiti turned Napoleon's lily white utopia of world domination into a black reality.

- Yes, the slaves of Haiti put a stop to Thomas Jefferson's ideology of annihilation of the black government.

- The spark for the Haitian revolution didn't originate at the

French revolution, but on the coasts of Africa with the kidnapping of Negroes since 550 AD. Haitian slaves never gave up their dream of freedom or their love for Alkebulan, the Motherland.

- All the tumult and conflicts in Haiti, from January 1st, 1804 to the present time, are the collateral consequences, the continued repercussions and after shocks of slavery. This is the creation of the western world with its 128 divisions of skin shade and ancestry.

- Dark skinned Haitians don't hate light skinned ones; like democrats and the Tea Party, they just have a difference of opinions. But it's a black thing better left alone, because whites could not understand it.

- Your look so fake, insincere, empty and phony when patronizing the many accomplishments of Francois Dominique Toussaint Breda L'Ouverture, Jean-Jacques Dessalines and Martin Luther King Jr. It is just plain pathetic. At the end of the day, you admired them so much that you froze Toussaint to death in a jail cell in France. You pumped Dessalines and Martin Luther King Jr full of bullets.

You hated us and have never been our friends.

PRESENTLY - The US is a country where scams, Ponzi and pyramid schemes are as common as a car driven down the streets, and the only solution so far remains to blame it all on black Nigeria.

- Europeans decry the infighting between the African tribes as savage encounters, as they continue to supply weapons to both sides of the created conflicts. Yet, westerners regard their bombing of the same Africans as a beautiful expression of their technology, and a great humanitarian gesture.

- The kidnapping of young Nigerian girls by the group known to the western world as Boko-Haram will never be blamed on Britain, which created the conditions for the Islamic group to form.

- Police forced Muslim women in Austria to remove their facial coverings, on a Sunday in 2017, as an anti-burqa law came into effect. A woman wearing a niqab facial veil, which only leaves the eyes uncovered, was seen being told to remove her veil by two police officers in Zell am See, a city south of Salzburg.

The so-called "burqa ban" prohibits facial coverings, including niqabs and burqas, and also places restrictions on surgical masks, ski masks and clown make-up worn in public. However, police officers may dress like ISIS militants.

White women wearing a burqa are called nuns, black women wearing a burqa are called terrorists. No word yet, if they will ask the nuns to strip.

- If Britain, US and France can claim places in Africa, there is no reason Russia can not claim Mount Everest.

- European countries remain the safest places in the world for war criminals, guilty of crimes against humanity, to live in. They are out of the reach of justice and can live without fear of being indicted, arrested, or jailed. Heck, hardened criminals run most of these nations and keep adding to their impressive genocidal records.

- Africa is still on the auction block with the old slave traders becoming the new negro killers. In an obscene and racist scheme of world depopulation, the American Eugenics Movement is slaughtering Africans who live in a country bigger than Europe, India, China and the US put together; with fewer people by size than India. Yet, many idiots continue to promote the idea that Africa has an overpopulation problem.

- The slaughter of indigenous people is ongoing as the New

York Times reported at least 10 members of an uncontacted tribe in Brazil's Amazon Basin were allegedly killed last August 2017 by illegal gold miners, according to Survival International. The organization, which advocates for indigenous rights, said the massacre included women and children and may have wiped out one-fifth of the tribe. Members of the tribe were gathering eggs along a river in the Javari Valley, in the country's remote west, when they came across the miners. The miners later boasted about the slaughter at a bar in the nearest town and even showed off a hand-carved paddle they claimed to have stolen as a trophy. Leila Silvia Burger Sotto-Maior, Funai's coordinator for uncontacted and recently contacted tribes, told the Times "They even bragged about cutting up the bodies and throwing them in the river." At least two other tribes in the region have seen their land invaded and are now surrounded by ranchers and others, Survival International reported. "The invaders are landowners, hunters, miners. Many indigenous are being killed in isolation, but we don't know the exact dates or number of deaths."

HEINZ ALFRED is the worse terrorist scum to ever soiled humanity. "Control oil and you control the world, control food and you control people" will forever remain the most bastardly demonic genocidal concept ever devised by a human maggot (my excuse to the natural maggots). The quote, which became the motto for the American Eugenics movement, came from the sewer rat, a German born Rothschild Zionist named Henry Heinz Alfred Kissinger who is responsible for many war crimes, crimes against humanity, and more deaths than Genghis Temujin Khan, Hitler, Stalin, Mao, Pol Pot, Franco and Mussolini combined.

Henry Heinz Kissinger's idiotic concept of world domination thru the control of the food supply is flawed and is bound to fail soon. The GMO agenda, from the American Eugenics Movement, was implemented to kill more negroes, using companies that can produce enough engineered food, medicine and "diplomacy". People who can not even spell agriculture and know absolutely nothing about producing crops are deciding behind a desk, while they have sidelined real farmers. It is up to par with every other western idea and schemes. The momentous efforts of the agri-business system of assisted genocides are very telling of the lack of intelligence and foresight of the self-chosen decision makers for humanity. Once again, when greed is coupled with stupidity, the only offspring possible is utter failure.

There is a better way than the moronic monopoly of concentrating crops destined for the world in the US only. Why not share the bounty with Africa and the rest of the world, instead of that selfish "all for me and none for you" attitude?

Fairness enriches both; him that gives, and him that takes.

The main injustice of the American Eugenics Movement is that it wants to eliminate people based on the lives that its own policies have negatively affected and altered (please see Deadly faith @Amazon.com/books). Their goal, instead, should be to remove the people responsible for these policies that have failed humanity and disrupted the lives of so many.

(For a more detailed account of the struggle facing the black people and nations, please see "2 burgers and a beer" @Amazon.com/books)

# AVE CAESAR

"Man's capacity for justice makes democracy possible, but man's inclination to injustice makes democracy necessary," (Reinhold Niebuhr)

Since time immemorial, humans have always respected the rights of the individual. Along with rights came responsibility which dictates certain behaviors as acceptable to a society and the ones that were prohibited. From there, the rule of law was born. It was a matter of time before the rules were changed and redefined to remove all the rights from an individual and sell them to distinct groups. In due time, after many legal maneuvers, an opportunity arose to transfer the consequences of prohibited actions, from the individual who could be indicted, to a corporation or government which became immune to prosecution. Thus, democracy, which originally meant "rule of the people", was sabotaged and became the new fake front used by a few shysters to cover their deeds. Murders and genocides became "legal" many times defined by the groups, and could therefore be recklessly conducted on behalf of the "selected and specific groups" with no fear of reprisal or prosecution.

In a real democracy, the people exercises its power by electing representatives from among themselves to form a governing body to protect the safety and well being of said people. With great power comes great responsibility. A legal constitution regulated all actions of the government, federal and accepted civil laws. We expect all citizens to benefit equally from agencies and programs created by the government they elected.

THE RED VECTOR. When the law favors the rich and powerful, then uses its illegal power to permeate different countries, a dysfunctional world ensues where people are abused and live in fear of their government or a central imperial master.

The real threat to the national security of a country is not terrorism, but an abusive greedy government riddled with corruption.

The American dream has turned into greed, inequality and racism.

Greed creates more corruption, corruption creates more greed; it's a vicious and destructive cycle. Many have succumbed to greed; it is getting harder and harder to find an honest politician, because what money can not buy, money can usually rent. When a greedy government, influenced by money from lobbyists, shows a conscious disregard for the welfare of the people and becomes willfully blind to their grievances, justice can no longer prevail or even exist. The citizenry gets screwed.

Justice is the finding of the truth. The truth can not be selective. When the road to justice is polluted, certain people rise above the law? History has seen many such tyrants and genocidal lunatics at all levels of a dysfunctional society.

There are cases after cases of madmen and women slaughtering innocent people at the altar of their delusional utopia.

There are cases after cases of people like Rush Limbaugh, pastor Zachery Tims, and other drug dealers and users, who may sell and use hard drugs when the average negro gets thrown in jail for 10, 20 years for minor possession of marijuana over 20 grams?

There are cases after cases of so-called important people who may avoid paying taxes. The Panama papers involved 300,000 corporations with 15,600 shell companies involved in illegal activities, money laundering, tax evasion, fraud, evading international sanctions. Many members of the US government and their lobbyists are on the list of the culprits. What has been done to correct and rectify the crimes? Nothing. Nobody went to jail. Any black citizen would have been subjected to wage garnishment and or jail time. Why are the rich Aryans allowed to avoid paying taxes, with offshore accounts like the Panama papers, while they throw Ms Lauryn Noelle Hill and Wesley Trent Snipes in jail?

They ignored justice in so many other ways, especially with an added dose of racism. Why does an unarmed Negro deserve the death penalty for ignoring a police officer's order to move to the sidewalk when the blue cowards backed down from the armed white people at the Cliven Bundy ranch, without firing a shot?

Cops can see invisible guns in any unarmed Negro's hand, yet are blind to armed white supremacists walking down a street in Charlottesville. (More about that later)

THE PRECEPT. There is no other instance in any business, anywhere in the world, beside American politics, where an employee, once hired, decides on the wages and benefits s/he wants, hijacks the company, makes the rules, keeps the owner out of the business, and if the owner dares question the work being done, s/he is dragged into a court by the employee or sent to jail. There will be no meeting about it, because the employee also rules that the employer, the people, should not have a say in what s/he does. To further supplement a largely undeserved income, the employee also decides that it is acceptable to take bribes and sell the already paid for services to the highest bidder, foreign or domestic. Talk about a criminal scheme and enterprise.

People don't run for public office to help anyone but themselves, and they run because the position allows them to use the office for personal gain. The real lure of a position in Congress is the rewarding side business that comes with it. From lucrative "speaking engagement", paid speeches, well-paid lobbyist positions and outright bribes, while the country and Constitution are out of sight, on the back burner. "So much money floating around, so little time to collect it" is the patriotic motto of the US Congress.

The US Congress is the only body in the entire world, which can challenge and defeat a cesspool when it comes to contents. One day, I started watching a video of Congress in session. After about 15 minutes, I realized that watching paint dry, grass grow, or molasses running uphill in the winter would be a better use of my time. The tremendously diligent and proficient work, they were doing, could only be put in perspective by looking at many of our honorable leaders who were busy picking their noses and eating the boogers, when not falling asleep in their chairs, listening to their own BS.

Not a day goes by without an incident from lawmakers who think they are above the laws they enact.

CASE. In March 2016, they arrested Kyle Tasker, a politician, and sentenced him (May 10th) to 3-10 years in prison, after he pleaded guilty to charges of drug possession and trying to lure a 14-year-old girl into a sexual encounter.

AFTER CASE. Scott Rothstein is an example of how a crooked lawyer, of Ponzi scheme fame, can enjoy the American dream with the complicity of law enforcement, mayor, governor, prosecutor, etc...

AFTER CASE. Michael T. Flynn, National Security Advisor, was forced to resign on February 13, 2017 over conversations he had with Russian envoys about sanctions during the transition, possibly violating the Logan Act.

AFTER CASE. Jeff Sessions, Attorney General, lied under oath to the Senate Judiciary Committee on January 10, 2017, stating that he "did not have communications with the Russians." On March 1, 2017, he has amended his statement to the opposite. They have not charged him with perjury, which is a felony.

Attorney General Jeff Sessions is facing calls from

lawmakers to once again appear before the Senate Judiciary Committee and answer questions on his participation in Russia's alleged interference in the US presidential election.

AFTER CASE. The Paradise papers exposed that Commerce Secretary Wilbur Ross failed to disclose ties to Vladimir Putin's son-in-law during the confirmation hearing for his Cabinet post.

AFTER CASE. A U.S. senator called for a criminal investigation of executives from credit bureau Equifax Inc. for stock sales after a massive data breach this summer and said their actions were comparable to insider trading. Senator Heidi Heitkamp is either a hypocrite or an idiot, Congress does the exact same thing.

Thinkprogress.org reported on 10/24/2017. "In the dead of night, Republicans vote to give lawsuit immunity to banks. Tuesday night, as many Americans were preparing to go to bed, an evenly divided Senate voted to give broad lawsuit immunity to credit card companies, auto lenders, credit reporting companies like Equifax, and many other financial firms. Vice President Mike Pence (R) broke the 50- 50 tie in the Senate, and the House approved the lawsuit immunity measure. We expect President Trump to sign it. The resolution passed by the Senate overrides a rule created by the Consumer Financial Protection Bureau (CFPB), which prevents many financial firms from engaging in two abusive practices."

AFTER CASE. It's 10/21/2017, and we are finally at the high point of the Mueller investigation into the Russian meddling in the last US elections. After many titillating months of innuendos, the Networks have announced that a first indictment and arrest will come on Monday 10/23/2017. Like the coverage of the hurricanes, they rounded up all the idiots available to talk about it. Speculations abound from former and retired political analysts who have no ties to the investigations in progress. The saying "no comment on any ongoing investigation" went out of the window, as morons lined up in front of the cameras to predict what the masses can not wait to hear two days later.

They don't know, have absolutely no idea who the suspect is and what the charges will be, yet are willing to talk for 2 damn days, fill the airwaves for two solid days with "no valid information."

AFTER CASE. Paul Manafort, who joined the Trump's presidential campaign in 2016, has been indicted along with Rick Gates and George Papadopoulos. On October 30th, 2017, Paul Manafort and Rick Gates surrendered to the FBI on 12 felony charges of conspiracy against the US, money laundering, failing to register as foreign agents and making false statements for actions that took place.

Arrested after he arrived at Dulles International airport, on July 27th, 2017, George Papadopoulos pleaded guilty to lying and started singing like a happy canary. The plea agreement shows he is cooperating with the investigating team of Robert Swan "Bob" Mueller III, the Special Counsel for Russia investigation.

Paul Manafort, who has been indicted and arrested on treason charges for the Russian collusion in the last US election, is requesting a bail hearing and he wants to use his Trump Tower condo as collateral for his bail. The judge replied he needs to know more about Manafort's finances before he will consider the request. And Manafort is more of a flight risk than a common pigeon in the park.

Rumor has it that next to be indicted will be Michael Thomas Flynn, Trumps's former National Security adviser, followed by Trump's son-in-law Jared Corey Kushner, the current senior adviser.

This is a perfect example of American democracy at work

and the level of respect reserved for the rule of law. Anyone who still has any doubt about the American justice system can just imagine Paul Manafort as black and poor. Would a negro be allowed to post bail after an indictment on treason charges? If you are white and rich in America, you are above the law and justice; you may do as you please. Shoot people, urge a foreign country to hack into the computers of a US political candidate, even collude with a foreign nation that you keep accusing of being unfriendly and you were in a senseless war against from 1947 to 1991, to tamper with US election.

AFTER CASE. Dr. William Bradford resigned from the US Department of Energy Office of Indian Energy amid reports he had made racial slurs directed at Barack Obama. Bradford had claimed that some comments resulted from identity theft and not his.

AFTER CASE. Roy Moore has no intention of quitting his 2017 race for U.S. Senate in Alabama despite a swirling scandal involving accusations. He assaulted a 14-year-old and pursued teenage girls when he was in his 30s. Moore's senior campaign adviser Brett Doster said: "No. Nothing is getting him out. He's not going anywhere."

A former prosecutor who worked in Alabama with GOP Senate nominee Roy Moore in the early 1980s told CNN on Saturday that it was common knowledge that Moore dated teenagers, and people thought it was weird. "It was common knowledge that Roy dated high school girls. Everyone we knew thought it was weird", former Etowah County deputy district attorney Teresa Jones told CNN national correspondent Alexander Marquardt. "We wondered why someone his age would hang out at high school football games and the mall. But you really wouldn't say anything to someone like that."

Jones worked as deputy district attorney for Etowah County, Ala., from 1982 to 1985. Moore worked in the same office as deputy district attorney from 1977 to 1982.

AFTER CASE. In the wake of heated protests in St. Louis following the acquittal of the cop who murdered Anthony Lamar Smith, a self-described Christian lawmaker from Pennsylvania endorsed running over protesters who block roads. While sharing a news story about the St. Louis protests, Pennsylvania Rep. Aaron Bernstine (R) tweeted that "if anyone EVER tries to stop my car on a highway with negative intentions… I will not stop under any conditions."

In subsequent tweets, Bernstine called protesters "thugs and snowflakes" and vowed he "won't be assaulted in the name of free speech." Aaron is one of the esteemed leaders running the country, and he swore to defend the Constitution.

AFTER CASE. On 06-15-2017, rep. Eric Schleien, a family value proponent, was charged with one count of sexual assault and 2 counts of simple assault on a 16-year-old girl.

AFTER CASE. They convicted senator Ted Stevens of seven corruption charges in a trial that threatened to end the 40-year career of Alaska's political patriarch in disgrace. Despite being a convicted felon, he is not required to drop out of the race or resign from the Senate. If he wins re-election, he can continue to hold his seat because there is no rule barring felons from serving in Congress.

AFTER CASE. On 11/02/2017, the Court of Criminal appeals of Texas has upheld the death sentence imposed upon a former Justice of the Peace, Eric Williams, who was convicted of capital murder in connection to the deaths of 2 prosecutors and one of their wives. He was planning on killing 2 more.

AFTER CASE. Seattle Mayor Ed Murray announced his resignation after a fifth man, one of his cousins, came forward and accused him of sexual abuse. Four men had previously accused Murray of sexually abusing them. One, Delvonn Heckard, sued the mayor in April, saying Murray had paid him for sex when Heckard was a teen. Jeff Simpson is another man who accused Murray, who had been Simpson's foster parent in Oregon. This year, Oregon's Department of Human Services discovered old files that included a child-welfare investigator's conclusion that Murray sexually abused Simpson in the early 1980s.

Murray grew up in working-class neighborhoods in and around Seattle as one of seven children in an Irish Catholic family and became one of the state's most prominent political figures.

AFTER CASE. David Porter of the Associated Press reported on Wednesday, Sept. 6, 2017: NEWARK, N.J. U.S. Sen. Bob Menendez "sold his office for a lifestyle he couldn't afford" by accepting luxury trips and other favors from a wealthy doctor seeking political influence, a government prosecutor told jurors Wednesday during opening statements of the Democrat's corruption trial.

Menendez's attorney responded that gifts from Florida ophthalmologist Salomon Melgen, Menendez's longtime friend, didn't equate to a bribery agreement. Menendez's meetings with government officials, though they could have aided Melgen's business interests, were "what members of Congress do" and were meant to influence future policy, attorney Abbe Lowell said.

Menendez and Melgen were indicted in 2015 and face multiple fraud and bribery charges in a case that could threaten Menendez's political career and potentially alter the makeup of a deeply divided U.S. Senate if he's convicted.

During the government's opening statement, Justice Department attorney Peter Koski described Menendez pressuring government officials to help Melgen with securing visas for his foreign girlfriends and intervening in a lucrative port security contract in the Dominican Republic and a multimillion- dollar Medicare dispute.

Individually and through his company, Melgen also contributed hundreds of thousands of dollars to Menendez's legal defense fund and entities that supported his 2012 re-election, Koski said.

Many of Menendez's meetings and interactions with the officials occurred in proximity to Melgen's donations or trips by Menendez he paid for, Koski claimed. "He went to bat when Dr. Melgen asked, and Dr. Melgen asked frequently," said Koski, who discounted defense lawyers' contentions that the trips were innocent gifts between friends. "There's no friendship exception to bribery. There's no friendship exception to breaking the law."

Among the gifts prosecutors say Melgen gave Menendez were flights on Melgen's private jet, vacations at Melgen's private villa in the Dominican Republic frequented by celebrities like Beyonce and Jay Z, and a three-night stay at a luxury Paris hotel valued at nearly $5,000.

AFTER CASE. If anyone is rich enough and not yet connected to a powerful source, s/he can exercise the option of pay-for-play, just like the Clintons were peddling and getting rich off.

America's government is a "pay to play" system, and that is basically a government run by corruption and bribery. Justice is for sale to the highest bidder, foreign or domestic. Hillary lost the last election for no other reason than that her corruption was off the chart, out of control. They brought her to heel.

Frankly, the Clinton's email dossier, Trump's collusion with the Russians, it's all part of the scheme to keep the American taxpayers from pulling their pants back up. Barely 1/10 of 1% of Americans know the meaning of the word "dossier".

THE MORON CASE. Secretary of State Rex Tillerson said he has never considered leaving his position and affirmed his commitment to President Trump's agenda in a statement. An NBC report said that after the speech, Tillerson called Trump a "moron". When asked specifically if he had called the president a moron, Tillerson did not deny it, saying, "I'm not going to deal with petty stuff like that."

After Tillerson's statement, CNN said it had confirmed through its own sources the "moron" remark, and MSNBC reporter Stephanie Rule elaborated that the exact phrase Tillerson used was "fuc*ing moron."

Tillerson also said that he never wanted the job as secretary of state and didn't seek the post. "My wife told me I'm supposed to do this", said the former ExxonMobil CEO when asked why he had accepted the position as America's top diplomat.

FROM THE TOP DOWN. On 10/08/2017, Jeremy Berke wrote that president Donald Trump told Secretary of State Rex Tillerson that American businesses were being unfairly penalized by federal laws prohibiting the bribing of foreign officials. In 2012, Trump told CNBC that The Foreign Corrupt Practices Act, which bars US companies from using bribes for a competitive advantage, is a "horrible, horrible law" that stifles American businesses working abroad. It puts us at a "huge, huge disadvantage."

Trump's position took aback Tillerson, who had initially called the meeting with Trump to introduce the president to a prospective deputy. "Tillerson told Trump that America didn't need to pay bribes, that we could bring the world up to our own standards," a source with knowledge of the meeting told The New Yorker. (America only pays bribes when it's convenient and to boomerang money back to American politicians.)

Tillerson then relayed an anecdote to Trump from his time as the CEO of Exxon Mobil, when he met with a senior Yemeni official to discuss a deal. During the meeting, Yemen's oil minister reportedly handed him a business card, with the account number to a Swiss bank account written on the back. "5 million dollars", the Yemeni official reportedly told him. "I don't do that, Exxon doesn't do that", Tillerson responded. Tillerson told the Yemenis that they'd have to play the deal by the book if they wanted Exxon's business. A month later, they agreed.

Abolishing federal laws barring foreign bribes has been a pet issue for Trump, whose family real estate company has been involved in deals around the globe. In February 2017, the Trump's administration killed a rule that forces energy companies listed on the US stock exchanges to disclose their payments to foreign officials. Congress got rid of the rule.

THE REASON FOR THE SEASONED. There can be no change in Congress, because the old farts trained the new members through a meticulous initiation process. The principal theme is "to play by the established rules if you want any of your pork projects to even be looked at or considered."

We have moved from people-loving Pharaohs who ruled from divine power and intercession to money-loving leaders who use bribe, force, threat, and intimidation. Much like going from Spirituality, to the ogre of the Old Testament. Ethics and the rule of law can always take a back seat to a free vacation in Colorado.

LEGISLATORS. Members of Congress make and amend the laws, which means they decide what is legal and when. Why is it so hard, then, to discern the intricacies of the seriously legalized institutional corruption in the US Congress, in the form of bribery, extortion, cronyism, nepotism, parochialism, patronage, influence peddling, graft, and embezzlement? Why is it so hard to prosecute anyone in Congress? Sometimes, government officials deliberately use ambiguous language that makes it difficult to distinguish between legal and illegal actions.

The greed of many members of Congress placed them on the payroll of lobbyists who have interests that conflict with the primary purpose of the institution. Most of the lobbyists are former members of Congress themselves or their close pals.

An example of the influence of lobbyists over Congress is the vitamin industry, which is still unregulated. Companies are totally free to put anything they desire in supplements they label vitamins. Anything from inert and useless compounds to harmful and deadly ones. Free from any kind of regulation, something that was secured by bribes from very generous lobbyists, the vitamin industry, in total disregard for public safety, is dumping billion of dollars worth of countless toxic products on the market for the gullible masses to ingest. All that is needed is a disclaimer in small print that warns: "the Food and Drug Administration" has not evaluated these statements."

Another example is the tolerated legal corruption of lobbyists affecting political campaigns with contributions from wealthy donors and big corporations, to get tax cuts, subsidies, enact special laws and have unlimited access to legislators. Companies, corporations are writing or influencing the laws of the land.

Meanwhile, Congress people are more interested in publicizing their feats when they should attend to the need of the people. How can Congress side with the people they are supposed to represent when they take their orders from lobbyists? Most people are living from paycheck to paycheck; for many, hope is just a daily horizon.

SHUFFLE BOARD. Too many cooks in the kitchen spoil the broth, too many crooks in government ruin the world. They processed every foreign aid in a way to boomerang money back to the original senders. One may wonder if a war is not a created opportunity to divert money. Creating chaos and shuffling funds around, guarantee that no one can trace and find any sizeable sum of missing money. This only means the Feds and their member banks are transacting money outside the law. It's basically money laundering, which is supposed to be a criminal activity.

No one has any idea how much money they diverted during the Gulf war in Iraq. Some estimate about 8.7 billions from the loot sent for reconstruction, during 2 shipments of respectively 19, then 26 billions of taxpayers' dollars. The Pentagon lost 2.3 trillions of taxpayers' money around September 10th of 2001, and it can not account for another 6.5 trillions worth of Army general fund transaction and data. We have spent 500 billions dollars in Iraq and the country still doesn't have electricity.

No one has any idea how much money they diverted to Afghanistan, even when the trail of the money is still fresh. Someone can find out where that money went. Nobody asked or answered a question. Nobody cared, except the people who got rich. The Karzai's clan and many American politicians are still smiling and spending, living high on the sweat of American taxpayers.

Corruption is evident when congress has a carte blanche to spend, back by the stupidity of taxpayers willing to pay for it. Congress doesn't abide by any set or approved budget, doesn't refrain from dipping in other budgets or mis-appropriating funds altogether.

FOOLISH SPENDER. The average American citizen is a direct reflection of his government. He blows money he doesn't have on shit he doesn't need. Then, when totally broke, he borrows from the big vault in his mind, if he wants more crap. Never mind, it gets to a point where he is just making the minimum payment that doesn't even cover the interest charges.

One can count on the goofy smile that is usually offered when an idiot claims: "I can't be broke, I still have checks." The entire world is in awe of how much time we spend shopping, eating and blowing away money we don't have. People have come to see a credit card as an integral part of their saving accounts. They inherited it from the same British system to borrow money they don't have to wage wars they couldn't afford. But this time, we are smarter, because we have figured out a way to pay a credit debt with another credit card.

It's going to take many authentic geniuses to balance the books after this generation rides into the sunset.

LEGALIZED CORRUPTION. The Supreme Court of the land ruled that corporate money is considered "free speech", which legalizes corruption. It becomes legal for corporations to put up an insane amount of money to buy favors and produce ads smearing officials who don't bow to them. When offering something of value to a government official, intending to influence what that official does, is not considered bribery, but "free speech" by the Supreme Court which is not immune to bribes itself, corruption becomes the true law of the land. Justice becomes a luxury only corporate interest can afford by pouring huge amounts of money into the bank account of candidates and judges. And we all know very well that corporations don't hand out cash to senators and judges to show their patriotism.

This new expression of free speech was verified during the candidacy of Barack Hussein Obama for president, when the NRA and AAA went all out with smear campaign ads and lies that Obama planned a ban on weapon and ammunition. They deluged voters with a barrage of ads claiming that Obama would ban handguns on his first day in office, if elected. Obama was elected, re-elected, and never proposed a ban on handguns.

UNETHICAL MOVES. Today, members of Congress may do something that their constituents can not legally do: use inside information to trade on commodities they are supposed to regulate, from trading funds, IPOs, health care stocks (even during the health care reform debates), etc... Congress has, over the years, granted lots of favors to Wall Street, and there has never been an investigation of violation of congressional rules or ethics.

When they exit Congress, former members get very lucrative lobbying jobs from the corporations they helped along the way. Forty-three percent of the 198 members, who have left Congress since 1998 and were eligible to lobby, have become registered lobbyists. They get to lobby their friends still in Congress.

YES, ANOTHER WAY. On September 28th, 2017, President Trump accepted Health and Human Services Secretary Tom Price's resignation, the White House said, ending days of presidential criticism over Price's use of private airplanes. Price "offered his resignation earlier today, and the President accepted," White House press secretary Sarah Sanders said in a brief statement. In his resignation letter, Price told Trump he regrets how "recent events have created a distraction" from the president's agenda*, including unsuccessful efforts to repeal and replace President Barack Obama's health care law. The announcement came less than two hours after Trump called Price a "very fine man," but once again expressed his irritation about how Price racked up roughly $1 million in flight costs on private and military aircraft since taking office in February. Politico first revealed that Price billed taxpayers for the more costly flights, instead of flying commercial airlines, which would be cheaper.

(Note*: this is a common excuse for a free get out of jail card. Another example of white privilege in the US.)

On Thursday, Price said he would repay the government about$52,000 of the over 1 million for his domestic travel on chartered planes. He apologized for taking the flights.

In February 2017, USA TODAY reported on two separate stock transactions by Price involving companies that would have benefited from the Patient Access to Durable Medical Equipment Act he introduced in May 2016. A week after he introduced the bill, Price purchased up to $15,000 worth of shares in Blackstone, which owns the privately held home medical equipment company Apria. Price bought and sold health care company stocks often enough as a member of Congress to warrant probes by both federal securities regulators and the House ethics committee. Between 2012 and February, Price traded shares worth more than $300,000 in about 40 health-related companies, according to a Wall Street Journal analysis. Price was on the House Ways and Means Committee's subcommittee on health, working on measures that could affect his investments.

Price is the latest high-ranking official to leave the Trump administration, joining a list that includes White House Chief of Staff Reince Priebus, senior strategist Steve Bannon, press secretary Sean Spicer, and National Security Adviser Michael Flynn. The president also dismissed FBI Director James Comey.

HEALTHCARE. Members of Congress have access to the best healthcare coverage in the world, for free. They pay nothing because the taxpayers are stupid enough to pick the tab.

Meanwhile, the average citizen is up the creek without a paddle when it comes to healthcare coverage.

WASHINGTON (AP) Millions of people who buy individual health insurance policies and get no financial help from the Affordable Care Act are bracing for another year of double-digit premium increases, and their frustration is boiling over. Some are expecting premiums for 2018 to rival a mortgage payment.

What they pay is tied to the price of coverage on the health insurance markets created by the Obama-era law, but these consumers get no protection from the law's tax credits, which cushion against rising premiums. Instead, they pay full freight and bear the brunt of market problems such as high costs and diminished competition.

On Capitol Hill, there's a chance that upcoming bipartisan hearings by Sens. Lamar Alexander, R-Tenn., and Patty Murray, D-Wash., can produce legislation offering some relief. But it depends on Republicans and Democrats working together despite a seven-year health care battle that has left raw feelings on both sides. The most exposed consumers are middle- class people who don't qualify for the law's income-based subsidies. They include early retirees, skilled tradespeople, musicians, self-employed professionals, business owners, and people whose small employer doesn't provide health insurance.

A policy, with a deductible of $6,000, costs $740 a month in premiums, and it's expected to be around $1,000 monthly, a 35 percent increase.

DIRE PROGNOSTIC. While the faith-based economy is in a tailspin, with hundreds of thousands losing their homes, millions out of work, 16 millions American children going to bed hungry every night, constituents struggling to keep a roof over their heads and food on the table, retired seniors denied a measly cost-of-living adjustment, our representatives in Congress gave themselves an automatic pay raise, every single year. Countless of insane benefits, perks and entitlements are not enough to get them to do any legislative work or keep them from siphoning money off lobbyists. Fundraising or campaigning for their next election are way more important than attending to the people's business, the job we hired them for. It is absolutely useless to think that reforms can solve the current corruption problem in Congress, not when the public is so aloof. 545 millionaires get to have fun and run the country into the ground.

What makes it even more corrupt, above everything else, is that the bribes offering, money spending companies write the laws. Remember the bail-out when the banks received 700 billions dollars to redress their greed and irresponsibility, while the American taxpayer got the shaft? Remember the bail-out when the US automakers received another 700 billions dollars allowed by EESA, while the American taxpayer got the shaft? And it's all the same, down to when citizens are issued traffic tickets to enhance revenue, when raising taxes would be unpopular.

Every administration comes in with its own cabinet made up of cronies who are supposed to "take care" of a clique. All positions, at all levels of decision making, are filled to repay big donors who contributed enormous sums to the campaign of the winner. This is happening in a country where it is said to be illegal to buy a vote, yet as soon as the inaugural ceremonies are over, clowns jumped on the political trapezes to collect bribes, fill back orders and cash pledges received on the campaign trail.

ALL FOR ME. Corruption governed even the awarding of any government contracts, like all specially labeled pork projects. Those involved deemed multi layered corruption, with no accountability or oversight, so successful that they expanded the program to pollute the entire world. Here is a glaring example:

WASHINGTON (AP) Matthew Daly reported that members of Congress from both parties, on Tuesday 10/24/2017, called for an investigation into a $300 million contract awarded to a small company based in Interior Secretary Ryan Zinke's hometown of Whitefish, Montana. The Puerto Rico Electric Power Authority awarded the contract to Whitefish Energy Holdings to help crews restore transmission and distribution lines damaged or destroyed during Hurricane Maria. The "two-year-old company had just two full-time employees" when the storm hit last month, but says it is contracting with hundreds of workers for the Puerto Rico project.

RING AROUND CORRUPTION. When they exposed a corrupt act in public, all it takes is for one hand-picked fall guy to step forward and say: I take full responsibility for... (fill in the blanks). That's it. No indictment, no trial, no probation, no jail time. This process assures that the system can freely move on to the next scheme.

When corruption is rampant at all levels, the scales of justice are no longer on the level. When justice is kept behind closed doors, with armed guards in front of them, the people prevented from and/or denied access to justice. When people are abused, desperate, and out of options, they take the easiest road to a reprieve, including killing themselves or others. That's why we find so many instances of violence in the American society. Not a week goes by without someone, somewhere, flying off the handle and sending innocent victims 6' underground.

Others contribute another way to an already decaying society. It may be hard for many to believe that drug dealers don't wake up one day to become the stellar and beloved pillars of the community they operate in, out of pure luck; they work their way up inside a corrupt system with the help and protection of the elected "defenders" of said community.

Every day, news in the US are very telling of a society in decay, of corruption going amuck, of racism becoming more and more virulent. That's why most Americans are hoping for a third World War to end it all, out of hopelessness, the last act of a desperate people.

TRICKLE DOWN CORRUPTION. The most potent effect of corruption is the dumbing down of the people living in fear of the elected rulers. Anything is used to foster the hatred that can distract the populace. The old national pastime, called racism, has been reinforced for Americans to trash each other, yet the supremacist bullies can't even notice how much they too are being screwed.

Natural rights which come with birth are being sold, every day, in offices by clerks of the government. One has to go to a government agency and purchase his natural right to hunt, fish, and exist. Many Americans just take the chance to hunt and fish without a license and hope they don't get caught. So we have a populace which is not allowed to freely feed itself. And that's not all.

PERSONAL EXPERIENCE. The last time I went to the Department of Motor Vehicles in 2016, to renew my license, I was asked if I wanted to be an organ donor. My answer was a resounding no. I told the lady that I wanted to go out with all the parts I came in with. In total disregard for my wish, she forced me to be an organ donor, overriding my personal decision not to be an organ donor. When I came back home, I instructed my son to sue the pants off them, if they removed anything from my carcass, after I die.

RACIST INBRED. Another pastime is to viciously trash and denigrate people receiving government help. In the US, there are countless of idiots ready to bash the unemployed at a moment's notice. And Americans are so stupid that the morons just assume that Negroes are. Americans will argue vehemently that there is not one white person on welfare or public assistance. Once again, blacks are perceived as welfare recipients, but not the plantation owners who sat on the porch indulging in moonshine and opium, while the Negroes did all the work during slavery.

The unemployed are not responsible for job creation; 545 leaders are. It is because of the poor performance of the elected officials that one stops being a working father, mother, brother, sister, to become a burden on the also struggling employed members of the community which resent their misfortunes.

SIGNS AFTER SIGNS. We can see the daily desperation of the people in the many comments posted online about any subject.

The racism, bile, malice, bitterness, antipathy, hostility, meanness, venom, animosity and anger are frightening expressions of the dysfunctional mentality of the mostly white keyboard warriors. They also directed their nasty disposition at the country; I have never seen so many unpatriotic illegal immigrants wishing and hoping for the utter failure of a stolen country they pretend to love. That is the tragedy of our American society.

Meanwhile, politicians have gone from the public adoration for JFK to the abject rejection of Jason Chaffetz who is throwing in the towel. The saying goes: if you can't stand the heat, get out of the kitchen. Called a coward and told to do his job by his constituents, Jason Chaffetz removed his political apron. He will make plenty of money as an analyst on TV or will open his own "consulting" business. When one is in over his head and responsibility becomes a burden, there is one choice left and it's renouncing power and flee.

Lately, the ire of the masses was clearly evident at several town hall meetings between senators and their angry constituents. Public officials like Tim Bishop, Allen Boyd, Thomas Perriello, Bruce Braley, Dan Maffei, Bill Cassidy, Jim Sessions, Tom McClintock, Darrell Issa, Duncan Hunter, Susan Davis, Scott Peters, Marsha Blackburn, Dennis A. Ross, Charles E. Grassley, Diane Black among others, all got an earful.

The media scrambled to report on many screaming citizens, signs carrying mobs, protesters dragged out by the cops, and congress people fearful for their safety. It got so bad that a few law makers needed police protection to get to their cars in the parking lot and are now afraid to hold any more houses of horrors meetings. Many old gizzards tried in vain to out-talk and yell at angry constituents before asking for their removal. There is no doubt that many legislators will continue to have town hall meetings, ignoring the fact that if at first you don't succeed, skydiving is not for you.

While they always give the white protesters free air time to voice their displeasure, the black protesters are just shut down and relegated to a few comments by a Zionist influenced media always willing to use name-calling. White illiterate commentators do the talking for all black protests.

Unfortunately, the exasperation may reach a boiling point, sometimes. On June 14th, 2017, a white gunman opened fire at a GOP baseball practice, wounding 5 people including house majority whip Steve Scalise and 2 police officers. No media outlet or internet warrior called him a homegrown terrorist, SOB, POS, thug or even criminal. A white man shot 2 cops and a politician, yet the cops are still slaughtering unarmed Negroes. It requires very little effort to hate a man whom you have wronged.

The vice president of the US came up with a brilliant solution when he asked the nation for prayers, ignoring the fact that if Jesus was awake, watching and cared, the whole shooting incident would have been prevented. Jesus was on the side of the shooter.

MATRIX OF FORCE. This state of affairs forced the scared and fearful legislators to ask for additional security, a wider "blue" line between them and their constituents. In response to earlier demand and consideration, we can observe an alarming trend where armed groups, under the label of law enforcement, have been requesting more sophisticated weapons of war to deal with a civilian population... sophisticated weapons of mass destruction, paid for by the taxpayers that these legal gangs are arming themselves against. A collateral damage which occurred when many vital decisions were taken away from the people by their representatives, in violation of the Constitution.

Imagine the impact of such military weapons, taking part in the 1921 Tulsa race riot, when police flew airplanes and dropped nitroglycerin and dynamite on 600 black businesses, burned 1500 houses and destroyed a 35 square blocks area of the black community of Tulsa, also known as the Greenwood district, or the black Wall Street. The same police force, which is executing negroes in broad daylight in the streets of the US today, has received enough weapons of war to fill 185 pages.

From a Beretta M9, Heckler & Koch MP5A3, FGM-148 Javelin, M83 smoke grenade, the local cops have access to tanks and all-terrain vehicles to patrol the paved streets of the US, military aircrafts, grenade launchers, heavily armed tactical vehicles, all in all, 4.3 billion dollars worth of weapons of mass destruction.

Except for the ones with past military experience, the average cop has no training on the equipment, or guidance, relying instead on what they taught themselves playing in the woods with fellow Klansmen, pretending to hunt Negroes.

CCJST. Let's take a closer look at law enforcement. As they enacted many laws to incarcerate more blacks, the demand for correctional and police officers increased. After spending $600 plus supplies, many sponsored recruits grabbed their GED and headed to the local community colleges to get a meager introduction to crime fighting from the Commission on Criminal Justice Standards and Training. Upon graduation four months later, after the review board interviews, a few recruits found out that the promised jobs were not full time or available to people without a political connection and specific ideological affiliation.

The silver lining came with the realization that many civilian jobs, paying double the LEO's starting salary, were available. Still, many graduates forwent the money for the uniform and perceived power.

A GUN AND A BADGE. Police departments and the Armed Forces are the only true buffer between politicians and constituents, between law-abiding citizens and criminals. That doesn't always work. We entrust them to enforce the biased laws of the land, and people believe the nonsense that they are here to protect and serve the public.

Do banks serve the public and interest of customers when they pay .02% interest on the money you deposit and charge you 25% interest on a credit card purchase?

We already know that cops don't deter or prevent crimes, because we still have plenty of crimes happening every day, and sometimes the police persons are the perpetrators of crimes like murder, extortion, execution, rape, theft, free use of drugs from evidence lockers. The only true service they provide is criminal record keeping and recording; that's why they usually show up after a crime, to document it. And that function is enough to warrant special benefits, which may be construed as corruption, like the personal bicycles purchased with taxpayer's money because the cops were planning on riding the streets to get closer to the people in the community. They also received horses and motorcycles because we would see them as friendly and cool.

What ever happened to these programs? They still get free use of taxpayers financed patrol cars because it could be a great crime deterrent to have a patrol car parked in any gated neighborhood.

Meanwhile, the police academy teaches to stay off duty, when off the clock, and to transfer information on any crime in progress to working units.

Another benefit for the LEO is that local businesses provide free or reduced priced food to law enforcement personnel. Many cops just grab whatever items they desired from a shelf at a convenience store, show the food they "appropriated" to the cashier before exiting without paying; a silent promise they will include the store in question on their patrol route. The mafia charging protection money did the same. Today, businesses in the US are giving 10% off of regular price to vets, law enforcement and uniformed personnel, which really means they are charging the regular Joe 10% more.

Special car stickers are another sign of corruption that allows cops to be above the law. Recognized by all departments, they affix stickers to identify personal vehicles, thus making it possible for cops not to be tagged for infractions like parking infractions or moving violations. Something that is extended to family members of police and correction officers.

When these corrupt government employees retire, we appoint them to lucrative positions in the private sector, or security companies where they can collect overdue bribes and kickbacks. Sometimes, they achieve the same goal by remaining in a civilian position within the government. That's if they can avoid friendly fire.

TRYING TO PASS. 6/22/2017 The Associated Press reported that an off-duty African-American police officer was shot Wednesday night by a white colleague in St. Louis, while both officers were attempting to aid first responders after a high-speed car chase ended in a crash, the St. Louis Metropolitan Police Department told Yahoo News.

Authorities said the injured officer was in his home when he heard a crash. He decided to help officers who had already arrived at the scene, who had exchanged fire with the suspects. His colleagues initially ordered the unnamed officer, who was also armed, to the ground, but after recognizing him, they invited him to approach them.

"At this time, a responding officer, 36-year-old white male with over 8 years of service, just arriving in the area observed this and 'fearing for his safety' and apparently not recognizing the off-duty officer, discharged a shot, striking the off-duty officer in the arm," the police department said by email.

The unnamed wounded officer is 38 years old and an 11-year veteran of the same department. According to the officer's lawyer, Rufus Tate Jr., the friendly fire shooting was part of a trend of police violence toward African-American men.

"In the police report, you have so far, there is no description of the threat he perceived," Tate told Fox 2 Now. "So we have a real problem with that. But this has been a national discussion for the past two years. There is this perception that they automatically feared a black man."

"Per department policy, they will place seven officers on administrative leave," the department said. "The Force Investigative Unit responded," it added, and an investigation will take place.

End of story, with a most likely quiet financial settlement to the black officer.

ELSEWHERE. In 2009, a white officer shot and killed Omar J. Edwards, a 25-year-old New York City police officer on a Harlem street while in street clothes.

And in Providence, Rhode Island, an off-duty black police sergeant, Cornel Young Jr., was killed by two uniformed white colleagues in 2000 while he was trying to break up a fight in a parking lot. Young was the son of the department's highest-ranking black officer at the time.

WHEN THE SHOE IS ON THE OTHER FOOT. On July 15th, 2017, an Australian woman became the latest victim of a police shooting. Immediately following the incident, elected officials, the media and American populace became enraged and exploded in putrid comments when someone leaked the preliminary facts that the shooter was a black cop. Not only did they reveal the officer's name, but they also made his national origin, religion, and the content of his employee records public. Within hours of the shooting, the identity and record of black Somali-American officer Mohamed Noor were available to the deranged public*. Without completing an investigation, they directed all the blame personally towards the black officer.

(Note: *Even today, they still shield the identities of the white cops responsible for the slaughter of countless unarmed black men and women in secrecy.)

Speaking publicly, Minneapolis Police Chief Janeé Harteau said the killing of Australian woman Justine Ruszczyk didn't need to happen. The 40-year-old "didn't have to die," Harteau said of the July 15, 2017 shooting incident. "It goes against who we are as a department, how we train and our expectations for our officers."

Does that mean the negroes who got shot deserved to die? No one ever said anything close to those words about any of the murders of unarmed black men, women, and children. Not one single article contained one single derogatory word about the white victim. This shows the level of racism that exists and permeates the white Confederate society of the United British States of America.

Nekima Levy-Pounds, a civil rights lawyer and activist running for mayor of Minneapolis, said Chief Harteau "needed to be fired." Ms. Levy-Pounds said it had been "a slap in the face to people of color" that the chief spoke out about the death of Ms. Damond, who was white, after defending officers involved in past shootings of black people. She is attempting to paint this as an isolated case based on one officer's poor judgment as opposed to a systemic pattern, Ms. Levy-Pounds said.

State investigators continue to probe Ms. Damond's death. Both Ms. Hodges and Chief Harteau have said she should not have been shot. "Justine didn't have to die," chief Harteau said, citing information released by state officials investigating the case. (In the cases of white officers who butchered unarmed black men and women, everyone is told to WAIT for the result of the delayed investigations.)

The racism that can be found in the US is unique; there is no other place on the planet that can match the virulent, deadly American hatred of dark-skinned people. The national reaction was amazing to one white woman who received the posthumous attention that all victims of police violence deserve after so many Negroes have been executed and slaughtered by the jack booted Confederate Klansmen, skinheads of the police force. No one dared to utter one bad thing about Justine; she was not a thug, hoe, SOB, POS, super predator... everything she was or did was lily white and perfect. They changed her last name from Ruszczyk to Damond, making it easier for dumb white Americans to pronounce. The American populace denigrated murdered negroes and dragged their names through the mud. Countless of keyboard warriors volunteered hundred of thousands of reasons negroes deserved to die. Everything said about the departed white woman was peachy. Many asked: why did US police shoot an Australian woman? The chief of police lost her job, and she didn't pull the trigger; They also made her personal life public, on display in the news.

The following is one of the many media reports, after the death of Australian Justine Ruszczyk, from Amy Forliti and Steve Karnowski of the Associated Press. They are all alike in their renderings and treatment of the involved.

MINNEAPOLIS (AP) Minneapolis police Chief Janee

Harteau resigned Friday at the request of the mayor, who said she lost confidence in the chief following last week's shooting death of an unarmed Australian woman by a police officer. In a statement released Friday, Harteau said: "I've decided I will step aside to let a fresh set of leadership eyes see what more can be done for the MPD to be the very best it can be." Minneapolis Mayor Betsy Hodges said she asked for the chief's resignation. "I've lost confidence in the Chief's ability to lead us further... it is clear that she has lost the confidence of the people of Minneapolis as well," Hodges said. "For us to continue to transform policing, and community trust in policing, we need new leadership at MPD." (Mayor Hodges is the same person who lauded, on Facebook, the graduation and hiring of Officer Mohamed Noor in the Minneapolis police force.)

Harteau, who worked her way up from the bottom of the department to police chief, said she was proud of the work she accomplished, but the shooting of 40-year-old Justine Damond by one of her officers, and other incidents, "have caused me to engage in deep reflection". She added, "Despite the MPD's many accomplishments under my leadership over these years and my love for the City, I have to put the communities we serve first".

Harteau was out of the city on personal time for nearly a week following Saturday's shooting of Damond, a 40-year-old life coach and bride-to-be who was killed by an officer responding to her 911 call of a possible rape. The state is investigating the shooting. In Harteau's first remarks on the case on Thursday, when she returned to work, she was sharply critical of Somali- American officer Mohamed Noor while defending his training. "The actions in question go against who we are in the department, how we train and the expectations we have for our officers," Harteau said Thursday. "These were the actions and judgment of one individual."

That wasn't enough for some City Council members. Linea

Palmisano, who represents the ward where Damond died, told her fellow council members Friday that she was "done with image control and crisis management." She said the department has systemic problems, and it was time to consider a change in leadership. Palmisano added: "The time for talk is done. It is time for action." A department spokesperson said Harteau would not be available for an interview after Friday's announcement.

Harteau has spent her career with the department, starting as a beat cop in 1987, when she was just 22. She worked her way up the ranks and in 2012, was appointed chief, becoming the city's first female, first openly gay and first Native American police chief. But she's had a rocky tenure in the top post. Her relationship with Hodges was strained, particularly after the fatal shooting of 24-year-old Jamar Clark during a confrontation with two white police officers in 2015. The black man's death, amid heightened tensions around the U.S., sparked protests citywide that included an 18-day occupation outside the police station on the city's north side. A U.S. Department of Justice review faulted poor communications between the mayor and the chief.

The chief and mayor butted heads again in April when Hodges blocked Harteau's promotion of Lt. John Delmonico to lead the Fourth Precinct, after the chief had already made the public announcement. Delmonico had been a critic of Hodges when he headed the police union.

And Harteau, being out of town when Damond was killed, didn't help either. Harteau, who said she was backpacking in an area with limited cellphone reception, told reporters Thursday evening that it would have been "challenging" to return but that she had kept in touch with her command staff.

Harteau and her longtime patrol partner, Holly Keegel, were featured in a 1990 episode of the reality TV series "Cops." The partners endured years of harassment from some male colleagues, and it escalated to the point where they felt endangered because they weren't getting help when they would call for backup. The Minnesota Department of Human Rights upheld their discrimination and sexual harassment complaint, which led to changes in training and to discipline against some officers.

Harteau and Keegel got married in 2013 after gay marriage became legal in Minnesota. Harteau told the Star Tribune a year later that they had separated amid the strains of her being chief.

Three years earlier, they honored the chief as the grand marshal of the city's annual Pride Parade. But she found herself on the defensive in June when organizers asked law enforcement to minimize their participation because of tensions over the recent acquittal of St. Anthony police officer Jeronimo Yanez in the fatal shooting of another black man, Philando Castile, in the St. Paul suburb of Falcon Heights last summer.

She said she was "beyond disappointed" that they did not consult beforehand with her, but later persuaded the organizers to welcome LGBT officers after all.

SHOP AND COMPARE. Compare the above story to the following one.

DETROIT. In 1967 Mary Jarrett Jackson explained: "There were some white girls there, with three black men at the Algiers Motel. They were there willingly. That upset the police. The officers divided those kids up and took them into different rooms, beat them up and did some awful things to their bodies by ramming things into their genitalia, up their anus. It was awful to look at those kids beaten as they were, shot in the head. The way they brutalized those black men, I did the forensic work on that. There was lots of evidence, but they didn't want that brought out in court. It should have been prosecuted to the fullest extent of the law. "

The slaughter of three black men caused the anger of the black community to explode after decades of social injustice, police brutality, and institutional racism. In the end, the Detroit Free Press reported: 43 black people were dead, over 1,100 black people injured, over 7,000 blacks arrested, and over 2,500 businesses destroyed.

The families of the three slain teens (17-year-old Carl Cooper, 19-year-old Aubrey Pollard and 18-year-old Fred Temple), fought for years to get justice. To this day, they don't believe they ever got it.

HANDS UP, DON'T SHOOT. People say that the system is not bad, that the problems arise from corrupt cops. If you put a rotten egg in a recipe, does only part of the dish is foul?

The news and social media abound of real life videos of white cops shooting and killing unarmed black men and children when the situation did not warrant it. They never charge them because the US still considers Negroes as commodities. They have summarily executed hundreds of black males for no other reason than their black skin. Earlier this year, a video showed a white South Carolina cop shooting a 50-year-old unarmed black man in the back as he was running away from him. The explanation is always the same: the cop was afraid for his life. How could the cop be afraid for his life when the unarmed black man was running away from him? The most important pieces of data in a cop's memory bank, after a deadly shooting, are "I was afraid for my life," "he was reaching for my, or a gun". It's something that is drilled into you the minute the police academy starts, when the indoctrination of the "us vs. them" ideology starts.

In yet another case, more training from the police academy was evident from a court testimony from a murderous police officer: "I meant to stop the threat," he told jurors. "I didn't shoot to kill him. I didn't shoot to wound him. I shot to stop his actions." He remembered his training well... too well. That's the textbook training from the police academy. Long before going to the firing range, that they pounded potential defense into everyone's head.

LINE OF DUTY. They killed more cops in the line of duty last year (2016) than in any year since 2011, leading many, including some in the FBI, to falsely connect the increase in violence with the rise of the Black Lives Matter movement. Earlier this month, the FBI declared that "black identity extremists" are a violent threat to officers, but data released by the Bureau on Monday shows white people are actually much more of a threat to cops. In 2016, cop-killing suspects included 59 individuals, out of which only 15 were black. These suspects were responsible for the intentional shooting or running down of sixty-six officers.

The message has always been the same: "if you are black, all the police officers have to do is say they were in fear of their life and they get away with murder because the victim is black," the local NAACP said in a statement. The acquittals mean a police officer can create a dangerous situation, then cite that dangerous situation as the reason for killing someone. Justice is not only elusive, it's nonexistent when a dark-skin is involved. The pain of always being denied justice is almost too much to bear, as Confederate white supremacists use recycled words in their inability to come up with anything of value to express and justify their old ideology.

In 2014, another South Carolina police officer shot an unarmed African American whom he had stopped in a parking lot for a seatbelt violation. Imagine that, the death penalty for not wearing a seat belt. Would that have been the case if the driver was white?

White officers, too often, act out of animosity towards blacks, because they still see them as commodities, run-away slaves, thugs, drug dealers, or, in the words of Hillary Clinton, super predators. It is racism, pure and simple. When a person's skin color triggers a reaction, it is racism, there is no other word to conceal the action. One can stretch and wiggle to find other words to describe the murders of blacks in the US, but it is what it is... institutional racism. It permeates all levels of the white society, from the bottom to the top, complete with buzzwords, libels, derogatory words, etc... The shooting is just a confirmatory bias to reinforce the belief that the black man has served his purpose in the US and is no longer needed in plantations or wanted in the white society.

Blacks are at a point where the complaints are just complaints. There is no one to hear or willing to listen to them. Jailing and killing young black males has the same effect as when the slave traders removed the strong young black males from Africa. It's to induce the depopulation and destabilization of the black community.

Like pedophiles to the Catholic priesthood, jack booted skinheads, neo-Nazis, Klansmen have flocked to the Confederate police departments.

JUSTICE FOR ALL? When corruption is coupled with racism, then idiots like Joe Arpaio and his shadow David Clarke come out of the woodwork to create an even deadlier dysfunctional police force.

Frank Nucera Jr, the chief of police in Bordentown, New Jersey, systematically abused black residents, denied them their civil rights and even likened them to ISIS, said federal prosecutors who charged him, on Wednesday 11/01/2017, with a hate crime. He used racial slurs and police dogs to threaten and intimidate black Americans. He expressed his wish and dream of lining blacks and mowing them down with bullets. Just like his ancestor King Leopold II of Belgium did in the Congo. In September 2016, he slammed a black 18-year-old's head into a metal door jamb. He is now facing 20 years in prison for his racist abuses. But, since it happened to Negroes in the US, a country so very passionate about the rule of law, Frank Nucera Jr. will most likely walk, or receive probation for a job well done.

IN-JUSTICE. The "leaders in charge" have learned to ignore the black chants and demands; they know they are in control, and they are fairly confident that, like a hurricane, the noise will be over soon, after a couple of days. If blacks continue to protest the injustices, they send executioners to silence the chants and demands. The reason blacks don't get any respect is because they are still regarded as 3/5 of a human, by the white supremacist ideology that is prevalent in the US, especially among Christians who received the instructions from their God.

Even the ignorant clichés are still in use. In July 2017, a St. Petersburg mayoral candidate in Florida said that African-American supporters of his rival should "go back to Africa" if they don't like it in the U.S.

Until last September 19, 2017, Tyler Roysdon suited up as a volunteer firefighter in Franklin Township, a small town in southwestern Ohio, about 40 miles north of Cincinnati. But, according to station WHIO, a recent Facebook back-and-forth caught the 20-year-old writing that in a burning building he would choose to save a dog before an African American because "one dog is more important than a million niggers" he wrote.

LEGAL WRECK. They rigged the justice system to treat blacks as runaway slaves and commodities. A survey revealed that 92 percent of white police officers believe the United States has already assured equal rights for African-Americans. They rigged it to protect police officers and to ensure that blacks keep being butchered by police officers. Everywhere along the way, the officer's action is protected by racist judges, prosecutors who are in place primarily to protect what the officers do, and grand juries which are mostly populated by relatives of law enforcement personnel, and or people affiliated with law enforcement. Police officers who know will slaughter more Negroes because the justice system will protect them.

US prosecutors have found it difficult to convict police officers in high-profile shooting cases involving black victims, despite recent incidents being captured on video. Anger over the failure to find the officers guilty has sometimes boiled over, leading to violent protests. One needs only to read a few online comments from the white public about the murder of a negro to understand why the US is a white supremacist country.

JUSTICE DELAYED AND DENIED. Another day, another story, another way to add insult to injury. The news media reported that four African American members of the LGBTQ community, who marched in the PRIDE parade in Columbus, Ohio and who felt the burden of their race and their sexuality, protested the Philando Castile ruling by calling for seven minutes of silence. The result is that they arrested them as whites looked on, appearing to be cheering their fate.

That's the black reality in a country with a supposed Constitutional provision for redress of grievances. And they arrested them for being silent, just like the vocal protesters. That's one of the many ways they silence Negroes in the US.

They can do all the studies that money can buy, they can invent and create a new dictionary, it is what it is. Most shoot-don't- shoot live scenarios are affected by the skin color of the target. They have made a few studies that reveal that split-second decisions are sometimes a factor. They are not; if that was the case, why wasn't there a shoot-out at the Bundy ranch where armed white people were there for a gunfight with the cops? So all these studies are just BS trying to calm the negroes until they shoot the next one.

It is a fact that all white people perceive all black males as threatening. They take white jobs, drive cars usually reserved for whites, heck, many even "date" white women. It is a cultivated perception that is now embedded in the screwed up white psyche.

EINSATZGRUPPEN. Let's be honest, in 99.99% of the cases where blacks have been butchered, the officer's life was not in danger and he wasn't threatened in any way, shape or form. But the easiest route in American society is to kill the Negro, and let the system explain why. This is the collateral damage when powers are given by the state to a racist cop to use deadly force.

This occurs in direct violation of federal law, which prohibits discrimination in police work. Any police department receiving federal funding is covered by Title VI of the Civil Rights Act of 1964 (42 U.S.C. § 2000d) and the Office of Justice Programs statute (42 U.S.C. § 3789d[c]), which prohibit discrimination on the basis of race, color, national origin, sex, and religion. These laws prohibit conduct ranging from racial slurs and unjustified arrests to the refusal of departments to respond to discrimination complaints. Yet none of that can stop a murderous cop from the reckless slaughter of a negro.

This is above and beyond the fact that key federal criminal statute makes it unlawful for anyone acting with police authority to deprive or conspire to deprive another person of any right protected by the Constitution or laws of the United States, Section 18 U.S.C. § 241. Another statute, commonly referred to as the police misconduct provision, makes it unlawful for state or local police to engage in a pattern or practice of conduct that deprives persons of their rights, 42 U.S.C.A. 14141.

IT BROKE ME. Trevor Noah's emotional reaction to the assassination of Philando Castile said it all. "What they're basically saying is, in America, it is officially reasonable to be afraid of a person just because we are black," said Noah of the newly released dashcam video of the horrific murder of Philando Castile.

"You hear the stories, but you watch that and forget race. Are we all watching the same video? The video where a law-abiding man followed the officer's instructions to the letter of the law, and then was killed regardless? People watched that video and then voted to acquit?"

"It's one thing to have the system against you, the district attorneys, the police unions, the courts, that's one thing. But when a jury of your peers, your community, sees this evidence and then decides that even this is self-defense? That is truly depressing. Because what they're basically saying is in America, it is officially reasonable to be afraid of a person just because we are black. And that's the truth of what we saw with this verdict."

CLASS A, GROUP A. Much of the respect for law enforcement rests in the false belief that cops reduce crimes and are the "blue" line between law-abiding citizens and the criminal elements of society. If that was true, why do criminals still prey on law-abiding citizens? Another common misconception is that if the police forces were not here, violence and lawlessness would be rampant; it would be like the Old West. The Old West never existed, except in Hollywood films and movies. There was no police department before 1830 when the city of Boston established the first; how did the law-abiding citizens survive before that date?

The actual job of a flatfoot is to record crime and prevent civil disorder. Law enforcement is part of the Armed Forces, an embedded front line military unit charged with civil policing. That notion was clearly explained at the police academy by GB, an instructor who added: "You will always have backup. When you are faced with a situation, other cops from your department will show up. If more help is needed, the Sheriff's Office will be there. If that's not enough, the Armed Forces will be your backup. All the while, you will have the support of all branches of the government to do your job."

The police academy encourages and reinforces white supremacist ideologies. It's a place where recruits can collect many jewels, like if we see a black man in a white neighborhood at a certain time, he is there to "case" the houses; if we see a white man in a black neighborhood at the same hour, he is there to buy drugs. This is the indoctrination provided to reach the frame of mind of today's American police officer. They also pound the "us vs them" program into everyone's head at the academy.

SMILE. While training for defensive tactics, recruits learned to control a detained suspect with "the thumb and shoulder restraint". The thumb technique involves the officer's right hand firmly grasping the suspect's left thumb, moving it backwards toward the forearm of the suspect, twisting the wrist behind his back while maintaining body control with the left hand over the suspect's upper arm or opposite shoulder. While demonstrating the technique, they advised recruits to be aware of the presence of any news camera or recording being made. The officer should always project calmness, look at the cameras and repeat non- stop: "please cooperate with me, sir, please cooperate with me." To make it look like the suspect is resisting arrest, the suspect's thumb can be twisted harder to make it seem like he is not cooperating, when in reality, he is just in pain, trying not to get his finger dislocated.

And of course, another jewel from the academy is that the trunk of the squad car is an ideal place to store handy items like Chinese throwing stars (in the old days), knives, drugs and old confiscated guns that can be used if "things get out of control."

AMBER ALERT. Now the job is a lot easier as the cops sit on their butts and let the public do law enforcement work for free, with amber alerts. They don't even patrol the neighborhoods anymore; they cruise by sometimes. It won't be long for an emergency call to go like, "Your call is very important to us. We will be with you shortly." 2 hours later, someone in India or Pakistan will answer the phone call.

Anyone who wants to be impressed by the ability of law enforcement to solve crimes should visit the story of Henry Lee Lucas.

TRICK QUESTIONS. A clique of all white officers, in charge of hiring recruits at an all-white police department, asked me the following question: "You are on duty and come across a police officer who stole a loaf of bread, because he is hungry and needs to feed his starving children. What would you do?" The look on their faces revealed that they didn't like my answer.

One genius, after looking at my certificate of naturalization, asked: "Are you a boat people?" I replied, "no sir, I am too young to have been on the Mayflower." They didn't like that answer either. Afterwards, one of them received a demotion for copying the document that clearly warned in red letters, "It is punishable by U. S. Law to copy, print or photograph this certificate."

By the time the third question headed my way, I didn't want the position and was already eye-balling the exit door. The smartest of the bunch asked: "The Supreme Court decides that murder is legal. You come across a human sacrifice by a gang of Rastafarians. What would you do?" The idiotic racism was too much. I discarded the first thought to make fun of him. The highest court of the land deemed murder legal? Then, I brushed away the desire to educate and help him understand Rastas don't indulge in human sacrifices, don't wear dreadlocks and certainly don't smoke ganja. So, I took the nicest way out by pretending to not understand the question: "You mean, I am on duty, and come across a gang of Rastas, behaving like the Donner Party or your ancestors in Jamestown, Virginia?" Every time I remember the look on his face, I end up with a smile, followed by a laughing fit.

Exit stage left.

MORE RACISM. Lately, the local law enforcement agencies have been used to extend the ranks and reach of ICE in targeting only Mexicans for arrest and deportation. White citizens can waltz in from Aryan breeding farms like: Andorra, Hungary, Norway, Australia, Iceland, Portugal, Austria, Ireland, San Marino, Belgium, Italy, Singapore, Brunei, Japan, Slovakia, Chile, Latvia, Slovenia, Czech Republic, Liechtenstein, South Korea, Denmark, Lithuania, Spain, Estonia, Luxembourg, Sweden, Finland, Malta, Switzerland, France, Monaco, Taiwan, Germany, Netherlands, United Kingdom, Greece, and New Zealand. The cops and any other employee of the government know or should know that it is illegal to discriminate on the basis of race, color, religion and country of origin. Why are the white illegal immigrants not targeted by ICE?

PRIVILEGE 101. To think that police corruption can be stymied within a department is childish and laughable. Cops, being members of the military, are off the limits and reach of the legal system of the mafia they serve together. A member of the team is above any sanction by the team. As members of the team, they are partly to blame for a crime, and as a member of the team, they can not be fully responsible for that crime. Everyone else is doing the same thing, and no finger pointing is allowed in the clubhouse. From manufactured trumped-up charges, planted weapons and drugs, altered evidences, bungled investigations, false arrests, police work is never done. Then comes the legal finesse required to cover all that up.

The false image of the mission to protect and serve the public is maintained with billboards offering safety tips or requesting tips about criminal activities to help solve crimes, and sometimes truly awful television commercials, like the laughable and silly stunt pulled by the Lake County (Florida) Sheriff Office, dressed like ISIS militants, taunting and challenging local heroin dealers to a gunfight.

EXTRA MONEY. Corruption is very profitable in law enforcement. A controversial law enforcement practice allows police to confiscate property from individuals without ever convicting them of a crime, and often without even charging them. Many cops got rich from that scheme. Under this process, local police agencies could evade stricter state laws on civil forfeiture by deferring to more lax federal standards. And there are always many more ways to increase a cop's salary.

The police protective services provided to Benny Hinn and other big shot evangelists are very telling of the privilege accorded to cops by the corrupt elite. The cops get overtime pay and the elite get to flaunt their power and status backed by armed servants on the taxpayers' tab. What good is an armed cop in front of a church where god is supposed to be in charge? An omnipotent God can not even handle the traffic in front of his own church? Damn!

OMERTA. When it comes to police work, one point stressed by an FBI research is the importance of responsibility to prevent corruption. Yet the FBI, a federal law enforcement agency, is never too thrilled to investigate corrupt police officers, because they are part of the same gang. Cops don't want to turn in other cops, for the simple reason they don't want to be a rat, a zero or a cry-baby. There is also the unspoken threat and warning that if you tattle on "one of yours," your back will not only be covered, but you may have to watch your back. There is a fraternal understanding among police officers known variously as "the Code of Silence" and "the Blue Curtain" under which officers regard testimony against a fellow officer as betrayal.

Just like Scientology.

Even when honest cops are willing to blow the whistle, there may be no one willing to listen. Everyone remembers the movie based on real life with Al Pacino about the code of silence. Police officer Frank Serpico's startling testimony against fellow officers not only revealed systemic corruption but highlighted a longstanding obstacle to investigating these abuses.

FBI LEADERSHIP FILES. All departments have goals and the officers follow the lead of their higher ups on the second floor. One of these goals is to maintain the public trust. As one researcher explained, "principled leaders do not act to protect their own egos, try to put on a good appearance without substance in their decisions or efforts, or attempt to intimidate those under them. Instead, principle-based executives who work with their subordinates can take an important step toward creating an ethical climate by developing an agenda that explains the moral purposes of the department".

It looks good on paper, as we well know what happens in reality. There are subordinates who have a close-knit relationship with the leadership in all departments, and these "favored" individuals also have subordinates they are close to, joke with and work with daily. That's not considering rogue officers who will do as they want and try to influence the newly hired.

One example was a particular officer who insisted on driving the wrong way down a one-way street and laughed, because "who is going to write me a ticket?" He never got a reprimand. While ethical supervisors help maintain an ethical workplace, the opposite also remains true: uncaring and incompetent officials actually can promote misconduct and racism. Like politicians, police chiefs keep their jobs.

ACADEMY 101. So a recruit receives a 4 months long training, 250 hours of Constitutional and basic law enforcement standards at the academy with all the basic rules and regulations to start an on-the-job training.

While the academy is just an introduction to law enforcement, it is nevertheless the hiring department policies that will affect his job performance. That's where they set the standards for officers to follow. Departments tend to hire people who will fit within their respective organization, individuals who share the same attitudes, ideology, perceptions, assumptions, values, core beliefs, ways of living, and traditions. Individual departments become micro family units, where cops see each other as closer than their own blood relatives. There are parking lots for personnel, full of the same type of cars. That's why many police departments will hire mostly Europeans, while one mumbled something like "the lowest minority we will hire is an American Indian." Whatever that means. So, when an officer runs afoul of the law, just look at his department. Cops who shoot negroes work in a mainly predominant white department or one with a couple of token blacks.

MADE MEMBER. Once the probationary period is over, the recruit becomes a member of the new family. The instructions received at the academy of "us versus them" become real, and a new mentality creates an allegiance stronger than that to the mission of the department or even the profession. Just like the mafia.

There was a preventable accident in a small country town, where a Spanish speaking drunk driver crashed into a truck driven by a deputy sheriff who died at the scene. A white police officer, who responded to the emergency call, was so severely distraught that he wanted to shoot the drunk driver instead of arresting him.

This is the level of allegiance between cops, the "us versus them" mentality.

Even the department administrators are not immune to the ire of a scorned cop. Two cops were seriously pissed off at a sergeant after he scolded one of them in public, in front of a group of civilians. And we could see the difference of opinion as they clearly articulated, afterwards, that they had each other's back, and the sergeant didn't have their backs.

SWAT. The other notion that law enforcement work is a daily life and death struggle is a joke. The only unit which sees a bit of action is the SWAT, and the rare situations are very controlled with perimeters and overwhelmingly armed officers. Imagine the swat team showing up to foil a bank robbery with tanks and armored personnel carriers. That's if they get there on time, before the getaway. In cases with hostages, the scenarios involve taking long-range shots, most of the time without target acquisition. That's how the captives end up with the bullets sometimes. Countless of officers never had to pull their guns out of the secured holsters during their entire careers. When some of them do, it's to murder unarmed blacks, with the public at large always willing to justify their actions. Cops are the most tolerated public employees, regardless of their actions. Especially desperate lonely women will give a carte blanche to any "handcuffs carrying man in uniform".

SHARE THE LOOT. One of the contributing factors in corruption is the system of perks that officers who "perform" to the ideals of the department will receive. Anything that promotes his department, arrests, seized weapons, recovered drugs, issued traffic tickets are very important in an officer getting a promotion or a raise in pay. Numbers count and somehow are a telltale sign of how well an officer is doing his job. An officer will make an arrest or issue citations to increase his quota with no care in the world. So the actual job entails getting results at all costs, arresting as many people as possible, then let the judges and lawyers sort it out.

And blacks suffer the brunt of these abusive and illegal actions because they all "look alike and guilty." This little debacle is another excuse used by law enforcement, something that can be heard on the news after a murder: we arrested the bad guys and the court system let them out. Once again, the officers are the heroes of the day, even when they arrested a guy who had nothing to do with the crime in question. Unless totally outrageous, this behavior will be tolerated within the department, with the harshest punishment being a few days off with pay or relegated to desk duty*.

(*In one of his Harry Callahan movies, Clint Eastwood received a scalding from his supervisor who assigned him to "desk duty." His reply: "desk duty is for a**holes.")

A NEGRO A DAY. There are many rotten apples in law enforcement, not just one or two... whole orchards. The question that begs an answer is why are they not removed from their position? The answer is very simple, the entire system is corrupt, as any corrupt officer who is fired can get a job at another department.

To go back to the scenario of the officer stealing a loaf of bread to feed himself and his hungry kids, some acts are seen as minor and only require a warning or counseling. But was it the first time that the officer "appropriated" a loaf of bread? Or a sandwich at a convenience store? Or wrote a ticket to boost his chances at a promotion? Or arrested the first black man he saw? Or accepted sexual favor to dismiss a speeding ticket? Or murdered an unarmed negro? That's the side business of law enforcement.

When a partner is corrupt, it becomes very easy for a recruit to become as corrupt. In a study conducted by the International Association of Chiefs of Police, 7 of the top 10 issues determined as critically important to officers actively working in law enforcement involved ethics and integrity.

It is often said that while officers are human and will continue to make mistakes, ethical misconduct can not and should not be tolerated. Then why are unethical police officers allowed to remain on the force after outlandish misconduct? Whenever a criminal officer breaks the law, the solution always flows in his favor as re-assignment, relocation, time off with pay, etc... While the cadre will deplore certain illegal and criminal acts by police officers, it lacks the courage to deal with those who are responsible for the failures. Once again, the basic tenet of Criminal Justice is ignored: justice is the finding of the truth.

RECENTLY. On July 29, 2017 4:38 PM, Donovan Harrell reported: A Washington D.C. police officer accused of wearing a racist shirt while on duty was suspended Friday after an investigation.

Law4BlackLives, a lawyer group that supports Black Lives Matter*, filed a complaint against the officer, after a photo of him wearing the shirt began circulating on social media. "This t-shirt is symptomatic of a dangerous and insidious combination of racism and a crass abuse of power that has infiltrated the police department," the complaint read. D.C. Police didn't release the officer's name, but the lawyer group identified the officer as Vincent Altiere in the complaint.

(Note*: Isn't it funny that white supremacists hate the original #black lives matter, yet are not beyond copying blacks, like "blue lives matter" and "white lives matter".)

According to The Washington Post, the black shirt has the words "Seventh District," which is a district that has a few of the city's most violent areas, including Anacostia, Barry Farm and Washington Highlands.

The centerpiece of the shirt is the Grim Reaper holding a rifle with the Washington D.C. flag attached to it. Above the flag lies the words "powershift," which refers to the officers assigned to areas with high amounts of crime, The Washington Post reported.

On the 'O' in "powershift" is a type of cross identified by the

Anti-Defamation League as the same type of cross belonging to a neo-Nazi website.

Last, the shirt has a phrase that says "Let me see that waistband jo," which the advocacy group said refers to the police practice of demanding to see individuals' waistbands, mainly people of color, to check for weapons.

INCIDENTS IN THE NEWS. The news media sometimes has no choice but to report on the rotten apples. Once again, it's not done in the truth's interest, but to somehow maintain the illusion that the system polices itself and is always willing to remove the bad seeds.

- BALTIMORE AGAIN On Jul 19, 2017, 4:24pm EDT the following article was updated by German Lopez. "It's not especially rare to hear stories of a police officer abusing his power. But it is pretty rare to see a story in which the cop actually records himself doing it."

That's what seemed to happen in Baltimore recently, when a police officer appeared to accidentally record himself planting drugs at a crime scene. In the January 2017 video, reported by Fox Baltimore, officer Richard Pinheiro puts a bag of pills under some trash in an alley. He then walks to the street. He then switches on his camera, walks back to the alley, and acts like he just found the drugs for the first time.

Here's the crucial mistake that Pinheiro apparently made: He apparently didn't realize that body cameras often save the last 30 seconds of footage before they're manually activated. So they caught all of that preparation for his big faux discovery on tape.

"I'm going to check here," Pinheiro says as the camera is activated. "Hold on." He then walks to the scene and acts like he's looking around. Finally, he comes to the spot where he put the pills, picks them up, and says, "Yo!" The other officers appear to play along with his fake discovery, as if this is all routine and normal.

The defendant connected to the drugs would have gone to trial this week. But according to BuzzFeed, the prosecutor dropped the charges after the defendant's public defender discovered and saw the video. Although, in a troubling development, the prosecutor apparently used Pinheiro as an eyewitness in a separate case, even after learning of his misconduct in the video. Seriously. This really happened.

- Several other law enforcement agencies raided The Brooklyn, Illinois, including the Illinois State Police, and the St. Clair County Sheriff. Local news crews witnessed police from different agencies carrying equipment, computers, weapons, and records out of the building and driving away with them.

- (From an FBI analytical look, facts abound about the CPD). The Chicago Police Department has a long legacy of corruption, a checkered history of police scandals and an embarrassingly long list of police officers who have crossed the line to engage in brutality, corruption and criminal activity.

As of late, they have convicted 295 Chicago police officers of serious crimes, such as drug dealing, beatings of civilians, destroying evidence, protecting mobsters, theft and murder. The listing of police convicted of crimes undoubtedly underestimates the problem of corruption in the Chicago Police Department (CPD). The list does not include undetected and unreported illegal activity, serious misconduct resulting in internal disciplinary action, and officers who retire rather than face charges.

A report showed that, first, corruption has long persisted within the CPD and continues to be a serious problem. There have been 102 convictions of Chicago police since the beginning of 2000.

Second, police officers often resist reporting crimes and misconduct committed by fellow officers. The "blue code of silence", while difficult to prove, is an integral part of the department's culture and it exacerbates the corruption problems. A breakthrough almost happened last November when a federal jury found that the City of Chicago and its police culture were partially responsible for officer Anthony Abbate's brutal beating of a female bartender. After the civil trial to assess damages, the victim's attorney declared, "We proved a code of silence at every level in the Chicago Police Department".

Third, over time, a large portion of police corruption has shifted from police officers aiding and abetting mobsters and organized crime to officers involved with drugs dealers and street gangs. Since the year 2000, they convicted 47 Chicago law enforcement officers of drug and gang-related crimes. The department's war on drugs puts police officers, especially those working undercover, in dangerous situations where they must cooperate with criminals to catch criminals. These endeavors require that CPD superiors provide top leadership and oversight to keep officers on the straight and narrow.

Fourth, internal and external sources of authority, including police superintendents and mayors, have up to now failed to provide adequate anti-corruption oversight and leadership.

Despite all these facts, the ACLU declared: Our faith in the criminal justice system depends on the knowledge that everyone is playing by the rules. But they are not.

- (AP News) Georgia police have opened an internal investigation after dash-cam footage captured a police officer appearing to say to a nervous driver during a stop, "Remember, we only kill black people." The footage, obtained by Channel 2 Action News, shows Lieutenant Greg Abbott of the Cobb County Police Department asking a driver to pick up her cellphone during a DUI stop in July 2016. The incident only came to light this week following an open-records request by the channel.

The female driver said she was hesitant to move her hands because she had "just seen way too many videos of cops...," suggesting that she may have been afraid of getting shot. Abbott responded, "But you're not black. Remember, we only shoot black people. We only kill black people, right? All the videos you've seen, have you seen the black people get killed?"

Cobb County Police Chief Mike Register told Channel 2 that they had put Abbott on administrative duties pending the outcome of the investigation. "No matter what context they said it [in], it shouldn't have been said," said Register, who was not the police chief at the time of the incident. The attorney for the woman in the case, Suri Chadha Jimenez, said she thought the officer was being sarcastic but added that "it makes you cringe when you hear it" and called the comments "unacceptable."

- A St. Louis police officer who called Black Lives Matter activists "the klan with a tan" and "domestic terrorists" on Facebook is reportedly under an internal investigation by the police department. Officer Deron Riley, a 16-year veteran of the SLMPD with an annual salary of nearly $60,000, posted an image of Black Lives Matter protesters with the racially offensive captions as a comment on Facebook.

- Protests erupted over the acquittal of killer cop Jason Stockley, a white former police officer charged with murder and suspected of planting a gun on the man he killed.

- (CNN/Meredith) Video of a former sheriff's deputy in Milton, Florida intentionally crashing his patrol car into his ex-wife's home, has been released. The state attorney's office released the dash cam video this week. The incident happened in November 2016. Timothy Taylor reverses out of the home's driveway, then steers the cruiser to face the home. Taylor lets a car pass just before he speeds up and slams into the front of the house.

Taylor admitted to Milton Police he was under the influence of prescription drugs. He said he tried to commit suicide because of marital problems. Taylor pleaded no contest to DUI and criminal mischief charges. They sentenced him to two years' probation.

- Wearing his uniform and sitting in his Palm Beach Sheriff's issued car, a deputy waited for his ex-girlfriend. When he found her walking her dog, he stepped out of his car and shot her before shooting and killing himself, police said Friday 10/13/2017. The shooter, Michael DeMarco, 55, had been with the sheriff's office since 1995, according to Palm Beach Sheriff's Office spokeswoman Teri Barbera. His relationship with the woman, a bank worker, began in May and ended three weeks before the shooting. Boynton Beach Police investigators are not releasing the name of the woman because of a state law exempting victims of domestic violence.

- ST. LOUIS (AP) The American Civil Liberties Union of Missouri filed a lawsuit against the city of St. Louis on Friday over what it called "unlawful and unconstitutional action" during demonstrations that followed the acquittal of a white former police officer in the death of a black man.

The suit accuses police of misconduct by using chemical weapons, interfering with video of police activity and violating due process. It seeks an order requiring police to act within the bounds of the U.S. Constitution.

- Oklahoma City police officers, who opened fire on a man in front of his home as he approached them holding a metal pipe, didn't hear witnesses yelling that he was deaf, a department official said Wednesday. Magdiel Sanchez, 35, wasn't obeying the officers' commands before one shot him and another tased him Tuesday night, police Capt. Bo Mathews said at a news conference. He said witnesses were yelling "he can't hear you" before the officers fired, but the officers didn't hear them. "In those situations, very volatile situations, you have a weapon out. You can get what they call tunnel vision, or you can really lock in to just the person who has the weapon that'd be the threat against you."

Being deaf in the US will also get someone the death sentence. This is one situation in the shoot-don't-shoot training scenarios.

- Alex Dobuzinskis reported in Los Angeles (Reuters) A decades- old investigation in the U.S. state of Georgia into the murder of a black man in 1983 culminated in the arrest of five white people on Friday, including two law enforcement officers charged with hindering the probe, officials said. The body of Timothy Coggins, 23, was found on Oct. 9, 1983, in a grassy area near power lines in the community of Sunnyside, about 30 miles south of downtown Atlanta. He had been "brutally murdered" and his body had signs of trauma, the Spalding County Sheriff's Office said in a statement. Investigators spoke to people who knew Coggins, but the investigation went cold, Spalding County Sheriff Darrell Dix said at a news conference. This past March, fresh evidence led investigators from the Georgia Bureau of Investigation and Spalding County to re-examine the case.

Dix did not provide details on the evidence, saying they received more tips after authorities, over the summer, announced to the media the case was re-opened. Some witnesses confessed they lived with knowledge about the case for years, but were afraid to come forward, Dix said. "It has been an emotional roller coaster for everybody that was involved," Dix said. Police arrested five people on Friday in connection with the slaying. Frankie Gebhardt, 59, and Bill Moore Sr, 58, were each charged with murder, aggravated assault and other crimes. Authorities did not immediately say where Gebhardt and Moore lived. Gregory

Huffman, 47, was charged with obstruction and violation of oath of office, Dix said. Huffman was a detention officer with the Spalding County Sheriff's Office, but his employment was terminated after he was arrested. Lamar Bunn, a police officer in the town of Milner, which is south of Spalding County, was also arrested and charged with obstruction, as was Sandra Bunn, 58. She is Lamar's mother, according to Atlanta television station WXIA.

Investigators are convinced the murder was racially motivated, Dix said. "There is no doubt in the minds of all investigators involved that the crime was racially motivated and that if the crime happened today, it would be prosecuted as a hate crime," the Sheriff's Office said. Several members of Coggins' family appeared at the news conference where authorities announced the arrests. The family held out for justice all this time, said Heather Coggins, a niece of the victim. "Even on my grandmother's deathbed, she knew that justice would one day be served," she said. It was not immediately clear if any of the five arrested people had an attorney, and they could not be reached for comment. Dix promised more arrests in the case, as the investigation continues.

- UTAH POLICE On July 26, 2017, a nurse in Salt Lake City was aggressively arrested for obeying hospital policy and refusing to allow a police detective to draw blood from a severely injured patient, according to several reports. In a viral video that emerged this week, Alex Wubbels, the head nurse at the University of Utah Hospital's burn unit, keeps her cool while Detective Jeff Payne insists that he be given permission to collect the blood sample of a patient, despite not having a warrant.

The July 26 footage, filmed on Payne's body camera, captures Wubbels explaining that "three things that allow us to [give blood samples] are if you have an electronic warrant, patient consent or patient under arrest, and you have neither of those things… the patient can't consent. He told me repeatedly that he doesn't have a warrant, and the patient is not under arrest."

"So, I'm just trying to do what I'm supposed to do, that's all," she adds.

Wubbels appears professional throughout the exchange and has her supervisor on speakerphone so the detective can listen. You can hear the supervisor telling Payne that he's making a "huge mistake" in threatening Wubbels and by claiming that she's interfering with his police duties when she's simply following protocol. For Payne's part, he was reportedly explicitly told by his lieutenant to arrest Wubbels if she refused to let him take a sample of blood, according to The Salt Lake Tribune. In fact, a 2016 Supreme Court ruling suggests that the nurse was right to not allow Payne to get a blood alcohol test without a warrant. As The Washington Post noted in its report Friday, the U.S. Supreme Court "has explicitly ruled that blood can only be drawn from drivers for probable cause, with a warrant." Wubbels appeared to do everything correctly.

The supervisor barely finishes what he's saying when Payne shouts, "We're done!" repeatedly at Wubbels. He then chases her down and handcuffs her. A sobbing Wubbels screams "Help me!" and "You're assaulting me!" while being pushed out of the hospital and toward a police car. "I just feel betrayed, I feel angry … I'm a health care worker. The only job I have is to keep my patients safe," Wubbels said, according to the site. "A blood draw, it just gets thrown around there like it's some simple thing. But blood is your blood. That's your property. And when a patient comes in a critical state, that blood is extremely important and I don't take it lightly."

Since the horrifying arrest, they have suspended Payne from the department's blood draw unit. They expected him to remain on active duty as the investigation was conducted. They have not charged Wubbels. She said in a news conference Thursday, accompanied by her lawyer Karra Porter, that she is not ruling out taking legal action. "I just feel betrayed, I feel angry, I feel a lot of things," Wubbels said during the conference. "And I'm still confused."

The hospital stands by Wubbels, indicating that she did everything she was supposed to in a statement it gave to The New York Post. "She followed procedures and protocols in this matter and was acting in her patient's best interest," the statement reads. "We have worked with our law enforcement partners on this issue to ensure an appropriate process for moving forward."

Salt Lake County District Attorney Sim Gill ordered a criminal investigation Friday into the actions of Detective Jeff Payne. Salt Lake City Mayor Jackie Biskupski and Police Chief Mike Brown apologized for Payne's actions and promised investigations from Internal Affairs and the Civilian Review Board.

- A southern Illinois sheriff's deputy is accused of twice assaulting a woman in her home. St. Clair County Deputy Robert Sneed is charged with two counts of official misconduct and is on paid administrative leave. He posted a $2,500 bond this month, the Belleville News-Democrat reported. Court records show Sneed pulled the woman over in February and followed her to her home in Cahokia after telling her she needed to show him her car's title. Cahokia is a St. Louis suburb on the Illinois side of the Mississippi River. Police say Sneed sexually assaulted the woman in her home and suggested she could be jailed if she didn't comply.

- KEY WEST, Fla. - A Monroe County corrections deputy was arrested Tuesday after stealing prescription pills from a family friend while she was babysitting for him, according to the Monroe County Sheriff's Office. The victim of the theft is Key West police Officer David Kouri.

Kouri called the deputies in the morning and told them that Ashlie Hernandez, 27, had taken prescription medications while babysitting for him Monday night in his home, sheriff's spokeswoman Becky Herrin said. Kouri said he knew how many pills were in the bottles because he had just filled the prescription and had not yet taken any of them. He also told deputies he counted the pills and found that some were missing, Herrin said.

As part of the investigation, Kouri called Hernandez to discuss the theft, Herrin said. It was during that phone call Hernandez told Kouri that her boyfriend had taken the drugs. She then told Kouri that she had some drugs and they agreed to meet in the parking lot of the Key West Police Department so she could return the pills, Herrin said. The pair met at about 4 p.m. and soon after, Hernandez handed over a plastic bag with the pills inside, Herrin said. Detectives stopped her, and she admitted to taking the pills, Herrin said. They arrested Hernandez on charges of possession of a controlled substance without a prescription and theft of a controlled substance.

- A Florida police department is investigating officer Michael Hamill who posted anti-Zionist remarks on his Facebook page that were unearthed after his superiors commended the cop in an official post for helping the community after Hurricane Irma. The photo went viral on social media because of the cops' good looks. The positive attention was short-lived.

Someone located Hamill's personal Facebook page, which was filled with anti-Semitic remarks that predated him joining the Gainesville force in 2016. Hamill wrote in 2013: "Who knew that reading Jewish jokes before I go to bed would not only make me feel better about myself but also help me sleep better as well? Here is one for everybody. What's the difference between boy scouts and Jews? Anybody know? Well, it is because boy scouts come back from their camps."

In a second Facebook post two years earlier, Hamill ranted about people who abuse government resources and said they should be dealt with the Hitler way. "Stupid people annoy me. Put them in an oven and deal with them the Hitler way. Haha," he wrote.

- WHITE PRIVILEGE. Did Patrick Kelly, a Chicago police officer with a troubled history, shoot Michael D. LaPorta in the head, leaving him permanently disabled? On 10/26/2017 a federal jury found Kelly shot LaPorta on Jan. 12, 2010, while off-duty in his home after a night of drinking. Then, the jury held the city of Chicago responsible for the shooting with a crushing $44.7 million verdict. This isn't the first time Kelly cost the city money. Earlier this year, Chicago settled for $500,000 a separate lawsuit filed by a woman who said she suffered a miscarriage after Kelly used a Taser on her three times in August 2013. In fact, ahead of LaPorta's shooting, 19 complaints had been registered against Kelly in six years, according to the LaPorta family's lawsuit. At least eight more allegedly followed, including claims of excessive force, racial bias, domestic violence and battery.

A Chicago Police Department spokesperson said they stripped Kelly of his police powers this month and is under investigation based on the court proceedings for making a false oral or written report. Kelly called 911 after the shooting, calmly telling a dispatcher, "I have a friend that committed suicide … He's dead right now." But soon, his tone changed, and he abruptly blurted out the words, "he's still breathing!"

Kelly invoked his constitutional right not to incriminate himself 31 times when he took the stand last week. He did so moments before LaPorta testified from his wheelchair, denying that he shot himself and insisting about Kelly, "I know he shot me."

Kelly earlier settled with LaPorta's family for $300,000, records show.

- BOYNTON BEACH (AP) - Authorities say a Florida sheriff's deputy shot and wounded a woman and then fatally shot himself, on 10/12/2017. The Palm Beach County Sheriff's Office said in a news release that the shooting happened shortly after 8 a.m. Thursday in a gated Boynton Beach neighborhood. They have not released the names and races of those involved. The sheriff's office said they took the woman to a hospital, and she is in critical condition. The deputy died at the scene. No further details were immediately available.

- NEWARK AIRPORT. They arrested three Customs and Border Protection officers assigned to a specialized screening team at Newark Airport Wednesday for assaulting fellow officers, allegedly pinning the victims to what they knew as a "rape table," according to court records.

Tito Catota, Parmenio Perez and Michael Papagni are charged with forcibly assaulting, impeding, intimidating, and interfering with two men identified in court documents as "Victim One" and "Victim Two" while the victims were on duty as CBP officers.

"The defendants, who were members of a unit responsible for identifying dangerous contraband and threats to national security, allegedly subjected their own colleagues to senseless physical abuse, all while on duty at Newark Liberty International Airport," acting U.S. Attorney William Fitzpatrick said.

- Authorities said Tuesday a former Cleveland police officer who allegedly cut off his GPS tracker and went on the run one week before he would have gone on trial for rape and kidnapping has killed himself after a standoff with police. The U.S. Marshals Service looked for Tommie Griffin, 52, who was wanted the Cuyahoga County Sheriff's Office for the bond violation, according to Pete Elliott of the U.S. Marshals Service. They tracked Griffin to a house in Cleveland, where Cleveland Police SWAT was called in, Elliott said Tuesday. Police tried to call him out of the house, but received no response from him. When police entered, they found Griffin dead from an apparently self-inflicted gunshot wound to the chest, police said.

They arrested Griffin for rape, assault and kidnapping after allegedly attacking his girlfriend in January, The Associated Press said. He allegedly pistol-whipped her and fired two shots next to her, the AP said. They had scheduled Griffin's trial to begin on Oct. 30.

HISTORICAL FACT. The news from the UK is that police corruption can be traced back to the world's first police force in London, England, where several accounts of police corruption have been documented since the force's inception.

Imogen Calderwood reported on 08/05/2016. They have kicked out of the force, a sadistic police officer who was recorded repeatedly raping a woman after she installed a sleep app on her iPhone. PC Michael Graham, 49, was jailed for 16 years for his campaign of physical and sexual abuse against the victim on his houseboat in Uxbridge, West London. He controlled his victim for months by telling her no one would believe her because he was a Met Police officer. Booting him out of the police force, Assistant Commissioner Helen King praised the victim's 'courage and resilience' in reporting Graham to his colleagues. At trial, the court heard how the officer tied the victim up, slapped her and choked her and also boasted that he would end up killing her.

He also branded her a 'slut' and a 'cu*t.'

INSTITUTIONAL CORRUPTION. Police corruption is a simple phenomenon, which does readily submit to simple analysis. Any newspaper or any police-related publication, on any given day, will have an article about a police officer that got busted committing some kind of corrupt act. Police corruption has skyrocketed with the cocaine trade, with officers acting alone or in-groups to steal money from dealers or distribute cocaine themselves. They have caught large groups of corrupt police officers in New York, New Orleans, Washington, DC, and Los Angeles. When police officers are exposed violating the law, people are often shocked and outraged, even when the corruption is universal. A police officer in the US is as much on the take as one in India, Afghanistan, Iraq, France, Zimbabwe or Kenya.

In the US, police corruption can include brutality, physical or verbal harassment, violation of the Fourth Amendment rights against unreasonable search and seizure, evidentiary rules forbidding the use at trial of evidence tainted by unconstitutional police actions (fruits of the poisonous tree), and the establishment of the so-called Miranda warning requiring officers to advise detained suspects of their constitutional rights, discriminatory arrest, selective enforcement of the law, discrimination, sexual harassment, intimidation, receiving or fencing stolen goods, false testimony in court, pay off from prostitutes, drug addicts or pushers and professional burglars.

There are many instances where police officers collaborated with drug dealers who pay protection money to be left alone to conduct their business. That's when the officers were not selling the drugs themselves.

"Color of law" violations include false arrest and the use of excessive force by police, according to the FBI's website. And that's not all.

CASE IN POINT. A particular incident happened at a police station in Eatonville, Florida. On a Sunday afternoon, a cop answered a call about drugs being peddled in a city street. Upon his arrival at the scene, the alleged drug dealers took off on foot. The officer in question failed to give pursuit, opting instead to inspect the car left behind. He found a small amount of illegal drugs, $400 in cash and a gun. He processed the scene and wrote his report.

Missing from the details were the $400 which "he took home for safekeeping." Early the following Monday, the chief who had set up the decoy bust confronted and arrested him, because the local drug dealers were complaining about being robbed by the cop. Two hours later, they released him, pending "further investigation." Luckily, this case didn't fall through the cracks and they eventually fired this cop. It's worth mentioning that he was previously broke before they hired him, then paid $120,000 cash for a house after just 2 months working a 20 hours part-time job.

FOX NEWS REPORT. Authorities arrested a sheriff's deputy in Florida, who was caught on home surveillance video last month reportedly stealing from a recently deceased man, on Thursday 10/19/2017. Deputy Jason Cooke of the Palm Beach Sheriff's Office was charged with burglary and grand theft with a firearm, WPBF reported. They released him on house arrest after he paid a $28,000 bond. They accused Cooke of robbing a house that belonged to Moe Rosoff, an 85-year-old man who had injured himself in a blackout during Hurricane Irma and later died, ABC 10 News reported.

Rosoff's family had reportedly asked authorities on Sept. 12 to do a welfare check on their father, who was braving the storm alone. Three deputies found the elderly man on the floor of his home and brought him to the hospital before he eventually died.

The family alleged that the accused deputy heard the garage entry code over his police radio and went to the victim's house, knowing he wouldn't be there, ABC reported. Unbeknownst to the suspect, surveillance cameras at the house turned on when he entered, CBS 12 reported. The family later saw the video and turned it over to the police on Sept. 20. They claim the deputy wandered around the house and stole money, jewelry and medication. They also suggested that Cooke received "preferential treatment" from the sheriff's office, noting that they did not arrest the suspect until five weeks after they initially turned over the video, CBS 12 said.

Police allowed Cooke, who reportedly only admitted to the crime after seeing the surveillance video, to attend a 30-day drug rehabilitation program before facing arrest, the family said. Police found several types of prescription drugs inside Cooke's patrol car, not all of which reportedly belonged to the victim. The family alleged that this was potentially not the deputy's first crime and that he "posed a significant threat to the public's safety," CBS 12 reported.

"In our opinion, had we not had this video, this cop would still be out there posing a threat of danger to the community he swore to protect and committing more crimes," the family said in a statement. "It is our hope that the justice system treats this cop like any other criminal out there and that he doesn't receive further preferential treatment because he is a police officer."

"Unfortunately, sometimes an employee makes a bad decision which leads to misconduct," the sheriff's office said in a statement following Cooke's arrest. "This misconduct was reported, investigated and subsequently determined to be criminal in nature, resulting in the charges." According to the family, the suspect was placed on paid administrative leave, CBS 12 said.

ANOTHER REALITY. Everyone remembers the Knapp Commission in 1972 and the many NYPD corruption cases. The problem was supposedly solved until it resurfaced in 1992 when five officers were arrested on drug-trafficking charges. Millions of cases of corruption and illegal activities are treated as individual rarity every single time.

An article in the New York Times asked: "Police agencies, to eliminate corruption have tried everything from increasing salaries, requiring more training and education, and developing policies which should focus directly on factors leading to corruption. What have all these changes done to eliminate or even decrease the corruption problem? Little or nothing." Internal Affairs unit is just that: internal affairs.

FOLLOW THE LAW. The only remedy to police brutality, false arrest and imprisonment, malicious prosecution, and wrongful death is found in state law, which permits victims to sue police departments for damages in civil actions. A few law firms have defied the odds by taking on corrupt cops: civil rights attorney Jasmine Rand who has represented the families of Trayvon Martin and Michael Brown in their cases and local counsel Shelley Stangler, who has handled many civil rights suits, the Black lawyers for Justice and the Southern Center for justice. But the rest of the story remains that the local community ends up paying the price for police corruption. Once again, the taxpayers receive the shaft in the form of a higher tax rate to replenish the city coffers and cover the money awarded to the victims.

BAD LEGACY. All the illegal actions are happening despite the legal safeguards, codes of conduct, civilian complaint review boards, criminal and civil statutes. Enforcement is the responsibility of the Justice department, and they are part of the same gang. More and more, they give law enforcement more immunity from prosecution, just like judges and legislators.

That's also why the US Supreme Court decisions have continually asserted the general rule that they must give officers the benefit of the doubt that they acted lawfully in carrying out their day-to-day duties. It doesn't matter to the court that these officers are card-carrying members of the KKK or other hate groups.

When people use weapons illicitly and taint it with racism, they murder negroes. As cops continue to kill negroes, it will become harder and harder for them to patrol black communities without the fear of someone willing to exact revenge.

DRUG PEDDLERS. What the corrupt cops cannot

understand is that every crime by an officer erases all the trust obtained from the community. That's if they cared. In Cleveland, the FBI arrested 42 officers from five law enforcement agencies on charges of conspiracy to distribute cocaine; something the CIA got away with when they "legally" introduced crack in the black neighborhoods. The federal General Accounting Office (GAO) found evidence of growing police involvement in drug sales, theft of drugs and money from drug dealers, and perjured testimony about illegal searches.

Traditionally, police corruption had been understood to involve individuals acting alone, but the new trend revealed officers working in small groups to protect and assist each other, like the Los Angeles Police Department's Rampart precinct and particularly its elite anti-gang unit, CRASH (Community Resources Against Street Hoodlums). Following local and federal investigations, CRASH was dismantled, some 70 officers were investigated, and several either pleaded guilty to or were convicted of crimes ranging from drug theft and peddling to assault, fabricating arrests, and filing false reports.

Police corruption has occasionally led to rioting. In an ironic reversal of fate, citizens now require protection from the very people appointed to protect and serve.

UNCHANGED LEGACY. On 10/07/2017, as stated earlier, the FBI's counterterrorism unit continued the white agenda of racial superiority when it has identified a new group, "black identity extremists," as a growing threat to the safety of law enforcement. Let us get this straight. This is a list of black people that the FBI is afraid might retaliate against ongoing police violence? Do they have a list of violent white police officers? It takes very little effort to hate a man whom you have wronged.

The need for more jails and punishments comes from the fact that, in our modern world, there is no venue for redress of grievances. The poor, the exploited, African, non-European, anyone with dark-skin, immigrant Asian laborer, native American, Japanese-American, Mexican, the sick or anyone classified outside the gentrified genetic lines drawn up by the raceologists of the American Eugenics Movement do not influence the laws. The unfortunate people, who have been marginalized by the racist ruling elite for having presumed defects or inheritable undesirable traits (negative eugenics), are SOL. They do not view it as the fault of the "decision makers" that they were born with the wrong perceived genes, or in the wrong country.

The eugenicists don't understand that their standards must be at least as high as those of the person whom they sit in judgment. Whatever the law of the land, the rich man must obey as much as the poor man. We must accord the black man the same legal protocol as we accord the white man.

How many innocent negroes need to be murdered or exonerated after 10, 20, 40 years in jail, for the world to understand the racist scheme going on? Bureaucracy and muddled language have raped the original fair system of justice and the rule of law everywhere in the world, so a few can enrich themselves and satisfy their demented lunatic ideology.

They must heed the words of Carl Sagan. "If a human disagrees with you, let him live. In a hundred billion galaxies, you will not find another."

REALITY. Corruption uses new wording to describe a world still divided between masters and slaves. The voices of millions upon millions of people marginalized by the ruling racist elite have been silenced, along with equal protection under the law. Justice now belongs to whoever can afford it and of a certain skin color. Only the powerful can broadcast their wishes and actions all over the world. They are the only ones allowed and able to use the propaganda machine to deflect any blame from themselves unto the abused. Countless lies and contradictory accounts make sure no one can get to the truth.

AMERICA THE BEAUTIFUL. The parasitic white man in the US will be the victim of his own doing. When he thought he was exploiting blacks, he was building his own undoing. The new administration created three distinct classes in the country; a tiny mixed center, with poor blacks and poor whites constantly at each other's throat, never finding a common ground to coexist, flanked by two extremist sides. On one side are the extremist whites who are hanging on to a colonial confederate white supremacy utopia and on the other side, people who have had enough.

A self-proclaimed, self-selected, sacred and powerful rich elite is trying per argumentum ad crumenam to manipulate a switch for a social remedy that would keep the peasants at peace, so they can maximize their profits. They used many social experiments. Now the prevalent one is to take jobs away from the blacks, in exchange for education, and try to get the whites to work. That should take care of the discontent and appease the white extremists who are ready to explode. But the whites do not want the jobs, because they have been brainwashed, and they encrusted in their psyche that they are above any manual labor. All the while, the elite is ignoring the reality that it is a very weak temporary lull, since Europeans have no chance of permanence on the planet.

OVER REACH. As every successful venture was being taken over, the Anglo-American empire became the new mafia running the world. Corruption is the only true weapon of choice as the grand wizard of the world wrestled the opium trade from Afghanistan, protection trade from the Mafia, cocaine trade from Columbia, marijuana trade from Mexico, smut trade from California and New York, and now it's going after the religious trade from Islam. We can see the same prevalent corruption in the elite approval and tolerance of anarchists, lunatics, war criminals and plain ignorant idiots.

The only western progress ever made is called corruption. Where ever Britain and the US are found, so will corruption and injustice in their highest forms. Nobody knows the business of corruption like the western world. That is its only accomplishment to date.

They implemented a new slavery with injustice and corruption. A purposely divided world in which legislative predators play their chosen games, side by side, simultaneously, from rigged elections, usurpation of power, threats, intimidation, to illegal acts, unconstitutional edicts, backed by corrupt judicial accomplices. The executive, legislative, and judicial branches have compromised and breached the separation and balance of powers.

The nation is in trouble when theft of cash from black and Hispanic travelers by the Volusia County Sheriff Office, on I-95, received the accolade from judge James Nelson. The sheriff's office could keep the stolen money.

All attempts to legally assemble in order to present a constitutionally guaranteed right to redress of grievances by negroes are countered with police repression, from Ferguson city, black lives matter protests, to any natural human reaction to the murder of another unarmed black man. And there have been many murders of unarmed black men. Negroes are killed because the cops see them as foreign enemy combatants who don't belong in the land that whites are claiming for themselves.

People have shown a tendency to accept undeserved punishment until they can take no more. The only time people will engage in a popular revolt or revolution is when their instinct for self-preservation is pushed to its limits. Souffrir que mourir, c'est la devise des hommes.

HOPE. There is an organization called NAAPB, founded by Jonathan Newton, that combats police corruption on a case-by-case basis. Recently, they fought for victims of a large-scale police conspiracy in Camden, New Jersey, in which officers planted drugs on innocent residents. They also advocate for transparency and accountability in law enforcement's use of civil asset forfeiture laws and funds. By ensuring the law is enforced legitimately and through honest means, they seek to strengthen the relationship between law enforcement agencies and their communities, helping citizens remain safe.

THE GAME IS RIGGED. Laws and rules are now enacted by the people who are benefiting from them. Businesses, corporations and companies are the facade hiding rich investors milking the public, the new and improved King Leopold II of Belgium.

They will blame income inequality and disparity on lack of education, even when most of the richest people are school dropouts who have mastered the art of corruption. The three wealthiest individuals have assets that exceed those of the poorest 10% of the world's population. How much education did they get?

As the gap widens between rich rulers and poor subjects, there is bound to be an equal increase in resentment from the people. The US government has switched allegiance from representing the people to being completely subservient to companies with generous lobbies.

SIGNS AFTER SIGNS. We can see the daily desperation of the people in the many comments posted online about any subject

The racism, bile, malice, bitterness, antipathy, hostility, meanness, venom, animosity and anger are frightening expressions of the dysfunctional mentality of the mostly white keyboard warriors. They also directed their nasty disposition at the country; I have never seen so many unpatriotic illegal immigrants wishing and hoping for the utter failure of a stolen country they pretend to love. That is the tragedy of our American society.

Meanwhile, politicians have gone from the public adoration for JFK to the abject rejection of Jason Chaffetz who is throwing in the towel. The saying goes: if you can't stand the heat, get out of the kitchen. Called a coward and told to do his job by his constituents, Jason Chaffetz removed his political apron. He will make plenty of money as an analyst on TV or will open his own "consulting" business. When one is in over his head and responsibility becomes a burden, there is one choice left and it's renouncing power and flee.

Lately, the ire of the masses was clearly evident at several town hall meetings between senators and their angry constituents. Public officials like Tim Bishop, Allen Boyd, Thomas Perriello, Bruce Braley, Dan Maffei, Bill Cassidy, Jim Sessions, Tom McClintock, Darrell Issa, Duncan Hunter, Susan Davis, Scott Peters, Marsha Blackburn, Dennis A. Ross, Charles E. Grassley, Diane Black among others, all got an earful.

The media scrambled to report on many screaming citizens, signs carrying mobs, protesters dragged out by the cops, and congress people fearful for their safety. It got so bad that a few law makers needed police protection to get to their cars in the parking lot and are now afraid to hold any more houses of horrors meetings. Many old gizzards tried in vain to out-talk and yell at angry constituents before asking for their removal. There is no doubt that many legislators will continue to have town hall meetings, ignoring the fact that if at first you don't succeed, skydiving is not for you.

While they always give the white protesters free air time to voice their displeasure, the black protesters are just shut down and relegated to a few comments by a Zionist influenced media always willing to use name-calling. White illiterate commentators do the talking for all black protests.

Unfortunately, the exasperation may reach a boiling point, sometimes. On June 14th, 2017, a white gunman opened fire at a GOP baseball practice, wounding 5 people including house majority whip Steve Scalise and 2 police officers. No media outlet or internet warrior called him a homegrown terrorist, SOB, POS, thug or even criminal. A white man shot 2 cops and a politician, yet the cops are still slaughtering unarmed Negroes. It requires very little effort to hate a man whom you have wronged.

The vice president of the US came up with a brilliant solution when he asked the nation for prayers, ignoring the fact that if Jesus was awake, watching and cared, the whole shooting incident would have been prevented. Jesus was on the side of the shooter.

MATRIX OF FORCE. This state of affairs forced the scared and fearful legislators to ask for additional security, a wider "blue" line between them and their constituents. In response to earlier demand and consideration, we can observe an alarming trend where armed groups, under the label of law enforcement, have been requesting more sophisticated weapons of war to deal with a civilian population... sophisticated weapons of mass destruction, paid for by the taxpayers that these legal gangs are arming themselves against. A collateral damage which occurred when many vital decisions were taken away from the people by their representatives, in violation of the Constitution.

Imagine the impact of such military weapons, taking part in the 1921 Tulsa race riot, when police flew airplanes and dropped nitroglycerin and dynamite on 600 black businesses, burned 1500 houses and destroyed a 35 square blocks area of the black community of Tulsa, also known as the Greenwood district, or the black Wall Street. The same police force, which is executing negroes in broad daylight in the streets of the US today, has received enough weapons of war to fill 185 pages.

From a Beretta M9, Heckler & Koch MP5A3, FGM-148 Javelin, M83 smoke grenade, the local cops have access to tanks and all-terrain vehicles to patrol the paved streets of the US, military aircrafts, grenade launchers, heavily armed tactical vehicles, all in all, 4.3 billion dollars worth of weapons of mass destruction.

Except for the ones with past military experience, the average cop has no training on the equipment, or guidance, relying instead on what they taught themselves playing in the woods with fellow Klansmen, pretending to hunt Negroes.

CCJST. Let's take a closer look at law enforcement. As they enacted many laws to incarcerate more blacks, the demand for correctional and police officers increased. After spending $600 plus supplies, many sponsored recruits grabbed their GED and headed to the local community colleges to get a meager introduction to crime fighting from the Commission on Criminal Justice Standards and Training. Upon graduation four months later, after the review board interviews, a few recruits found out that the promised jobs were not full time or available to people without a political connection and specific ideological affiliation.

The silver lining came with the realization that many civilian jobs, paying double the LEO's starting salary, were available. Still, many graduates forwent the money for the uniform and perceived power.

A GUN AND A BADGE. Police departments and the Armed Forces are the only true buffer between politicians and constituents, between law-abiding citizens and criminals. That doesn't always work. We entrust them to enforce the biased laws of the land, and people believe the nonsense that they are here to protect and serve the public.

Do banks serve the public and interest of customers when they pay .02% interest on the money you deposit and charge you 25% interest on a credit card purchase?

We already know that cops don't deter or prevent crimes, because we still have plenty of crimes happening every day, and sometimes the police persons are the perpetrators of crimes like murder, extortion, execution, rape, theft, free use of drugs from evidence lockers. The only true service they provide is criminal record keeping and recording; that's why they usually show up after a crime, to document it. And that function is enough to warrant special benefits, which may be construed as corruption, like the personal bicycles purchased with taxpayer's money because the cops were planning on riding the streets to get closer to the people in the community. They also received horses and motorcycles because we would see them as friendly and cool.

What ever happened to these programs? They still get free use of taxpayers financed patrol cars because it could be a great crime deterrent to have a patrol car parked in any gated neighborhood.

Meanwhile, the police academy teaches to stay off duty, when off the clock, and to transfer information on any crime in progress to working units.

Another benefit for the LEO is that local businesses provide free or reduced priced food to law enforcement personnel. Many cops just grab whatever items they desired from a shelf at a convenience store, show the food they "appropriated" to the cashier before exiting without paying; a silent promise they will include the store in question on their patrol route. The mafia charging protection money did the same. Today, businesses in the US are giving 10% off of regular price to vets, law enforcement and uniformed personnel, which really means they are charging the regular Joe 10% more.

Special car stickers are another sign of corruption that allows cops to be above the law. Recognized by all departments, they affix stickers to identify personal vehicles, thus making it possible for cops not to be tagged for infractions like parking infractions or moving violations. Something that is extended to family members of police and correction officers.

When these corrupt government employees retire, we appoint them to lucrative positions in the private sector, or security companies where they can collect overdue bribes and kickbacks. Sometimes, they achieve the same goal by remaining in a civilian position within the government. That's if they can avoid friendly fire.

TRYING TO PASS. 6/22/2017 The Associated Press reported that an off-duty African-American police officer was shot Wednesday night by a white colleague in St. Louis, while both officers were attempting to aid first responders after a high-speed car chase ended in a crash, the St. Louis Metropolitan Police Department told Yahoo News.

Authorities said the injured officer was in his home when he heard a crash. He decided to help officers who had already arrived at the scene, who had exchanged fire with the suspects. His colleagues initially ordered the unnamed officer, who was also armed, to the ground, but after recognizing him, they invited him to approach them.

"At this time, a responding officer, 36-year-old white male with over 8 years of service, just arriving in the area observed this and 'fearing for his safety' and apparently not recognizing the off-duty officer, discharged a shot, striking the off-duty officer in the arm," the police department said by email.

The unnamed wounded officer is 38 years old and an 11-year veteran of the same department. According to the officer's lawyer, Rufus Tate Jr., the friendly fire shooting was part of a trend of police violence toward African-American men.

"In the police report, you have so far, there is no description of the threat he perceived," Tate told Fox 2 Now. "So we have a real problem with that. But this has been a national discussion for the past two years. There is this perception that they automatically feared a black man."

"Per department policy, they will place seven officers on administrative leave," the department said. "The Force Investigative Unit responded," it added, and an investigation will take place.

End of story, with a most likely quiet financial settlement to the black officer.

ELSEWHERE. In 2009, a white officer shot and killed Omar J. Edwards, a 25-year-old New York City police officer on a Harlem street while in street clothes.

And in Providence, Rhode Island, an off-duty black police sergeant, Cornel Young Jr., was killed by two uniformed white colleagues in 2000 while he was trying to break up a fight in a parking lot. Young was the son of the department's highest-ranking black officer at the time.

WHEN THE SHOE IS ON THE OTHER FOOT. On July 15th, 2017, an Australian woman became the latest victim of a police shooting. Immediately following the incident, elected officials, the media and American populace became enraged and exploded in putrid comments when someone leaked the preliminary facts that the shooter was a black cop. Not only did they reveal the officer's name, but they also made his national origin, religion, and the content of his employee records public. Within hours of the shooting, the identity and record of black Somali-American officer

Mohamed Noor were available to the deranged public*. Without completing an investigation, they directed all the blame personally towards the black officer.

(Note: *Even today, they still shield the identities of the white cops responsible for the slaughter of countless unarmed black men and women in secrecy.)

Speaking publicly, Minneapolis Police Chief Janeé Harteau said the killing of Australian woman Justine Ruszczyk didn't need to happen. The 40-year-old "didn't have to die," Harteau said of the July 15, 2017 shooting incident. "It goes against who we are as a department, how we train and our expectations for our officers."

Does that mean the negroes who got shot deserved to die? No one ever said anything close to those words about any of the murders of unarmed black men, women, and children. Not one single article contained one single derogatory word about the white victim. This shows the level of racism that exists and permeates the white Confederate society of the United British States of America.

Nekima Levy-Pounds, a civil rights lawyer and activist running for mayor of Minneapolis, said Chief Harteau "needed to be fired." Ms. Levy-Pounds said it had been "a slap in the face to people of color" that the chief spoke out about the death of Ms. Damond, who was white, after defending officers involved in past shootings of black people. She is attempting to paint this as an isolated case based on one officer's poor judgment as opposed to a systemic pattern, Ms. Levy-Pounds said.

State investigators continue to probe Ms. Damond's death. Both Ms. Hodges and Chief Harteau have said she should not have been shot. "Justine didn't have to die," chief Harteau said, citing information released by state officials investigating the case. (In the cases of white officers who butchered unarmed black men and women, everyone is told to WAIT for the result of the delayed investigations.)

The racism that can be found in the US is unique; there is no other place on the planet that can match the virulent, deadly American hatred of dark-skinned people. The national reaction was amazing to one white woman who received the posthumous attention that all victims of police violence deserve after so many Negroes have been executed and slaughtered by the jack booted Confederate Klansmen, skinheads of the police force. No one dared to utter one bad thing about Justine; she was not a thug, hoe, SOB, POS, super predator... everything she was or did was lily white and perfect. They changed her last name from Ruszczyk to Damond, making it easier for dumb white Americans to pronounce. The American populace denigrated murdered negroes and dragged their names through the mud. Countless of keyboard warriors volunteered hundred of thousands of reasons negroes deserved to die. Everything said about the departed white woman was peachy. Many asked: why did US police shoot an Australian woman? The chief of police lost her job, and she didn't pull the trigger; They also made her personal life public, on display in the news.

The following is one of the many media reports, after the death of Australian Justine Ruszczyk, from Amy Forliti and Steve Karnowski of the Associated Press. They are all alike in their renderings and treatment of the involved.

MINNEAPOLIS (AP) Minneapolis police Chief Janee Harteau resigned Friday at the request of the mayor, who said she lost confidence in the chief following last week's shooting death of an unarmed Australian woman by a police officer. In a statement released Friday, Harteau said: "I've decided I will step aside to let a fresh set of leadership eyes see what more can be done for the MPD to be the very best it can be." Minneapolis Mayor Betsy Hodges said she asked for the chief's resignation. "I've lost confidence in the Chief's ability to lead us further... it is clear that she has lost the confidence of the people of Minneapolis as well," Hodges said. "For us to continue to transform policing, and community trust in policing, we need new leadership at MPD." (Mayor Hodges is the same person who lauded, on Facebook, the graduation and hiring of Officer Mohamed Noor in the Minneapolis police force.)

Harteau, who worked her way up from the bottom of the department to police chief, said she was proud of the work she accomplished, but the shooting of 40-year-old Justine Damond by one of her officers, and other incidents, "have caused me to engage in deep reflection". She added, "Despite the MPD's many accomplishments under my leadership over these years and my love for the City, I have to put the communities we serve first".

Harteau was out of the city on personal time for nearly a week following Saturday's shooting of Damond, a 40-year-old life coach and bride-to-be who was killed by an officer responding to her 911 call of a possible rape. The state is investigating the shooting. In Harteau's first remarks on the case on Thursday, when she returned to work, she was sharply critical of Somali- American officer Mohamed Noor while defending his training. "The actions in question go against who we are in the department, how we train and the expectations we have for our officers," Harteau said Thursday. "These were the actions and judgment of one individual."

That wasn't enough for some City Council members. Linea Palmisano, who represents the ward where Damond died, told her fellow council members Friday that she was "done with image control and crisis management." She said the department has systemic problems, and it was time to consider a change in leadership. Palmisano added: "The time for talk is done. It is time for action." A department spokesperson said Harteau would not be available for an interview after Friday's announcement.

Harteau has spent her career with the department, starting

as a beat cop in 1987, when she was just 22. She worked her way up the ranks and in 2012, was appointed chief, becoming the city's first female, first openly gay and first Native American police chief. But she's had a rocky tenure in the top post. Her relationship with Hodges was strained, particularly after the fatal shooting of 24-year-old Jamar Clark during a confrontation with two white police officers in 2015. The black man's death, amid heightened tensions around the U.S., sparked protests citywide that included an 18-day occupation outside the police station on the city's north side. A U.S. Department of Justice review faulted poor communications between the mayor and the chief.

The chief and mayor butted heads again in April when Hodges blocked Harteau's promotion of Lt. John Delmonico to lead the Fourth Precinct, after the chief had already made the public announcement. Delmonico had been a critic of Hodges when he headed the police union.

And Harteau, being out of town when Damond was killed, didn't help either. Harteau, who said she was backpacking in an area with limited cellphone reception, told reporters Thursday evening that it would have been "challenging" to return but that she had kept in touch with her command staff.

Harteau and her longtime patrol partner, Holly Keegel, were featured in a 1990 episode of the reality TV series "Cops." The partners endured years of harassment from some male colleagues, and it escalated to the point where they felt endangered because they weren't getting help when they would call for backup. The Minnesota Department of Human Rights upheld their discrimination and sexual harassment complaint, which led to changes in training and to discipline against some officers.

Harteau and Keegel got married in 2013 after gay marriage became legal in Minnesota. Harteau told the Star Tribune a year later that they had separated amid the strains of her being chief.

Three years earlier, they honored the chief as the grand marshal of the city's annual Pride Parade. But she found herself on the defensive in June when organizers asked law enforcement to minimize their participation because of tensions over the recent acquittal of St. Anthony police officer Jeronimo Yanez in the fatal shooting of another black man, Philando Castile, in the St. Paul suburb of Falcon Heights last summer.

She said she was "beyond disappointed" that they did not consult beforehand with her, but later persuaded the organizers to welcome LGBT officers after all.

SHOP AND COMPARE. Compare the above story to the following one.

DETROIT. In 1967 Mary Jarrett Jackson explained: "There were some white girls there, with three black men at the Algiers Motel. They were there willingly. That upset the police. The officers divided those kids up and took them into different rooms, beat them up and did some awful things to their bodies by ramming things into their genitalia, up their anus. It was awful to look at those kids beaten as they were, shot in the head. The way they brutalized those black men, I did the forensic work on that. There was lots of evidence, but they didn't want that brought out in court. It should have been prosecuted to the fullest extent of the law. "

The slaughter of three black men caused the anger of the black community to explode after decades of social injustice, police brutality, and institutional racism. In the end, the Detroit Free Press reported: 43 black people were dead, over 1,100 black people injured, over 7,000 blacks arrested, and over 2,500 businesses destroyed.

The families of the three slain teens (17-year-old Carl Cooper, 19-year-old Aubrey Pollard and 18-year-old Fred Temple), fought for years to get justice. To this day, they don't believe they ever got it.

HANDS UP, DON'T SHOOT. People say that the system is not bad, that the problems arise from corrupt cops. If you put a rotten egg in a recipe, does only part of the dish is foul?

The news and social media abound of real life videos of white cops shooting and killing unarmed black men and children when the situation did not warrant it. They never charge them because the US still considers Negroes as commodities. They have summarily executed hundreds of black males for no other reason than their black skin. Earlier this year, a video showed a white South Carolina cop shooting a 50-year-old unarmed black man in the back as he was running away from him. The explanation is always the same: the cop was afraid for his life. How could the cop be afraid for his life when the unarmed black man was running away from him? The most important pieces of data in a cop's memory bank, after a deadly shooting, are "I was afraid for my life," "he was reaching for my, or a gun". It's something that is drilled into you the minute the police academy starts, when the indoctrination of the "us vs. them" ideology starts.

In yet another case, more training from the police academy was evident from a court testimony from a murderous police officer: "I meant to stop the threat," he told jurors. "I didn't shoot to kill him. I didn't shoot to wound him. I shot to stop his actions." He remembered his training well... too well. That's the textbook training from the police academy. Long before going to the firing range, that they pounded potential defense into everyone's head.

LINE OF DUTY. They killed more cops in the line of duty last year (2016) than in any year since 2011, leading many, including some in the FBI, to falsely connect the increase in violence with the rise of the Black Lives Matter movement. Earlier this month, the FBI declared that "black identity extremists" are a violent threat to officers, but data released by the Bureau on

Monday shows white people are actually much more of a threat to cops. In 2016, cop-killing suspects included 59 individuals, out of which only 15 were black. These suspects were responsible for the intentional shooting or running down of sixty-six officers.

The message has always been the same: "if you are black, all the police officers have to do is say they were in fear of their life and they get away with murder because the victim is black," the local NAACP said in a statement. The acquittals mean a police officer can create a dangerous situation, then cite that dangerous situation as the reason for killing someone. Justice is not only elusive, it's nonexistent when a dark-skin is involved. The pain of always being denied justice is almost too much to bear, as Confederate white supremacists use recycled words in their inability to come up with anything of value to express and justify their old ideology.

In 2014, another South Carolina police officer shot an unarmed African American whom he had stopped in a parking lot for a seatbelt violation. Imagine that, the death penalty for not wearing a seat belt. Would that have been the case if the driver was white?

White officers, too often, act out of animosity towards blacks, because they still see them as commodities, run-away slaves, thugs, drug dealers, or, in the words of Hillary Clinton, super predators. It is racism, pure and simple. When a person's skin color triggers a reaction, it is racism, there is no other word to conceal the action. One can stretch and wiggle to find other words to describe the murders of blacks in the US, but it is what it is... institutional racism. It permeates all levels of the white society, from the bottom to the top, complete with buzzwords, libels, derogatory words, etc... The shooting is just a confirmatory bias to reinforce the belief that the black man has served his purpose in the US and is no longer needed in plantations or wanted in the white society.

Blacks are at a point where the complaints are just complaints. There is no one to hear or willing to listen to them. Jailing and killing young black males has the same effect as when the slave traders removed the strong young black males from Africa. It's to induce the depopulation and destabilization of the black community.

Like pedophiles to the Catholic priesthood, jack booted skinheads, neo-Nazis, Klansmen have flocked to the Confederate police departments.

JUSTICE FOR ALL? When corruption is coupled with racism, then idiots like Joe Arpaio and his shadow David Clarke come out of the woodwork to create an even deadlier dysfunctional police force.

Frank Nucera Jr, the chief of police in Bordentown, New Jersey, systematically abused black residents, denied them their civil rights and even likened them to ISIS, said federal prosecutors who charged him, on Wednesday 11/01/2017, with a hate crime. He used racial slurs and police dogs to threaten and intimidate black Americans. He expressed his wish and dream of lining blacks and mowing them down with bullets. Just like his ancestor King Leopold II of Belgium did in the Congo. In September 2016, he slammed a black 18-year-old's head into a metal door jamb. He is now facing 20 years in prison for his racist abuses. But, since it happened to Negroes in the US, a country so very passionate about the rule of law, Frank Nucera Jr. will most likely walk, or receive probation for a job well done.

IN-JUSTICE. The "leaders in charge" have learned to ignore the black chants and demands; they know they are in control, and they are fairly confident that, like a hurricane, the noise will be over soon, after a couple of days. If blacks continue to protest the injustices, they send executioners to silence the chants and demands. The reason blacks don't get any respect is because they are still regarded as 3/5 of a human, by the white supremacist ideology that is prevalent in the US, especially among Christians who received the instructions from their God.

Even the ignorant clichés are still in use. In July 2017, a St. Petersburg mayoral candidate in Florida said that African-American supporters of his rival should "go back to Africa" if they don't like it in the U.S.

Until last September 19, 2017, Tyler Roysdon suited up as a volunteer firefighter in Franklin Township, a small town in southwestern Ohio, about 40 miles north of Cincinnati. But, according to station WHIO, a recent Facebook back-and-forth caught the 20-year-old writing that in a burning building he would choose to save a dog before an African American because "one dog is more important than a million niggers" he wrote.

LEGAL WRECK. They rigged the justice system to treat blacks as runaway slaves and commodities. A survey revealed that 92 percent of white police officers believe the United States has already assured equal rights for African-Americans. They rigged it to protect police officers and to ensure that blacks keep being butchered by police officers. Everywhere along the way, the officer's action is protected by racist judges, prosecutors who are in place primarily to protect what the officers do, and grand juries which are mostly populated by relatives of law enforcement personnel, and or people affiliated with law enforcement. Police officers who know will slaughter more Negroes because the justice system will protect them.

US prosecutors have found it difficult to convict police officers in high-profile shooting cases involving black victims, despite recent incidents being captured on video. Anger over the failure to find the officers guilty has sometimes boiled over, leading to violent protests. One needs only to read a few online comments from the white public about the murder of a negro to understand why the US is a white supremacist country.

JUSTICE DELAYED AND DENIED. Another day, another story, another way to add insult to injury. The news media reported that four African American members of the LGBTQ community, who marched in the PRIDE parade in Columbus, Ohio and who felt the burden of their race and their sexuality, protested the Philando Castile ruling by calling for seven minutes of silence. The result is that they arrested them as whites looked on, appearing to be cheering their fate.

That's the black reality in a country with a supposed Constitutional provision for redress of grievances. And they arrested them for being silent, just like the vocal protesters. That's one of the many ways they silence Negroes in the US.

They can do all the studies that money can buy, they can invent and create a new dictionary, it is what it is. Most shoot-don't- shoot live scenarios are affected by the skin color of the target. They have made a few studies that reveal that split-second decisions are sometimes a factor. They are not; if that was the case, why wasn't there a shoot-out at the Bundy ranch where armed white people were there for a gunfight with the cops? So all these studies are just BS trying to calm the negroes until they shoot the next one.

It is a fact that all white people perceive all black males as threatening. They take white jobs, drive cars usually reserved for whites, heck, many even "date" white women. It is a cultivated perception that is now embedded in the screwed up white psyche.

EINSATZGRUPPEN. Let's be honest, in 99.99% of the cases where blacks have been butchered, the officer's life was not in danger and he wasn't threatened in any way, shape or form. But the easiest route in American society is to kill the Negro, and let the system explain why. This is the collateral damage when powers are given by the state to a racist cop to use deadly force.

This occurs in direct violation of federal law, which prohibits discrimination in police work. Any police department receiving federal funding is covered by Title VI of the Civil Rights Act of 1964 (42 U.S.C. § 2000d) and the Office of Justice Programs statute (42 U.S.C. § 3789d[c]), which prohibit discrimination on the basis of race, color, national origin, sex, and religion. These laws prohibit conduct ranging from racial slurs and unjustified arrests to the refusal of departments to respond to discrimination complaints. Yet none of that can stop a murderous cop from the reckless slaughter of a negro.

This is above and beyond the fact that key federal criminal statute makes it unlawful for anyone acting with police authority to deprive or conspire to deprive another person of any right protected by the Constitution or laws of the United States, Section 18 U.S.C. § 241. Another statute, commonly referred to as the police misconduct provision, makes it unlawful for state or local police to engage in a pattern or practice of conduct that deprives persons of their rights, 42 U.S.C.A. 14141.

IT BROKE ME. Trevor Noah's emotional reaction to the assassination of Philando Castile said it all. "What they're basically saying is, in America, it is officially reasonable to be afraid of a person just because we are black," said Noah of the newly released dashcam video of the horrific murder of Philando Castile.

"You hear the stories, but you watch that and forget race. Are we all watching the same video? The video where a law-abiding man followed the officer's instructions to the letter of the law, and then was killed regardless? People watched that video and then voted to acquit?"

"It's one thing to have the system against you, the district attorneys, the police unions, the courts, that's one thing. But when a jury of your peers, your community, sees this evidence and then decides that even this is self-defense? That is truly depressing. Because what they're basically saying is in America, it is officially reasonable to be afraid of a person just because we are black. And that's the truth of what we saw with this verdict."

CLASS A, GROUP A. Much of the respect for law enforcement rests in the false belief that cops reduce crimes and are the "blue" line between law-abiding citizens and the criminal elements of society. If that was true, why do criminals still prey on law-abiding citizens? Another common misconception is that if the police forces were not here, violence and lawlessness would be rampant; it would be like the Old West. The Old West never existed, except in Hollywood films and movies. There was no police department before 1830 when the city of Boston established the first; how did the law-abiding citizens survive before that date?

The actual job of a flatfoot is to record crime and prevent civil disorder. Law enforcement is part of the Armed Forces, an embedded front line military unit charged with civil policing. That notion was clearly explained at the police academy by GB, an instructor who added: "You will always have backup. When you are faced with a situation, other cops from your department will show up. If more help is needed, the Sheriff's Office will be there. If that's not enough, the Armed Forces will be your backup. All the while, you will have the support of all branches of the government to do your job."

The police academy encourages and reinforces white supremacist ideologies. It's a place where recruits can collect many jewels, like if we see a black man in a white neighborhood at a certain time, he is there to "case" the houses; if we see a white man in a black neighborhood at the same hour, he is there to buy drugs.

This is the indoctrination provided to reach the frame of mind of today's American police officer. They also pound the "us vs them" program into everyone's head at the academy.

SMILE. While training for defensive tactics, recruits learned to control a detained suspect with "the thumb and shoulder restraint". The thumb technique involves the officer's right hand firmly grasping the suspect's left thumb, moving it backwards toward the forearm of the suspect, twisting the wrist behind his back while maintaining body control with the left hand over the suspect's upper arm or opposite shoulder. While demonstrating the technique, they advised recruits to be aware of the presence of any news camera or recording being made. The officer should always project calmness, look at the cameras and repeat non- stop: "please cooperate with me, sir, please cooperate with me." To make it look like the suspect is resisting arrest, the suspect's thumb can be twisted harder to make it seem like he is not cooperating, when in reality, he is just in pain, trying not to get his finger dislocated.

And of course, another jewel from the academy is that the trunk of the squad car is an ideal place to store handy items like Chinese throwing stars (in the old days), knives, drugs and old confiscated guns that can be used if "things get out of control."

AMBER ALERT. Now the job is a lot easier as the cops sit on their butts and let the public do law enforcement work for free, with amber alerts. They don't even patrol the neighborhoods anymore; they cruise by sometimes. It won't be long for an emergency call to go like, "Your call is very important to us. We will be with you shortly." 2 hours later, someone in India or Pakistan will answer the phone call.

Anyone who wants to be impressed by the ability of law enforcement to solve crimes should visit the story of Henry Lee Lucas.

TRICK QUESTIONS. A clique of all white officers, in charge of hiring recruits at an all-white police department, asked me the following question: "You are on duty and come across a police officer who stole a loaf of bread, because he is hungry and needs to feed his starving children. What would you do?" The look on their faces revealed that they didn't like my answer.

One genius, after looking at my certificate of naturalization, asked: "Are you a boat people?" I replied, "no sir, I am too young to have been on the Mayflower." They didn't like that answer either. Afterwards, one of them received a demotion for copying the document that clearly warned in red letters, "It is punishable by U. S. Law to copy, print or photograph this certificate."

By the time the third question headed my way, I didn't want the position and was already eye-balling the exit door. The smartest of the bunch asked: "The Supreme Court decides that murder is legal. You come across a human sacrifice by a gang of Rastafarians. What would you do?" The idiotic racism was too much. I discarded the first thought to make fun of him. The highest court of the land deemed murder legal? Then, I brushed away the desire to educate and help him understand Rastas don't indulge in human sacrifices, don't wear dreadlocks and certainly don't smoke ganja. So, I took the nicest way out by pretending to not understand the question: "You mean, I am on duty, and come across a gang of Rastas, behaving like the Donner Party or your ancestors in Jamestown, Virginia?" Every time I remember the look on his face, I end up with a smile, followed by a laughing fit.

Exit stage left.

MORE RACISM. Lately, the local law enforcement agencies have been used to extend the ranks and reach of ICE in targeting only Mexicans for arrest and deportation. White citizens can waltz in from Aryan breeding farms like: Andorra, Hungary, Norway, Australia, Iceland, Portugal, Austria, Ireland, San Marino, Belgium,

Italy, Singapore, Brunei, Japan, Slovakia, Chile, Latvia, Slovenia, Czech Republic, Liechtenstein, South Korea, Denmark, Lithuania, Spain, Estonia, Luxembourg, Sweden, Finland, Malta, Switzerland, France, Monaco, Taiwan, Germany, Netherlands, United Kingdom, Greece, and New Zealand. The cops and any other employee of the government know or should know that it is illegal to discriminate on the basis of race, color, religion and country of origin. Why are the white illegal immigrants not targeted by ICE?

PRIVILEGE 101. To think that police corruption can be stymied within a department is childish and laughable. Cops, being members of the military, are off the limits and reach of the legal system of the mafia they serve together. A member of the team is above any sanction by the team. As members of the team, they are partly to blame for a crime, and as a member of the team, they can not be fully responsible for that crime. Everyone else is doing the same thing, and no finger pointing is allowed in the clubhouse. From manufactured trumped-up charges, planted weapons and drugs, altered evidences, bungled investigations, false arrests, police work is never done. Then comes the legal finesse required to cover all that up.

The false image of the mission to protect and serve the public is maintained with billboards offering safety tips or requesting tips about criminal activities to help solve crimes, and sometimes truly awful television commercials, like the laughable and silly stunt pulled by the Lake County (Florida) Sheriff Office, dressed like ISIS militants, taunting and challenging local heroin dealers to a gunfight.

EXTRA MONEY. Corruption is very profitable in law enforcement. A controversial law enforcement practice allows police to confiscate property from individuals without ever convicting them of a crime, and often without even charging them. Many cops got rich from that scheme. Under this process, local police agencies could evade stricter state laws on civil forfeiture by deferring to more lax federal standards. And there are always many more ways to increase a cop's salary.

The police protective services provided to Benny Hinn and other big shot evangelists are very telling of the privilege accorded to cops by the corrupt elite. The cops get overtime pay and the elite get to flaunt their power and status backed by armed servants on the taxpayers' tab. What good is an armed cop in front of a church where god is supposed to be in charge? An omnipotent God can not even handle the traffic in front of his own church? Damn!

OMERTA. When it comes to police work, one point stressed by an FBI research is the importance of responsibility to prevent corruption. Yet the FBI, a federal law enforcement agency, is never too thrilled to investigate corrupt police officers, because they are part of the same gang. Cops don't want to turn in other cops, for the simple reason they don't want to be a rat, a zero or a cry-baby. There is also the unspoken threat and warning that if you tattle on "one of yours," your back will not only be covered, but you may have to watch your back. There is a fraternal understanding among police officers known variously as "the Code of Silence" and "the Blue Curtain" under which officers regard testimony against a fellow officer as betrayal.

Just like Scientology.

Even when honest cops are willing to blow the whistle, there may be no one willing to listen. Everyone remembers the movie based on real life with Al Pacino about the code of silence. Police officer Frank Serpico's startling testimony against fellow officers not only revealed systemic corruption but highlighted a longstanding obstacle to investigating these abuses.

FBI LEADERSHIP FILES. All departments have goals and the officers follow the lead of their higher ups on the second floor.

One of these goals is to maintain the public trust. As one researcher explained, "principled leaders do not act to protect their own egos, try to put on a good appearance without substance in their decisions or efforts, or attempt to intimidate those under them. Instead, principle-based executives who work with their subordinates can take an important step toward creating an ethical climate by developing an agenda that explains the moral purposes of the department".

It looks good on paper, as we well know what happens in reality. There are subordinates who have a close-knit relationship with the leadership in all departments, and these "favored" individuals also have subordinates they are close to, joke with and work with daily. That's not considering rogue officers who will do as they want and try to influence the newly hired.

One example was a particular officer who insisted on driving the wrong way down a one-way street and laughed, because "who is going to write me a ticket?" He never got a reprimand. While ethical supervisors help maintain an ethical workplace, the opposite also remains true: uncaring and incompetent officials actually can promote misconduct and racism. Like politicians, police chiefs keep their jobs.

ACADEMY 101. So a recruit receives a 4 months long training, 250 hours of Constitutional and basic law enforcement standards at the academy with all the basic rules and regulations to start an on-the-job training.

While the academy is just an introduction to law enforcement, it is nevertheless the hiring department policies that will affect his job performance. That's where they set the standards for officers to follow. Departments tend to hire people who will fit within their respective organization, individuals who share the same attitudes, ideology, perceptions, assumptions, values, core beliefs, ways of living, and traditions. Individual departments become micro family units, where cops see each other as closer than their own blood relatives. There are parking lots for personnel, full of the same type of cars. That's why many police departments will hire mostly Europeans, while one mumbled something like "the lowest minority we will hire is an American Indian." Whatever that means. So, when an officer runs afoul of the law, just look at his department. Cops who shoot negroes work in a mainly predominant white department or one with a couple of token blacks.

MADE MEMBER. Once the probationary period is over, the recruit becomes a member of the new family. The instructions received at the academy of "us versus them" become real, and a new mentality creates an allegiance stronger than that to the mission of the department or even the profession. Just like the mafia.

There was a preventable accident in a small country town, where a Spanish speaking drunk driver crashed into a truck driven by a deputy sheriff who died at the scene. A white police officer, who responded to the emergency call, was so severely distraught that he wanted to shoot the drunk driver instead of arresting him.

This is the level of allegiance between cops, the "us versus them" mentality.

Even the department administrators are not immune to the ire of a scorned cop. Two cops were seriously pissed off at a sergeant after he scolded one of them in public, in front of a group of civilians. And we could see the difference of opinion as they clearly articulated, afterwards, that they had each other's back, and the sergeant didn't have their backs.

SWAT. The other notion that law enforcement work is a daily life and death struggle is a joke. The only unit which sees a bit of action is the SWAT, and the rare situations are very controlled with perimeters and overwhelmingly armed officers. Imagine the swat team showing up to foil a bank robbery with tanks and armored personnel carriers. That's if they get there on time, before the getaway. In cases with hostages, the scenarios involve taking long-range shots, most of the time without target acquisition. That's how the captives end up with the bullets sometimes. Countless of officers never had to pull their guns out of the secured holsters during their entire careers. When some of them do, it's to murder unarmed blacks, with the public at large always willing to justify their actions. Cops are the most tolerated public employees, regardless of their actions. Especially desperate lonely women will give a carte blanche to any "handcuffs carrying man in uniform".

SHARE THE LOOT. One of the contributing factors in corruption is the system of perks that officers who "perform" to the ideals of the department will receive. Anything that promotes his department, arrests, seized weapons, recovered drugs, issued traffic tickets are very important in an officer getting a promotion or a raise in pay. Numbers count and somehow are a telltale sign of how well an officer is doing his job. An officer will make an arrest or issue citations to increase his quota with no care in the world. So the actual job entails getting results at all costs, arresting as many people as possible, then let the judges and lawyers sort it out.

And blacks suffer the brunt of these abusive and illegal actions because they all "look alike and guilty." This little debacle is another excuse used by law enforcement, something that can be heard on the news after a murder: we arrested the bad guys and the court system let them out. Once again, the officers are the heroes of the day, even when they arrested a guy who had nothing to do with the crime in question. Unless totally outrageous, this behavior will be tolerated within the department, with the harshest punishment being a few days off with pay or relegated to desk duty*.

(*In one of his Harry Callahan movies, Clint Eastwood received a scalding from his supervisor who assigned him to "desk duty." His reply: "desk duty is for a**holes.")

A NEGRO A DAY. There are many rotten apples in law enforcement, not just one or two... whole orchards. The question that begs an answer is why are they not removed from their position? The answer is very simple, the entire system is corrupt, as any corrupt officer who is fired can get a job at another department.

To go back to the scenario of the officer stealing a loaf of bread to feed himself and his hungry kids, some acts are seen as minor and only require a warning or counseling. But was it the first time that the officer "appropriated" a loaf of bread? Or a sandwich at a convenience store? Or wrote a ticket to boost his chances at a promotion? Or arrested the first black man he saw? Or accepted sexual favor to dismiss a speeding ticket? Or murdered an unarmed negro? That's the side business of law enforcement.

When a partner is corrupt, it becomes very easy for a recruit to become as corrupt. In a study conducted by the International Association of Chiefs of Police, 7 of the top 10 issues determined as critically important to officers actively working in law enforcement involved ethics and integrity.

It is often said that while officers are human and will continue to make mistakes, ethical misconduct can not and should not be tolerated. Then why are unethical police officers allowed to remain on the force after outlandish misconduct? Whenever a criminal officer breaks the law, the solution always flows in his favor as re-assignment, relocation, time off with pay, etc... While the cadre will deplore certain illegal and criminal acts by police officers, it lacks the courage to deal with those who are responsible for the failures. Once again, the basic tenet of Criminal Justice is ignored: justice is the finding of the truth.

RECENTLY. On July 29, 2017 4:38 PM, Donovan Harrell reported: A Washington D.C. police officer accused of wearing a racist shirt while on duty was suspended Friday after an investigation.

Law4BlackLives, a lawyer group that supports Black Lives Matter*, filed a complaint against the officer, after a photo of him wearing the shirt began circulating on social media. "This t-shirt is symptomatic of a dangerous and insidious combination of racism and a crass abuse of power that has infiltrated the police department," the complaint read. D.C. Police didn't release the officer's name, but the lawyer group identified the officer as Vincent Altiere in the complaint.

(Note*: Isn't it funny that white supremacists hate the original #black lives matter, yet are not beyond copying blacks, like "blue lives matter" and "white lives matter".)

According to The Washington Post, the black shirt has the words "Seventh District," which is a district that has a few of the city's most violent areas, including Anacostia, Barry Farm and Washington Highlands.

The centerpiece of the shirt is the Grim Reaper holding a rifle with the Washington D.C. flag attached to it. Above the flag lies the words "powershift," which refers to the officers assigned to areas with high amounts of crime, The Washington Post reported.

On the 'O' in "powershift" is a type of cross identified by the Anti-Defamation League as the same type of cross belonging to a neo-Nazi website.

Last, the shirt has a phrase that says "Let me see that waistband jo," which the advocacy group said refers to the police practice of demanding to see individuals' waistbands, mainly people of color, to check for weapons.

INCIDENTS IN THE NEWS. The news media sometimes has no choice but to report on the rotten apples. Once again, it's not done in the truth's interest, but to somehow maintain the illusion that the system polices itself and is always willing to remove the bad seeds.

- BALTIMORE AGAIN On Jul 19, 2017, 4:24pm EDT the following article was updated by German Lopez. "It's not especially rare to hear stories of a police officer abusing his power. But it is pretty rare to see a story in which the cop actually records himself doing it."

That's what seemed to happen in Baltimore recently, when a police officer appeared to accidentally record himself planting drugs at a crime scene. In the January 2017 video, reported by Fox Baltimore, officer Richard Pinheiro puts a bag of pills under some trash in an alley. He then walks to the street. He then switches on his camera, walks back to the alley, and acts like he just found the drugs for the first time.

Here's the crucial mistake that Pinheiro apparently made: He apparently didn't realize that body cameras often save the last 30 seconds of footage before they're manually activated. So they caught all of that preparation for his big faux discovery on tape.

"I'm going to check here," Pinheiro says as the camera is activated. "Hold on." He then walks to the scene and acts like he's looking around. Finally, he comes to the spot where he put the pills, picks them up, and says, "Yo!" The other officers appear to play along with his fake discovery, as if this is all routine and normal.

The defendant connected to the drugs would have gone to trial this week. But according to BuzzFeed, the prosecutor dropped the charges after the defendant's public defender discovered and saw the video. Although, in a troubling development, the prosecutor apparently used Pinheiro as an eyewitness in a separate case, even after learning of his misconduct in the video. Seriously. This really happened.

- Several other law enforcement agencies raided The Brooklyn, Illinois, including the Illinois State Police, and the St. Clair County Sheriff. Local news crews witnessed police from different agencies carrying equipment, computers, weapons, and records out of the building and driving away with them.

- (From an FBI analytical look, facts abound about the CPD). The Chicago Police Department has a long legacy of corruption, a checkered history of police scandals and an embarrassingly long list of police officers who have crossed the line to engage in brutality, corruption and criminal activity.

As of late, they have convicted 295 Chicago police officers of serious crimes, such as drug dealing, beatings of civilians, destroying evidence, protecting mobsters, theft and murder. The listing of police convicted of crimes undoubtedly underestimates the problem of corruption in the Chicago Police Department (CPD). The list does not include undetected and unreported illegal activity, serious misconduct resulting in internal disciplinary action, and officers who retire rather than face charges.

A report showed that, first, corruption has long persisted within the CPD and continues to be a serious problem. There have been 102 convictions of Chicago police since the beginning of 2000.

Second, police officers often resist reporting crimes and misconduct committed by fellow officers. The "blue code of silence", while difficult to prove, is an integral part of the department's culture and it exacerbates the corruption problems. A breakthrough almost happened last November when a federal jury found that the City of Chicago and its police culture were partially responsible for officer Anthony Abbate's brutal beating of a female bartender. After the civil trial to assess damages, the victim's attorney declared, "We proved a code of silence at every level in the Chicago Police Department".

Third, over time, a large portion of police corruption has shifted from police officers aiding and abetting mobsters and organized crime to officers involved with drugs dealers and street gangs. Since the year 2000, they convicted 47 Chicago law enforcement officers of drug and gang-related crimes. The department's war on drugs puts police officers, especially those working undercover, in dangerous situations where they must cooperate with criminals to catch criminals. These endeavors require that CPD superiors provide top leadership and oversight to keep officers on the straight and narrow.

Fourth, internal and external sources of authority, including police superintendents and mayors, have up to now failed to provide adequate anti-corruption oversight and leadership.

Despite all these facts, the ACLU declared: Our faith in the criminal justice system depends on the knowledge that everyone is playing by the rules. But they are not.

- (AP News) Georgia police have opened an internal investigation after dash-cam footage captured a police officer appearing to say to a nervous driver during a stop, "Remember, we only kill black people." The footage, obtained by Channel 2 Action News, shows Lieutenant Greg Abbott of the Cobb County Police Department asking a driver to pick up her cellphone during a DUI stop in July 2016. The incident only came to light this week following an open-records request by the channel.

The female driver said she was hesitant to move her hands because she had "just seen way too many videos of cops...," suggesting that she may have been afraid of getting shot. Abbott responded, "But you're not black. Remember, we only shoot black people. We only kill black people, right? All the videos you've seen, have you seen the black people get killed?"

Cobb County Police Chief Mike Register told Channel 2 that they had put Abbott on administrative duties pending the outcome of the investigation. "No matter what context they said it [in], it shouldn't have been said," said Register, who was not the police chief at the time of the incident. The attorney for the woman in the case, Suri Chadha Jimenez, said she thought the officer was being sarcastic but added that "it makes you cringe when you hear it" and called the comments "unacceptable".

- A St. Louis police officer who called Black Lives Matter activists "the klan with a tan" and "domestic terrorists" on Facebook is reportedly under an internal investigation by the police department. Officer Deron Riley, a 16-year veteran of the SLMPD with an annual salary of nearly $60,000, posted an image of Black Lives Matter protesters with the racially offensive captions as a comment on Facebook.

- Protests erupted over the acquittal of killer cop Jason Stockley, a white former police officer charged with murder and suspected of planting a gun on the man he killed.

- (CNN/Meredith) Video of a former sheriff's deputy in Milton, Florida intentionally crashing his patrol car into his ex-wife's home, has been released. The state attorney's office released the dash cam video this week. The incident happened in November 2016. Timothy Taylor reverses out of the home's driveway, then steers the cruiser to face the home. Taylor lets a car pass just before he speeds up and slams into the front of the house.

Taylor admitted to Milton Police he was under the influence of prescription drugs. He said he tried to commit suicide because of marital problems. Taylor pleaded no contest to DUI and criminal mischief charges. They sentenced him to two years' probation.

- Wearing his uniform and sitting in his Palm Beach Sheriff's issued car, a deputy waited for his ex-girlfriend. When he found her walking her dog, he stepped out of his car and shot her before shooting and killing himself, police said Friday 10/13/2017. The shooter, Michael DeMarco, 55, had been with the sheriff's office since 1995, according to Palm Beach Sheriff's Office spokeswoman Teri Barbera. His relationship with the woman, a bank worker, began in May and ended three weeks before the shooting. Boynton Beach Police investigators are not releasing the name of the woman because of a state law exempting victims of domestic violence.

- ST. LOUIS (AP) The American Civil Liberties Union of Missouri filed a lawsuit against the city of St. Louis on Friday over what it called "unlawful and unconstitutional action" during demonstrations that followed the acquittal of a white former police officer in the death of a black man.

The suit accuses police of misconduct by using chemical weapons, interfering with video of police activity and violating due process. It seeks an order requiring police to act within the bounds of the U.S. Constitution.

- Oklahoma City police officers, who opened fire on a man in front of his home as he approached them holding a metal pipe, didn't hear witnesses yelling that he was deaf, a department official said Wednesday. Magdiel Sanchez, 35, wasn't obeying the officers' commands before one shot him and another tased him Tuesday night, police Capt. Bo Mathews said at a news conference. He said witnesses were yelling "he can't hear you" before the officers fired, but the officers didn't hear them. "In those situations, very volatile situations, you have a weapon out. You can get what they call tunnel vision, or you can really lock in to just the person who has the weapon that'd be the threat against you."

Being deaf in the US will also get someone the death sentence. This is one situation in the shoot-don't-shoot training scenarios.

- Alex Dobuzinskis reported in Los Angeles (Reuters) A decades- old investigation in the U.S. state of Georgia into the murder of a black man in 1983 culminated in the arrest of five white people on Friday, including two law enforcement officers charged with hindering the probe, officials said. The body of Timothy Coggins, 23, was found on Oct. 9, 1983, in a grassy area near power lines in the community of Sunnyside, about 30 miles south of downtown Atlanta. He had been "brutally murdered" and his body had signs of trauma, the Spalding County Sheriff's Office said in a statement. Investigators spoke to people who knew Coggins, but the investigation went cold, Spalding County Sheriff Darrell Dix said at a news conference. This past March, fresh evidence led investigators from the Georgia Bureau of Investigation and Spalding County to re-examine the case.

Dix did not provide details on the evidence, saying they received more tips after authorities, over the summer, announced to the media the case was re-opened. Some witnesses confessed they lived with knowledge about the case for years, but were afraid to come forward, Dix said. "It has been an emotional roller coaster for everybody that was involved," Dix said. Police arrested five people on Friday in connection with the slaying. Frankie Gebhardt, 59, and Bill Moore Sr, 58, were each charged with murder, aggravated assault and other crimes. Authorities did not immediately say where Gebhardt and Moore lived. Gregory Huffman, 47, was charged with obstruction and violation of oath of office, Dix said. Huffman was a detention officer with the Spalding County Sheriff's Office, but his employment was terminated after he was arrested. Lamar Bunn, a police officer in the town of Milner, which is south of Spalding County, was also arrested and charged with obstruction, as was Sandra Bunn, 58. She is Lamar's mother, according to Atlanta television station WXIA.

Investigators are convinced the murder was racially motivated, Dix said. "There is no doubt in the minds of all investigators involved that the crime was racially motivated and that if the crime happened today, it would be prosecuted as a hate crime," the Sheriff's Office said. Several members of Coggins' family appeared at the news conference where authorities announced the arrests. The family held out for justice all this time, said Heather Coggins, a niece of the victim. "Even on my grandmother's deathbed, she knew that justice would one day be served," she said. It was not immediately clear if any of the five arrested people had an attorney, and they could not be reached for comment. Dix promised more arrests in the case, as the investigation continues.

- UTAH POLICE On July 26, 2017, a nurse in Salt Lake City was aggressively arrested for obeying hospital policy and refusing to allow a police detective to draw blood from a severely injured patient, according to several reports. In a viral video that emerged this week, Alex Wubbels, the head nurse at the University of Utah Hospital's burn unit, keeps her cool while Detective Jeff Payne insists that he be given permission to collect the blood sample of a patient, despite not having a warrant.

The July 26 footage, filmed on Payne's body camera, captures Wubbels explaining that "three things that allow us to [give blood samples] are if you have an electronic warrant, patient consent or patient under arrest, and you have neither of those things… the patient can't consent. He told me repeatedly that he doesn't have a warrant, and the patient is not under arrest."

"So, I'm just trying to do what I'm supposed to do, that's all," she adds.

Wubbels appears professional throughout the exchange and has her supervisor on speakerphone so the detective can listen. You can hear the supervisor telling Payne that he's making a "huge mistake" in threatening Wubbels and by claiming that she's interfering with his police duties when she's simply following protocol. For Payne's part, he was reportedly explicitly told by his lieutenant to arrest Wubbels if she refused to let him take a sample of blood, according to The Salt Lake Tribune. In fact, a 2016 Supreme Court ruling suggests that the nurse was right to not allow Payne to get a blood alcohol test without a warrant. As The Washington Post noted in its report Friday, the U.S. Supreme Court "has explicitly ruled that blood can only be drawn from drivers for probable cause, with a warrant." Wubbels appeared to do everything correctly.

The supervisor barely finishes what he's saying when Payne shouts, "We're done!" repeatedly at Wubbels. He then chases her down and handcuffs her. A sobbing Wubbels screams "Help me!" and "You're assaulting me!" while being pushed out of the hospital and toward a police car. "I just feel betrayed, I feel angry … I'm a health care worker. The only job I have is to keep my patients safe," Wubbels said, according to the site. "A blood draw, it just gets thrown around there like it's some simple thing. But blood is your blood. That's your property. And when a patient comes in a critical state, that blood is extremely important and I don't take it lightly."

Since the horrifying arrest, they have suspended Payne from the department's blood draw unit. They expected him to remain on active duty as the investigation was conducted. They have not charged Wubbels. She said in a news conference Thursday, accompanied by her lawyer Karra Porter, that she is not ruling out taking legal action. "I just feel betrayed, I feel angry, I feel a lot of things," Wubbels said during the conference. "And I'm still confused."

The hospital stands by Wubbels, indicating that she did everything she was supposed to in a statement it gave to The New York Post. "She followed procedures and protocols in this matter and was acting in her patient's best interest," the statement reads. "We have worked with our law enforcement partners on this issue to ensure an appropriate process for moving forward."

Salt Lake County District Attorney Sim Gill ordered a criminal investigation Friday into the actions of Detective Jeff Payne. Salt Lake City Mayor Jackie Biskupski and Police Chief Mike Brown apologized for Payne's actions and promised investigations from Internal Affairs and the Civilian Review Board.

- A southern Illinois sheriff's deputy is accused of twice assaulting a woman in her home. St. Clair County Deputy Robert Sneed is charged with two counts of official misconduct and is on paid administrative leave. He posted a $2,500 bond this month, the Belleville News-Democrat reported. Court records show Sneed pulled the woman over in February and followed her to her home in Cahokia after telling her she needed to show him her car's title. Cahokia is a St. Louis suburb on the Illinois side of the Mississippi River. Police say Sneed sexually assaulted the woman in her home and suggested she could be jailed if she didn't comply.

- KEY WEST, Fla. - A Monroe County corrections deputy was arrested Tuesday after stealing prescription pills from a family friend while she was babysitting for him, according to the Monroe County Sheriff's Office. The victim of the theft is Key West police Officer David Kouri.

Kouri called the deputies in the morning and told them that Ashlie Hernandez, 27, had taken prescription medications while babysitting for him Monday night in his home, sheriff's spokeswoman Becky Herrin said. Kouri said he knew how many pills were in the bottles because he had just filled the prescription and had not yet taken any of them. He also told deputies he counted the pills and found that some were missing, Herrin said.

As part of the investigation, Kouri called Hernandez to

discuss the theft, Herrin said. It was during that phone call Hernandez told Kouri that her boyfriend had taken the drugs. She then told Kouri that she had some drugs and they agreed to meet in the parking lot of the Key West Police Department so she could return the pills, Herrin said. The pair met at about 4 p.m. and soon after, Hernandez handed over a plastic bag with the pills inside, Herrin said. Detectives stopped her, and she admitted to taking the pills, Herrin said. They arrested Hernandez on charges of possession of a controlled substance without a prescription and theft of a controlled substance.

- A Florida police department is investigating officer Michael Hamill who posted anti-Zionist remarks on his Facebook page that were unearthed after his superiors commended the cop in an official post for helping the community after Hurricane Irma. The photo went viral on social media because of the cops' good looks. The positive attention was short-lived.

Someone located Hamill's personal Facebook page, which was filled with anti-Semitic remarks that predated him joining the Gainesville force in 2016. Hamill wrote in 2013: "Who knew that reading Jewish jokes before I go to bed would not only make me feel better about myself but also help me sleep better as well? Here is one for everybody. What's the difference between boy scouts and Jews? Anybody know? Well, it is because boy scouts come back from their camps."

In a second Facebook post two years earlier, Hamill ranted about people who abuse government resources and said they should be dealt with the Hitler way. "Stupid people annoy me. Put them in an oven and deal with them the Hitler way. Haha," he wrote.

- WHITE PRIVILEGE. Did Patrick Kelly, a Chicago police officer with a troubled history, shoot Michael D. LaPorta in the head, leaving him permanently disabled? On 10/26/2017 a federal jury found Kelly shot LaPorta on Jan. 12, 2010, while off-duty in his home after a night of drinking. Then, the jury held the city of Chicago responsible for the shooting with a crushing $44.7 million verdict. This isn't the first time Kelly cost the city money. Earlier this year, Chicago settled for $500,000 a separate lawsuit filed by a woman who said she suffered a miscarriage after Kelly used a Taser on her three times in August 2013. In fact, ahead of LaPorta's shooting, 19 complaints had been registered against Kelly in six years, according to the LaPorta family's lawsuit. At least eight more allegedly followed, including claims of excessive force, racial bias, domestic violence and battery.

A Chicago Police Department spokesperson said they stripped Kelly of his police powers this month and is under investigation based on the court proceedings for making a false oral or written report. Kelly called 911 after the shooting, calmly telling a dispatcher, "I have a friend that committed suicide … He's dead right now." But soon, his tone changed, and he abruptly blurted out the words, "he's still breathing!"

Kelly invoked his constitutional right not to incriminate himself 31 times when he took the stand last week. He did so moments before LaPorta testified from his wheelchair, denying that he shot himself and insisting about Kelly, "I know he shot me."

Kelly earlier settled with LaPorta's family for $300,000, records show.

- BOYNTON BEACH (AP) - Authorities say a Florida sheriff's deputy shot and wounded a woman and then fatally shot himself, on 10/12/2017. The Palm Beach County Sheriff's Office said in a news release that the shooting happened shortly after 8 a.m. Thursday in a gated Boynton Beach neighborhood. They have not released the names and races of those involved. The sheriff's office said they took the woman to a hospital, and she is in critical condition. The deputy died at the scene. No further details were immediately available.

- NEWARK AIRPORT. They arrested three Customs and Border Protection officers assigned to a specialized screening team at Newark Airport Wednesday for assaulting fellow officers, allegedly pinning the victims to what they knew as a "rape table," according to court records.

Tito Catota, Parmenio Perez and Michael Papagni are charged with forcibly assaulting, impeding, intimidating, and interfering with two men identified in court documents as "Victim One" and "Victim Two" while the victims were on duty as CBP officers.

"The defendants, who were members of a unit responsible for identifying dangerous contraband and threats to national security, allegedly subjected their own colleagues to senseless physical abuse, all while on duty at Newark Liberty International Airport," acting U.S. Attorney William Fitzpatrick said.

- Authorities said Tuesday a former Cleveland police officer who allegedly cut off his GPS tracker and went on the run one week before he would have gone on trial for rape and kidnapping has killed himself after a standoff with police. The U.S. Marshals Service looked for Tommie Griffin, 52, who was wanted the Cuyahoga County Sheriff's Office for the bond violation, according to Pete Elliott of the U.S. Marshals Service. They tracked Griffin to a house in Cleveland, where Cleveland Police SWAT was called in, Elliott said Tuesday. Police tried to call him out of the house, but received no response from him. When police entered, they found Griffin dead from an apparently self-inflicted gunshot wound to the chest, police said.

They arrested Griffin for rape, assault and kidnapping after allegedly attacking his girlfriend in January, The Associated Press said. He allegedly pistol-whipped her and fired two shots next to her, the AP said. They had scheduled Griffin's trial to begin on Oct. 30.

HISTORICAL FACT. The news from the UK is that police corruption can be traced back to the world's first police force in London, England, where several accounts of police corruption have been documented since the force's inception.

Imogen Calderwood reported on 08/05/2016. They have kicked out of the force, a sadistic police officer who was recorded repeatedly raping a woman after she installed a sleep app on her iPhone. PC Michael Graham, 49, was jailed for 16 years for his campaign of physical and sexual abuse against the victim on his houseboat in Uxbridge, West London. He controlled his victim for months by telling her no one would believe her because he was a Met Police officer. Booting him out of the police force, Assistant Commissioner Helen King praised the victim's 'courage and resilience' in reporting Graham to his colleagues. At trial, the court heard how the officer tied the victim up, slapped her and choked her and also boasted that he would end up killing her.

He also branded her a 'slut' and a 'cu*t.'

INSTITUTIONAL CORRUPTION. Police corruption is a simple phenomenon, which does readily submit to simple analysis. Any newspaper or any police-related publication, on any given day, will have an article about a police officer that got busted committing some kind of corrupt act. Police corruption has skyrocketed with the cocaine trade, with officers acting alone or in-groups to steal money from dealers or distribute cocaine themselves. They have caught large groups of corrupt police officers in New York, New Orleans, Washington, DC, and Los Angeles. When police officers are exposed violating the law, people are often shocked and outraged, even when the corruption is universal. A police officer in the US is as much on the take as one in India, Afghanistan, Iraq, France, Zimbabwe or Kenya.

In the US, police corruption can include brutality, physical or verbal harassment, violation of the Fourth Amendment rights against unreasonable search and seizure, evidentiary rules forbidding the use at trial of evidence tainted by unconstitutional police actions (fruits of the poisonous tree), and the establishment of the so-called Miranda warning requiring officers to advise detained suspects of their constitutional rights, discriminatory arrest, selective enforcement of the law, discrimination, sexual harassment, intimidation, receiving or fencing stolen goods, false testimony in court, pay off from prostitutes, drug addicts or pushers and professional burglars.

There are many instances where police officers collaborated with drug dealers who pay protection money to be left alone to conduct their business. That's when the officers were not selling the drugs themselves.

"Color of law" violations include false arrest and the use of excessive force by police, according to the FBI's website. And that's not all.

CASE IN POINT. A particular incident happened at a police station in Eatonville, Florida. On a Sunday afternoon, a cop answered a call about drugs being peddled in a city street. Upon his arrival at the scene, the alleged drug dealers took off on foot. The officer in question failed to give pursuit, opting instead to inspect the car left behind. He found a small amount of illegal drugs, $400 in cash and a gun. He processed the scene and wrote his report.

Missing from the details were the $400 which "he took home for safekeeping." Early the following Monday, the chief who had set up the decoy bust confronted and arrested him, because the local drug dealers were complaining about being robbed by the cop. Two hours later, they released him, pending "further investigation." Luckily, this case didn't fall through the cracks and they eventually fired this cop. It's worth mentioning that he was previously broke before they hired him, then paid $120,000 cash for a house after just 2 months working a 20 hours part-time job.

FOX NEWS REPORT. Authorities arrested a sheriff's deputy in Florida, who was caught on home surveillance video last month reportedly stealing from a recently deceased man, on Thursday 10/19/2017. Deputy Jason Cooke of the Palm Beach Sheriff's Office was charged with burglary and grand theft with a firearm, WPBF reported. They released him on house arrest after he paid a $28,000 bond. They accused Cooke of robbing a house that belonged to Moe Rosoff, an 85-year-old man who had injured himself in a blackout during Hurricane Irma and later died, ABC 10 News reported.

Rosoff's family had reportedly asked authorities on Sept. 12 to do a welfare check on their father, who was braving the storm alone. Three deputies found the elderly man on the floor of his home and brought him to the hospital before he eventually died.

The family alleged that the accused deputy heard the garage entry code over his police radio and went to the victim's house, knowing he wouldn't be there, ABC reported. Unbeknownst to the suspect, surveillance cameras at the house turned on when he entered, CBS 12 reported. The family later saw the video and turned it over to the police on Sept. 20. They claim the deputy wandered around the house and stole money, jewelry and medication. They also suggested that Cooke received "preferential treatment" from the sheriff's office, noting that they did not arrest the suspect until five weeks after they initially turned over the video, CBS 12 said.

Police allowed Cooke, who reportedly only admitted to the crime after seeing the surveillance video, to attend a 30-day drug rehabilitation program before facing arrest, the family said. Police found several types of prescription drugs inside Cooke's patrol car, not all of which reportedly belonged to the victim. The family alleged that this was potentially not the deputy's first crime and that he "posed a significant threat to the public's safety," CBS 12 reported.

"In our opinion, had we not had this video, this cop would still be out there posing a threat of danger to the community he swore to protect and committing more crimes," the family said in a statement. "It is our hope that the justice system treats this cop like any other criminal out there and that he doesn't receive further preferential treatment because he is a police officer."

"Unfortunately, sometimes an employee makes a bad decision which leads to misconduct," the sheriff's office said in a statement following Cooke's arrest. "This misconduct was reported, investigated and subsequently determined to be criminal in nature, resulting in the charges." According to the family, the suspect was placed on paid administrative leave, CBS 12 said.

ANOTHER REALITY. Everyone remembers the Knapp Commission in 1972 and the many NYPD corruption cases. The problem was supposedly solved until it resurfaced in 1992 when five officers were arrested on drug-trafficking charges. Millions of cases of corruption and illegal activities are treated as individual rarity every single time.

An article in the New York Times asked: "Police agencies, to eliminate corruption have tried everything from increasing salaries, requiring more training and education, and developing policies which should focus directly on factors leading to corruption. What have all these changes done to eliminate or even decrease the corruption problem? Little or nothing." Internal Affairs unit is just that: internal affairs.

FOLLOW THE LAW. The only remedy to police brutality, false arrest and imprisonment, malicious prosecution, and wrongful death is found in state law, which permits victims to sue police departments for damages in civil actions. A few law firms have defied the odds by taking on corrupt cops: civil rights attorney Jasmine Rand who has represented the families of Trayvon Martin and Michael Brown in their cases and local counsel Shelley Stangler, who has handled many civil rights suits, the Black lawyers for Justice and the Southern Center for justice. But the rest of the story remains that the local community ends up paying the price for police corruption. Once again, the taxpayers receive the shaft in the form of a higher tax rate to replenish the city coffers and cover the money awarded to the victims.

BAD LEGACY. All the illegal actions are happening despite the legal safeguards, codes of conduct, civilian complaint review boards, criminal and civil statutes. Enforcement is the responsibility of the Justice department, and they are part of the same gang. More and more, they give law enforcement more immunity from prosecution, just like judges and legislators.

That's also why the US Supreme Court decisions have continually asserted the general rule that they must give officers the benefit of the doubt that they acted lawfully in carrying out their day-to-day duties. It doesn't matter to the court that these officers are card-carrying members of the KKK or other hate groups.

When people use weapons illicitly and taint it with racism, they murder negroes. As cops continue to kill negroes, it will become harder and harder for them to patrol black communities without the fear of someone willing to exact revenge.

DRUG PEDDLERS. What the corrupt cops cannot understand is that every crime by an officer erases all the trust obtained from the community. That's if they cared. In Cleveland, the FBI arrested 42 officers from five law enforcement agencies on charges of conspiracy to distribute cocaine; something the CIA got away with when they "legally" introduced crack in the black neighborhoods. The federal General Accounting Office (GAO) found evidence of growing police involvement in drug sales, theft of drugs and money from drug dealers, and perjured testimony about illegal searches.

Traditionally, police corruption had been understood to involve individuals acting alone, but the new trend revealed officers working in small groups to protect and assist each other, like the Los Angeles Police Department's Rampart precinct and particularly its elite anti-gang unit, CRASH (Community Resources Against Street Hoodlums). Following local and federal investigations, CRASH was dismantled, some 70 officers were investigated, and several either pleaded guilty to or were convicted of crimes ranging from drug theft and peddling to assault, fabricating arrests, and filing false reports.

Police corruption has occasionally led to rioting. In an ironic reversal of fate, citizens now require protection from the very people appointed to protect and serve.

UNCHANGED LEGACY. On 10/07/2017, as stated earlier, the FBI's counterterrorism unit continued the white agenda of racial superiority when it has identified a new group, "black identity extremists," as a growing threat to the safety of law enforcement. Let us get this straight. This is a list of black people that the FBI is afraid might retaliate against ongoing police violence? Do they have a list of violent white police officers? It takes very little effort to hate a man whom you have wronged.

The need for more jails and punishments comes from the fact that, in our modern world, there is no venue for redress of grievances. The poor, the exploited, African, non-European, anyone with dark-skin, immigrant Asian laborer, native American, Japanese-American, Mexican, the sick or anyone classified outside the gentrified genetic lines drawn up by the raceologists of the

American Eugenics Movement do not influence the laws. The unfortunate people, who have been marginalized by the racist ruling elite for having presumed defects or inheritable undesirable traits (negative eugenics), are SOL. They do not view it as the fault of the "decision makers" that they were born with the wrong perceived genes, or in the wrong country.

The eugenicists don't understand that their standards must be at least as high as those of the person whom they sit in judgment. Whatever the law of the land, the rich man must obey as much as the poor man. We must accord the black man the same legal protocol as we accord the white man.

How many innocent negroes need to be murdered or exonerated after 10, 20, 40 years in jail, for the world to understand the racist scheme going on? Bureaucracy and muddled language have raped the original fair system of justice and the rule of law everywhere in the world, so a few can enrich themselves and satisfy their demented lunatic ideology.

They must heed the words of Carl Sagan. "If a human disagrees with you, let him live. In a hundred billion galaxies, you will not find another."

REALITY. Corruption uses new wording to describe a world still divided between masters and slaves. The voices of millions upon millions of people marginalized by the ruling racist elite have been silenced, along with equal protection under the law. Justice now belongs to whoever can afford it and of a certain skin color. Only the powerful can broadcast their wishes and actions all over the world. They are the only ones allowed and able to use the propaganda machine to deflect any blame from themselves unto the abused. Countless lies and contradictory accounts make sure no one can get to the truth.

AMERICA THE BEAUTIFUL. The parasitic white man in the

US will be the victim of his own doing. When he thought he was exploiting blacks, he was building his own undoing. The new administration created three distinct classes in the country; a tiny mixed center, with poor blacks and poor whites constantly at each other's throat, never finding a common ground to coexist, flanked by two extremist sides. On one side are the extremist whites who are hanging on to a colonial confederate white supremacy utopia and on the other side, people who have had enough.

A self-proclaimed, self-selected, sacred and powerful rich elite is trying per argumentum ad crumenam to manipulate a switch for a social remedy that would keep the peasants at peace, so they can maximize their profits. They used many social experiments. Now the prevalent one is to take jobs away from the blacks, in exchange for education, and try to get the whites to work. That should take care of the discontent and appease the white extremists who are ready to explode. But the whites do not want the jobs, because they have been brainwashed, and they encrusted in their psyche that they are above any manual labor. All the while, the elite is ignoring the reality that it is a very weak temporary lull, since Europeans have no chance of permanence on the planet.

OVER REACH. As every successful venture was being taken over, the Anglo-American empire became the new mafia running the world. Corruption is the only true weapon of choice as the grand wizard of the world wrestled the opium trade from Afghanistan, protection trade from the Mafia, cocaine trade from Columbia, marijuana trade from Mexico, smut trade from California and New York, and now it's going after the religious trade from Islam. We can see the same prevalent corruption in the elite approval and tolerance of anarchists, lunatics, war criminals and plain ignorant idiots.

The only western progress ever made is called corruption. Where ever Britain and the US are found, so will corruption and injustice in their highest forms. Nobody knows the business of corruption like the western world. That is its only accomplishment to date.

They implemented a new slavery with injustice and corruption. A purposely divided world in which legislative predators play their chosen games, side by side, simultaneously, from rigged elections, usurpation of power, threats, intimidation, to illegal acts, unconstitutional edicts, backed by corrupt judicial accomplices. The executive, legislative, and judicial branches have compromised and breached the separation and balance of powers.

The nation is in trouble when theft of cash from black and Hispanic travelers by the Volusia County Sheriff Office, on I-95, received the accolade from judge James Nelson. The sheriff's office could keep the stolen money.

All attempts to legally assemble in order to present a constitutionally guaranteed right to redress of grievances by negroes are countered with police repression, from Ferguson city, black lives matter protests, to any natural human reaction to the murder of another unarmed black man. And there have been many murders of unarmed black men. Negroes are killed because the cops see them as foreign enemy combatants who don't belong in the land that whites are claiming for themselves.

People have shown a tendency to accept undeserved punishment until they can take no more. The only time people will engage in a popular revolt or revolution is when their instinct for self-preservation is pushed to its limits. Souffrir que mourir, c'est la devise des hommes.

HOPE. There is an organization called NAAPB, founded by Jonathan Newton, that combats police corruption on a case-by-case basis. Recently, they fought for victims of a large-scale police conspiracy in Camden, New Jersey, in which officers planted drugs on innocent residents. They also advocate for transparency and accountability in law enforcement's use of civil asset forfeiture laws and funds. By ensuring the law is enforced legitimately and through honest means, they seek to strengthen the relationship between law enforcement agencies and their communities, helping citizens remain safe.

THE GAME IS RIGGED. Laws and rules are now enacted by the people who are benefiting from them. Businesses, corporations and companies are the facade hiding rich investors milking the public, the new and improved King Leopold II of Belgium.

They will blame income inequality and disparity on lack of education, even when most of the richest people are school drop-outs who have mastered the art of corruption. The three wealthiest individuals have assets that exceed those of the poorest 10% of the world's population. How much education did they get?

As the gap widens between rich rulers and poor subjects, there is bound to be an equal increase in resentment from the people. The US government has switched allegiance from representing the people to being completely subservient to companies with generous lobbies.

# UGAIDI NA UJINGA

Our present society is in total decay. It is the worst that the planet has ever seen. 99.99% of Americans are on drugs, prescribed or otherwise; and that fact created the delusion, the drug induced paranoia that persists in the US, that the rest of the world is out to get them, for the crap they heaped upon other nations. For a long time, many have made it a game to subject other humans and creatures to the worst possible inhuman treatment. Nothing is safe from these lunatics, from humans being poisoned for the sake of corporations playing the money game so the CEOs can afford their mansions and lifestyle, to cats and dogs being over-bred so the puppies and kittens can be sold to make money for their owners to afford the drugs they need. Chickens and trees are being grown to provide a fleecing moment of satisfaction before being tossed in the trash pile. And what we can say about evangelists peddling their snake oil to secure a life of luxury? It is just sickening to see the wasteland that Mother Earth has become, because of the ignorance of one species that she allowed to thrive.

Merriam-Webster defines dysfunction as "abnormal or unhealthy interpersonal behavior or interaction within a group." If anyone needed any more proof or evidence of how stupid humans are, Mother Nature provided ample facts between August and September 2017.

THE ECLIPSE. Humans have watched eclipses from their first day on the planet until now, and during this long span of time, our scientific understanding of the physical world has grown enormously. As a result, detailed scientific physical explanations have replaced many of the older theories about the causes and effects of total solar eclipses. We no longer sacrifice virgins to appease the gods during an eclipse. But the casual observers of today remained the same idiots who got on their hands and knees to worship the first eclipses.

On Monday, August 21, 2017, all of North America was treated to an eclipse of the sun. The moon completely blocked the sun, and the corona was visible. Anyone within the path of totality, from Salem, Oregon to Charleston, South Carolina, could see one of nature's most awe-inspiring sights, a total solar eclipse. Observers outside this path could still see a partial solar eclipse where the moon covered part of the sun's disk. NASA created a website to provide a guide to this amazing event with activities, events, broadcasts, and resources.

While they broadcast the news for several days, warning people to use special glasses when looking at the eclipse, many chose not to follow the advice. It would have been a total embarrassment to the planet if "aliens landed on that day" and asked to meet the leader of the free world. They would have been told: "he is the one looking at the eclipse without glasses."

HURRICANES. Anyone with a pulse can see how ill prepared most people are when it comes to dealing with a hurricane which lasts a few hours, and no one seems to have kept any survival skills. People, totally baffled by a natural occurrence, reacted like a bunch of newborn humans.

From meteorologists yapping about things they are totally clueless about, reporters yapping about "possible" after effects to come, to forecasters who could never predict rain or sunshine on a normal day, to politicians trying to pay lip service to their constituents. The only thing missing was the prediction from Miss Cleo and the Psychic Friends Network. It doesn't help that the masses will partake in the hysteria designed to increase sales and buy crap they don't need. Dumb people are always willing to follow the lead of their clueless leaders. The biggest problem to come would not be from the hurricanes, but from the people.

When 3 Atlantic hurricanes, with 90-plus miles per hour wind, showed up on the local super, duper, quadruple, Doppler radar, apocalyptic scientists lost their minds. Philip Klotzbach, a research scientist at Colorado State University, took to Twitter to voice his ominous prophecy. According to the National Oceanic and Atmospheric Administration (NOAA), the last time three hurricanes were active at once was in 2010, when hurricanes Igor, Julia, and Karl were classified as hurricanes.

The message was being broadcasted that hurricanes Irma and Harvey were the products of climate change, and pseudo-scientists come out of the woodwork to blame global warming. To hear the non-stop inane rant of wanna-be doom and gloom weather prophets trying to justify their hallucination was sickening. Granted that many so-called natural perceived irregularities have been observed as of late, it doesn't reinforce the scheme that many want to use to get rich advocating. A 1 or 2 degrees hotter, hurricanes, volcanoes, tsunami, fruit trees setting blooms in November before a freeze, only means that Mother Nature is doing what she wants, regardless of any human interference or assumption. Mother Nature is not a photocopier that prints the same documents over and over. She is an independent lady who does what she wants, when, and the way she wants to do it. Tough luck if you are a testosterone overdosed macho man who can not accept that.

And they should not blame global warning on ALL humans, as all humans didn't contribute to it. First, they blamed it on the methane base emissions from cows, right before Al Gore screwed the world on his way to accumulating billions of dollars to pay for his mansions and personal jets. Now, his greedy buddies are following in his footsteps to make their own fortune, as climate change has become a cash cow. So far, they have said not one word about countless of companies which are the real culprits. Global warming (climate change) is not the real problem, it's just a facade. Where is the list of criminal corporations and their employees who knowingly poisoned the planet?

In the US, any disaster is a fun opportunity for government officials, at all levels, to brag and pat themselves on the back after the fact. The greatest country in the world where elected idiots can play politics after a natural disaster, when they can't figure out how to do their damn everyday job. The country transformed into a mega-church with the apocalyptic warnings coming from the governor, fire and police chiefs, Sheriff, all preaching and prophecizing about the impending doom and gloom. How do they get to prepare for disasters and accomplish so much when they are always wasting time in front of the cameras?

Although hurricanes usually last less than one day, millions of wannabe doomsday preppers rushed to local stores to load up on bread and overpriced bottled tap water, the two prime modern conveniences of our technological world. They extended the fun with the collateral need for another pastime: return items that were not used or even needed, from generators, bottled water, bread, propane tanks and glue guns. And toilet paper.

HARVEY. In Texas, Harvey first made landfall as a Category 4 hurricane. With rainfall topping 50 inches in some areas, Harvey devastated a swath of Texas stretching from the Houston area into Louisiana. "Our entire city is underwater," said Derrick Freeman, the mayor of Port Arthur, Tex. Who would think that everything would be under water during a hurricane, but the mayor thought it was necessary to remind his constituents of that fact?

As with any natural disaster in the US, it forced the city of Houston to warn residents about imposter Homeland Security agents who were telling people to evacuate their homes, in what the city said it believes was an effort to rob houses.

Thursday, August 31, 2017 marked the end of the worst of Hurricane Harvey, but they expect to take months to recover from the rain and flooding in Texas and Louisiana. People could be seen trying to navigate and escape waist deep muddy waters.

Emergency crews plucked people from rooftops using aircraft, dump trucks, and boats as the floodwaters rose. Scattered heaps of discarded appliances, wallboard and mattresses were seen throughout the city of 2.7 million people, the nation's fourth-largest. A chemical plant in Crosby reported two explosions, 25 miles northeast of Houston, and they asked residents within a 1.5-mile square radius to evacuate.

A week later, over 450,000 people either still do not have safe drinking water and need to boil their water first. A total of 52 of the state's public drinking water systems were still damaged, inoperable or destroyed, leaving 70,000 people without water, according to the U.S. Environmental Protection Agency and the Texas Commission on Environmental Quality.

Reuters reported that most damages in Houston came not from hurricane Harvey, but a deliberate flooding. Angry Houston residents shouted at city officials on Saturday over decisions to intentionally flood certain area neighborhoods during Hurricane Harvey, as they returned to homes that have been contaminated by overflowing sewers.

A town hall grew heated after City Council member Greg Travis, who represents parts of western Houston, told about 250 people that an Army Corps of Engineers official told him that certain gauges measuring water levels at the Buffalo Bayou, the city's main waterway, failed because of a decision to release water from two municipal reservoirs to avoid an overflow. Travis' words inflamed tensions at the town hall, held at the Westin Houston hotel. There were no representatives from the Army Corps at the town hall.

On Aug. 28, the Army Corps and the Harris County Flood Control District opened the Addicks and Barker reservoirs in western Houston to keep them from overflowing. They warned it would flood neighborhoods, some of which remained closed off two weeks later. Travis said the Army Corps official said they kept releasing water without knowing the extent of the flooding. "They didn't understand that the bathtub effect was occurring," he said. (There goes the BS about protection of life and property.)

Later, residents attempting to return to flooded homes had to contend with contaminated water and air, because the city's sewer systems overflowed during the floods. Fire chief Pena said alligators, rodents and snakes may also occupy homes because of the floods, and people returning home should wear breathing masks and consider getting tetanus shots.

"We couldn't survive the Corps. Why should we rebuild?" Debora Kumbalek, who lives in Travis' district in Houston, shouted during the town hall. Many residents face lengthy rebuilding processes, and the majority do not have flood insurance. Measly federal handouts may ease the frustration and coax to rebuild in a hurricane zone prone to flooding. Most residents failed to understand that they should move, not rebuild.

A few days after the hurricane, senators voted 80-17 Thursday in favor of a bill that provides billions of dollars in Hurricane Harvey relief while simultaneously funding the federal government through December. Sens. Bob Corker, Steve Daines, Mike Enzi, Joni Ernst, Deb Fischer, Jeff Flake, Lindsey Graham, Chuck Grassley, Ron Johnson, James Lankford, Mike Lee, John McCain, Jerry Moran, Rand Paul, James Risch, Ben Sasse, and Pat Toomey all voted against the bill. Three other Senators, Florida's little Marco Rubio, Alaska's Dan Sullivan and New Jersey's Bob Menendez, who is currently on trial for corruption and bribery, did not vote.

HOPE. But, amid the flood and desperation, there was hope in the air when a voice of reason rose louder than the devastation caused by the Army Corps of Engineers. Politicians, in the hurricane ravaged city of Houston, warned against donating to the

American Red Cross. Houston City councillor Dave Martin told a district meeting: "I beg you not to send them a penny" and repeatedly branded the Congress endorsed charity "the red loss." Speaking two weeks after the devastating hurricane, which left at least 70 people dead, Mr Martin claimed that the local government had done most of the arduous work in the aftermath of the disaster, as well as providing most resources. "Yet, every time I turn on the TV, I see the Red Cross taking in millions of dollars in donations," he said, branding the charity "the most inept, unorganized organization I've ever experienced. Don't waste your money. Give it to another cause," added Mr Martin, an independent member of the council who has a background working in private sector management.

Fortunately, against all odds, someone remembered that the Red Cross stole the millions donated to Haiti after the earthquake.

SOAKING WET GOD. For the hundreds of thousands enjoying themselves in the loony bin, Harvey was a religious test with the usual "It was the Lord's will. The Lord doesn't make mistakes." One American religious leader came up with the obvious holy reason the violent storm hit the US city of Houston: gay people. Kevin Swanson, a pastor in the Orthodox Presbyterian Church, claimed God brought the powerful hurricane and subsequent flooding on the Texan city because its mayor is aggressively pro-homosexual. "Jesus sends the message home, unless Americans repent, unless Houston repents, unless New Orleans repents, they will all likewise perish. That is the message that the Lord Jesus Christ* is sending home right now to America," Swanson told his radio show. He also reportedly said that Hurricane Irma, wreaking damage in the Caribbean and predicted to soon hit the US, could be stopped by banning abortion and gay marriage.

(Note*: This is the same biblical Jesus Christ who lived his entire life with 12 very close male buddies.)

No word if the good pastor was indulging in hallucinating drugs when he also asked for tax free donations.

Luckily, Jesus saved us from the hurricanes so we can continue to indulge in our passion: buy shoes with flashing lights for our children, "walk" our dog around in strollers, pick our nose and scratch our butt, and let's not forget the national pastime, inhaling 10 cheeseburgers as long as we wash them down with a diet soda.

US ZIONISM. Anyone who doesn't know or refuses to understand the influence of Israel on the US is an idiot.

(I excerpted the following paragraph from an article written by Erne Hume and first posted in 1999 before the Christian/Jewish Zionist Neocons took control of the base direction/decisions of the US government fronted by George W. Bush.)

The USA in 1999 is under that same degree of Jewish domination that Weimar Germany was under in 1929. Jews controlled 57% of the metal trade, 22% of grain, and 39% of textiles. Over 50% of the Berlin Chamber of Commerce were Jewish, as were a spectacular 1,200 of the 1,474 members of the German Stock Exchange. Of the 29 legitimate theaters in Berlin, 23 had Jewish directors. Authorship was almost a Jewish monopoly. In 1931, of 144 film scripts worked, Jews wrote 119 and produced 77 of them.

Look at Hollywood today, in 2017. Jews totally dominate the film industry. Although most of the films are vulgar, violent trash, the industry falls all over itself, giving each other awards for producing such. Propaganda and 'message' films flow out of Hollywood and across TV screens. The news and communications industry is a Jewish kingdom. How many Jewish bylines do you come across every single day? From the NY Times to your local paper, from NPR to radio talk show hosts, you are being 'informed' by a specific group of Zionist creeps, hell bent on Apartheid, genocide and the destruction of the US. Zionists hate America. Just Google the "Fink's bar diatribe".

The American financial industry is essentially a Jewish franchise. From the Federal Reserve to banks and mortgage and other financing industries, the ownership is most often Jewish. And the professions are so dominated by Zionists, it is shocking. Open the phone book Yellow Pages and read through the Physicians and Attorneys sections... and prepare to be stunned. Did you know an Israeli company does the entire billing for most of America's cell and regular phone systems? The company has total knowledge of who you talk to and for how long, at least.

Did you know an Israeli company created, installed and maintains the absolutely HIGHEST level of secure communications in the Pentagon and White House? Do you think someone might have built in a monitoring system?

So it's no surprise that Ray Downs reported the following on Oct. 20, 2017 (UPI) A Texas city is telling its residents that if they want aid to rebuild from the damage of Hurricane Harvey, they have to promise not to boycott Israel, which the American Civil Liberties Union said is unconstitutional.

In Dickinson, Texas, located just outside Houston, Hurricane Harvey hit residents hard in August and the local government there began accepting applications for grants to rebuild homes and businesses on Oct. 11. And the Dickinson government distributed aid via the Dickinson Harvey Relief Fund, which set-up the grants via the city's website.

But in order to be accepted for a grant to repair one's home or business in the south Texas suburb, one has to agree not to boycott Israel. According to the Dallas News, the application for the grant says applicants must agree to "not boycott Israel" and promise not to "boycott Israel during the term of this Agreement." The geopolitical ideology requirement for a Texas suburb rebuilding grant caught the attention of the ACLU, which said it violated the First Amendment.

"The First Amendment protects Americans' right to boycott, and the government cannot condition hurricane relief or any other public benefit on a commitment to refrain from protected political expression," said ACLU of Texas Legal Director Andre Segura. "Dickinson's requirement is an egregious violation of the First Amendment, reminiscent of McCarthy-era loyalty oaths requiring Americans to disavow membership in the Communist party and other forms of perceived 'subversive' activity."

However, many states, including Texas, have laws on the books that prohibit the state from contracting with companies that boycott Israel. Those state laws have been criticized as violations of the First Amendment, but a similar bill is also being pushed at the federal level.

FULL ARTICLE. Kyle Swenson reported on October 20, 2017 at 9:57 AM Nearly two months after Hurricane Harvey socked the Texas coastline, residents are still in the early stages of the costly and complicated cleanup process. Now in one Houston suburb, residents hoping to receive aid to help relaunch their lives have to factor Middle East political tensions into their recovery efforts. The city of Dickinson, Texas, about 30 miles southeast of Houston, recently posted applications online for relief grants "from the funds that were generously donated to the Dickinson Harvey Relief Fund," the city's website says. The application, however, includes a provision requiring applicants to promise not to boycott Israel.

Section 11 of the four-page document is titled, "Verification not to Boycott Israel." The text reads: "By executing this Agreement below, the Applicant verifies that the Applicant: (1) does not boycott Israel; and (2) will not boycott Israel during the term of this Agreement." The city attorney for Dickinson told a local television station he was only following a state law forbidding state agencies from doing business with Israel boycotters.

The aid grant application has triggered a strong rebuke from the American Civil Liberties Union. "The First Amendment protects Americans' right to boycott, and the government cannot condition hurricane relief or any other public benefit on a commitment to refrain from protected political expression," Andre Segura, ACLU of Texas Legal Director, said in a statement Thursday night. "Dickinson's requirement is an egregious violation of the First Amendment, reminiscent of McCarthy-era loyalty oaths requiring Americans to disavow membership in the Communist Party and other forms of 'subversive' activity."

The language is not out of nowhere. In May, Texas Gov. Greg Abbott signed the Anti-BDS (Boycott, Divestments, and Sanctions) bill into law. The statute "prohibits all state agencies from contracting with, and certain public funds from investing in, companies that boycott Israel," according to the governor's website. "Anti-Israel policies are anti-Texas," Abbott said at the bill's signing. "We will not tolerate such actions against an important ally*." How the law would apply to individuals seeking disaster relief, rather than businesses seeking contracts, is unclear.

(Note*: Obviously Texas Gov. Greg Abbott is ignorant of the attack on the USS Liberty and other anti-US actions from this "important" ally. It's safe to say that the epiphany will not happen until Texas Gov. Greg Abbott gently removes his head from his butt.)

The BDS movement started in 2005 as a nonviolent protest against Israhell's treatment of Palestinians. It involved a call to halt business with Israeli companies, as well as corporations doing business with Israel, as a way to put pressure on the Israeli government. Legislation in several states pushing back against BDS has followed, including proposals in the U.S. Congress. But as the ACLU pointed out in the organization's release on the Dickinson application, "The US Supreme Court ruled decades ago that political boycotts are protected by the First Amendment, and other decisions have established that the government may not require individuals to sign a certification regarding their political expression in order to obtain employment, contracts, or other benefits." Earlier, the ACLU filed a federal lawsuit challenging a similar anti-BDS law in Kansas. In an interview with ABC 13, Dickinson's city attorney David W. Olson said the city planned to follow the law and keep the provision in place until told to do otherwise.

FOLLOW UP. On Monday, 10/23/2017, Maryland Gov. Larry Hogan signed an executive order that prohibits the state from doing business with companies engaged in a boycott of Israel. Hogan took the executive action against the Boycott, Divestment and Sanction (BDS) movement, an effort started in 2005 by a coalition of Palestinian organizations in response to Israel's occupation of the West Bank territory.

This is the influence of Rothschild Zionism in the US, taking precedent over the Constitution of the United British States of America. It affects the everyday lives of American citizens and seeks to smash all democratic rights, working-class organizations, to protect a foreign gang of criminals. Something the Trump administration is so adamant about while raping and destroying the US Constitution? The anti-BDS laws are only enacted to bridge the US fringe extremist movement with the Zionist criminal elements and reinforce the white supremacy agenda.

A gang of hallucinating supremacist murderers are doing their best to create a fictitious land called Israhell, under the guidance of a fake fairy god who commanded them to eliminate all other nations in order to build a superior race.

And Hitler is the bad guy?

(It's safe to say that the epiphany will not happen until Maryland Gov. Larry Hogan gently removes his head from his butt.)

IRMA LA DOUCE. They predicted hurricane Irma to be extremely powerful and the strongest since Wilma in 2005, in terms of maximum sustained winds. The storm wrecked havoc and caused catastrophic damage in the Caribbean as a Category 5 hurricane.

Aiming for Miami, according to the local official geniuses in charge, Cat 5 Irma became the star of the moment and got the attention of elected officials and the news media. On September 4th, 2017 the governor of the State declared to his constituents "if you don't evacuate, no one will come to your rescue when the hurricane hits", while the director of FEMA described Irma as a disaster that will destroy the US. So there is at least one official who doesn't know the difference between the state of Florida and the US. Evacuation orders started on September 6th, and schools were ordered closed from September 7th to the 17th.

True to nature, the scared masses heeded the apocalyptic warnings and flocked to the local stores to purchase anything they could get their hands on. Apparently, the tap water from companies is better than the city's tap water at their house. Very few used the calm before the storm to fill the empty containers at their house with tap water they could use for drinking, cooking, and washing. Not one report from the media mentioned that hurricanes only last for a few hours, with the need for "survival" supplies in one or two days. Something that should have been in the house already.

After days of warning the populace about the ominous dangers of such hurricanes, the news corporations let the dogs out and released their most intelligent reporters, the ones who didn't know squat about hurricanes or anything else. Retired and former so-called experts were present in front of the cameras 24 hours a day, ready to spread their manure. The primary intent of such ad nauseum coverage from the network executives was to whip everyone in a frenzy, by inundating the airwaves with enough inane and worthless information to fill in every hour, minute, second of the day. Irma was still on a 2-days vacation in the Caribbean.

CBS4 had the best chance at winning the hurricane lottery; all they had to do was freeze a picture of Rudabeh Shahbazi on the screen and the hurricane would have calmed down to a gentle breeze. Viewers would have been happier and maybe, who knows, we could have achieved world peace.

Instead, many comedians reported on the hurricane while hiding behind buildings that could shield them from the gale force. They tethered other lesser clowns with colorful ropes to columns in the parking lot to prevent the hurricane from removing the trash. Here and there, some pearls of comedy entertained viewers as they watched these professional fools at work. The rapid-fire shocking reports came non-stop: "there is a tree down" (really, during a hurricane?) "the wind is strong," "everything is under water" (with all that rain?), "it's coming down now." One future award winner filmed his segment, on location, on a beach, to show and tell his viewers: "this is a beach where people would normally enjoy themselves".

Really, even during a hurricane?

One of the funniest comedic moments came when a news station boasted that its reporters on the field had a combined 20 years of experience reporting on hurricanes. Heck, my dog has been in the backyard for 20 years and it still can not open the gate.

Contrary to all the predictions, Irma veered to the West and missed the Miami area. Not before it provided plenty of entertainment venues, as one brilliant idiot came up with the idea of "shooting the hurricane with his guns" and found 59,000 of his like-minded brainless friends to join him online.

While the ocean was doing what oceans do best during a hurricane, a careless and clueless photographer decided that the Southern Most Point, in Key West, would be the best location to take pictures, as close to the waves as possible. He became the star of a YouTube video. Still, the lensman wasn't as smart as one storm chaser.

The wind was blasting everything in sight when a black man exited a car to "record" the wind gust; his smarter white buddy stayed in. They already projected the hurricane force to be around 115MPH and this "wanna-be scientist" needed to verify the info. It suffices to say that he lost the sumo wrestling match against Irma. The next day, however, he became an expert celebrity at a local TV station to share his findings. When asked what he discovered, his answer didn't disappoint: "it was a powerful hurricane." Hooray for knuckle heads!

But, in all honesty, the US would not be the great country it is, if there were no looting during a disaster. In towns, like Orlando and Miami, several videos showed many idiots and cowards breaking into stores to steal whatever they could. Active 1: Law enforcement caught and arrested many individuals who will probably be sentenced to probation and required to pay court costs.

In the end, Hurricane Irma weakened after making landfall in Cuba. Except for the Florida Keys, the total damage caused by Irma was not as great as government officials and forecasters had warned. After surveying the aftermath of Irma, Florida governor

Rick Scott said, "I thought we would see more damage." President Donald Trump commented on Twitter that the devastation in some places was "far greater than anyone thought."

Everywhere, city leaders were in front of the cameras detailing what happened and the measures being taken, while in the streets, Blacks and Mexicans actually started the clean-up work, trimming and cutting damaged trees to manageable sizes.

The clean-up will take 7 to 9 months, according to city officials; it would have taken a lot less time, but they deported most of the workers back to Mexico.

CITY LOVE. A few days later, the city sent the following love note to the residents: "Hurricane Irma blew into our lives last month, toppling trees, leaving many of us without power and water, and causing major damages throughout the entire state, but residents quickly knew they got lucky. For days, it appeared that the strongest hurricane in history was going to go right over our area, which would have caused catastrophic damage here. We still braced ourselves but were relieved when Irma veered to the West, leaving us with Cat 1 or Tropical Storm winds and rain instead of Cat 4 or more. While the city dealt with unforeseen water issues and power outages, city staff joined together with clean-up and recovery efforts. Volunteers and city staff distributed water and ice, crews worked around the clock to make repairs to the water plant and empty streets of debris. We hope at the time of reading this, we are stronger and moving forward, having endured a monster of a hurricane."

Once again, city officials lost or completely disregarded facts and common sense. Let's review this letter. A hurricane doesn't blow into anyone's life and Irma didn't even hit the Miami area. It's not that great to rejoice that the hurricane hit the West Coast of Florida instead of the eastside. After all these years of paying taxes and the salaries of city officials, residents should no longer accept "unforeseen water issues and power outages." While they forced taxpayers to boil water for days, fourteen nursing home residents died at the Rehabilitation Center at Hollywood Hills, because of the loss of electricity. The hurricane didn't even hit the area. No one from the city was cleaning streets of debris; as a matter of fact, clean-up will take close to 9 months. And finally, we did not endure a monster of a hurricane, just enough wind to fly a kite and intermittent rain.

BORICUA DE MI ALMA. An unfortunate drama unfolded after hurricane Maria, when president Trump picked a catfight with a Puerto Rican official. A pu**y grabbing white supremacist vs a hot mamacita with a bad attitude. The headlines were clear: San Juan mayor Carmen Yulín Cruz slams Donald Trump for 'terrible and abominable' Puerto Rico stunt. Cruz made headlines when she slammed the federal government for its slow response to the storm and pleaded for help from anyone able to provide it. "I am going to do what I never thought I would do. I am begging, begging anyone who can hear us to save us from dying," Cruz said in a tearful news conference. On Twitter, a narcissistic Trump claimed the mayor had been told by Democrats that she must be "nasty" to him.

In an escalating war of words with President Donald Trump, the mayor of San Juan, Carmen Yulín Cruz, slammed the president again for tossing rolls of paper towels to hurricane survivors in a beaming photo-op, calling the image "terrible and abominable." Trump traveled to Puerto Rico amid criticism that he neglected the storm-torn island after Hurricane Maria, which killed 34 people. Trump tossed the paper towels into the crowd of storm survivors and handed out flashlights at the Cavalry Chapel while joking, "You don't need them anymore," though most of the island remains without power. "This terrible and abominable view of him throwing paper towels and throwing provisions at people, it's really, it does not embody the spirit of the American nation, you know," mayor Carmen Cruz told MSNBC. "That is not the land of the free and the home of the brave, the beacon of democracy* that people have learned to look up to, you know."

(Note *: Does Carmen Yulín Cruz truly believe that the US has ever been the land of the free and the home of the brave, the beacon of democracy that people have learned to look up to?)

THE WALL PEOPLE. Mexico stepped up to the plate and said it will send aid to hurricane-ravaged Puerto Rico. That's the day after President Donald Trump's disastrous visit to the U.S. territory, during which he complained to victims that catastrophic damage to their island had thrown his budget "out of whack". The Mexican government said it would send 30 tons of bottled water and mosquito repellent, plus experts in power generation, transmission and distribution, Reuters reported.

Trump's relationship with Mexico has been troubled from his initial presidential campaign announcement when he demonized Mexicans as drug dealers and rapists, though added, "some, I assume, are good people." He frequently feuded with Mexico's government over who will pay for a wall he wants to build along the border the two countries share.

CALLOUS RACIST LEADER. Hurricane Maria killed dozens in Puerto Rico, left more than half of the island's 3.4 million residents without clean drinking water and 95% without power. Critics say Trump's overall response to this crisis has been inadequate and even inappropriate, especially in relation to his tweets attacking San Juan's mayor. The president's 17-minute visit to Puerto Rico included not only his comment about the cost of repairing the destroyed island, but a casual reference to Hurricane Maria not being "a real catastrophe like Katrina" because of what he considers a low overall death toll, which actually doubled in the hours after he left. At one point, the president awkwardly tossed paper towels at people in the crowd as if performing at a carnival.

And after families showed Trump the damage Hurricane Maria inflicted on their homes, the president said, "Have a good time", as he departed.

Later, from the comfort of his New Jersey golf resort, Trump lashed out again at the mayor of San Juan, Puerto Rico, and the ravaged island's residents, defending his administration's hurricane response by suggesting that Puerto Ricans had not done enough to help themselves. Trump tweeted "They want everything to be done for them when it should be a community effort". The president's comments were a breathtaking and racially inflected swipe at residents who have labored for more than a week to survive without electricity, running water, food or medical supplies. Media reports also have shown Puerto Ricans working together, a visible contradiction of the president's suggestion that they and their leaders had avoided helping themselves. Minutes after broadcasts showed Trump telling reporters at the White House that "we have done an incredible job", Cruz asserted on camera that the world could see Puerto Ricans being treated "as animals that can be disposed of."

Get off the golf course and go to jail.

The AP reported that "more Trump's absurdities marked the second straight weekend he has set off a national furor with tweets and comments that targeted nonwhites for criticism. Since last weekend, he has gone after African American athletes protesting police violence by declining to stand when the national anthem is played. He has demanded that the National Football League fire all such protesters. In some of his over 20 tweets on one day, the president sought to suggest that any criticism of the federal response was a criticism of the first responders, much as he cast NFL players' protests as directed against service members and veterans, not police violence. He also alleged that reporters, who have been in Puerto Rico documenting the hurricane's aftermath, had diminished the role of U.S. rescuers."

John Oliver joined the chaos when he branded President Donald Trump's response to the disaster relief efforts in Puerto Rico "horribly racist" on an episode. An incredulous Oliver said on his HBO show: "Really? Really? The primary obstacle to hurricane relief has been Puerto Rican laziness? You have got to hand it to Trump. Anyone can say horribly racist things about Hispanic people on a golden escalator," he added, "but it takes actual balls to do it while their fellow citizens are dying."

The only pinheads supporting Trump right now are from his white supremacist base, as all other idiots who used to have already figured out their mistake.

COMMON SENSE. Anyone who has a problem understanding the American version of democracy, the notion of freedom and independence, can readily reflect on the predicament of Puerto Rico, Barbuda and the other islands destroyed by hurricanes. It's easy to understand the course of action to take. Trump knew what to do!

Ramón Emeterio Betances is probably turning over in his grave, watching how his countrymen have sold their souls. Well, well, well...! Everyone still remembers that referendum about Puerto Rico becoming independent? Puerto Rico could have taken charge of its destiny. Instead, Puerto Ricans voted to be the stray dogs on the US porch, not even the front porch. When you surrender your freedom, you are doomed to accept whatever the massa gives you; decisions are made for you by the massa who will decide when to hand you the ration of salted meat and lemonade. As long as you willfully accept to be someone's bit*h, you have to shut the hell up and wait for your pimp's mood to change. It's in the fine prints of the contract you signed.

# UKUU WA NYEUPE

There are several accounts from everyday life in the US that do not shock anyone, anymore, anywhere. They are the sideshows that are expected from dysfunctional humans.

THE RAPTURE. Authorities in Casper received a call about a visibly drunk man claiming to be from the future, according to KTWO. Officers arrived to find Bryant Johnson warning that aliens would come next year and that people should leave as soon as possible. The white man claimed he was from the future and had traveled back in time from the year 2048 to warn civilization about the imminent arrival of aliens. Johnson was so concerned about his mission to save humanity that he requested to speak to the "president of the town."

Bryant Johnson should be in the White House or the least, Congress.

SICK DAY. They raped a female patient with a serious brain injury at Bronx-Lebanon Hospital, according to police sources. A registered nurse at the hospital was checking on the 32-year-old patient around 7:45 p.m. when she walked in on 37-year-old Keith Nembhard having sex with the incapacitated woman, police said. The victim's doctor told cops that the woman had a previous serious brain injury that rendered her incapable of consenting to sex, according to sources. The perpetrator, who knew the victim, was apprehended, arrested and charged with rape in the second degree, sources said.

MOTHER'S DAY. Two Caucasian Florida moms overdosed on heroin with their infant children in the backseat, police said. Kristen Leigh O'Connor, 28, and 29-year-old June Schweinhart were found overdosed in their vehicle after one of them called 911 for help, according to the Boynton Beach Police Department. Cops said that O'Connor told them she picked up Schweinhart in an SUV and the pair bought $60 worth of heroin from her old drug dealer. Both women's babies were in the car. "For whatever reason, they decided yesterday to buy heroin and then snorted it while inside the car with their children," the Boynton Beach Police Department wrote on Facebook about the incident. When one woman began convulsing, the other called police but then overdosed herself, authorities said.

FATHER OF THE YEAR. Sherin Mathews, who had a developmental disability, vanished in the early hours of Oct. 7th, 2017 after her father, Wesley Matthews, placed her outside of her home in an alleyway at 3 a.m. as punishment for not drinking her milk. When Mathews checked on Sherin 15 minutes later, she was gone; the father told police. The Richardson Police Department said investigators discovered a body around 11 a.m. Sunday in a culvert beneath a road and believe it to be the toddler.

THIN ICE. Meanwhile, on the new plantations, negroes are again restless. The debate over cultural appropriation was back on the forefront of several people's minds, particularly after Karuk artist Fox Spears pointed out on Twitter, Disney was selling Pocahontas costumes for the Halloween holiday, once again.

There are a lot better reasons for blacks to be offended. This is not one of them. It's ok to wear Pocahontas' costume; she was a traitor who defiled herself and her people by copulating with the white terrorist invader. My ancestor Anacaona is the only true native queen deserving of praise; she chose death over prostituting herself.

HOMEGROWN. In my previous books, I mentioned the US war on terrorism was a joke. British, American, Zionist and Greek are the people peddling the utopia of a superior race, especially the United British States of America, where dead white supremacists are celebrated. The Nazis didn't invent the concentration camps;

they emulated the agenda of the American Eugenics movement.

The long history of double standards when covering terrorism on US soil is another reality that can be attributed to racism. Previously, I duly noted that charges of terrorism are made according to a person's geographical and national origin, especially by skin color. In the US, terrorists would most certainly be white supremacists, instead of Arab Muslims.

Whenever a non-white attacker commits an act of violence, the media is quick to cry terrorism, even if they later rescinded it after the investigations yield the facts. The tail-wagging media never sees a white person as a terrorist, even when an act committed by the white terrorist falls within the purview of terrorism. There are many more instances of white terrorists spreading violence than non-white or Muslims. Yet, it would be very hard for someone to know or judge by the news media reports.

The US is a "democratic" country where a convicted white supremacist gets probation, or serves 5 years for murder, while a negro rots in jail for 20-30 years for possession of 20 grams of marijuana. That's if they do not shoot the Negro beforehand, for any reason, like driving or existing while black.

LAND OF THE FREE. It starts at the top, when president Donald Trump has been parroting the same nonsensical propaganda as his German ancestors did to the Soviets, trolling Mexicans and Muslims, while trying to unconstitutionally ban travel from certain countries. Yet he never mentions the white encounters, even when US Aryan supremacists kill police officers.

The Nation Institute's Investigative Fund exposed the fact that, between 2008 and 2016, the US has seen 201 homegrown terrorist incidents compared to 63 cases by extremist Muslims. Most homegrown terrorists are men and white. A fact that was ignored by or went over the head of the media and the Trump administration.

This is the way a society, under European supremacist control, saw things, thru thick biased lenses, from racist comments about any non-white incident, to the media doing its best to find whatever inane excuses can absolve any white supremacist. When they can not blame non-whites, they will even consider mental illness to get a white supremacist off the hook and tentatively justify his actions. When everything else fails, one can always count on the last ditch excuse: "he grew up in an unhealthy environment."

HOME OF THE BRAVES This is a country loaded with cowards where racism reeks at all levels of society.

On 10/17/2017, the parents of an African-American high school freshman at The woodlands High School in Texas said they are livid with their daughter's school district for not doing enough to discipline a student who sent her a racist message saying, "we should have hung all u niggers while we had the chance."

OKLAHOMA CITY On April 19, 1995, a truck-bomb explosion outside the Alfred P. Murrah Federal Building in Oklahoma City, Oklahoma, left 168 people dead and hundreds more injured. The blast was set off by white anti-government militant Timothy McVeigh, who in 2001 was executed for his crimes. His co-conspirator, Terry Nichols, received life in prison. Until September 11, 2001, the Oklahoma City bombing was the worst terrorist attack to take place on U.S. soil.

Nobody ever used words like white, supremacist, and homegrown terrorist to describe Timothy McVeigh or Terry Nichols.

SOUTH CAROLINA. When white homegrown terrorist

Dylann Roof killed 9 blacks in Charleston, South Carolina, in 2015, he was initially described by the media as a disturbed young man, until his klan and skinhead connections were discovered, days before a millionaire white supremacist posted his bail. During the entire media reporting process covering the slaughter, Dylann Roof was never called a terrorist, white supremacist, SOB, thug, POS, racist, murderer or any other labels usually reserved for blacks.

Still waiting on one single courageous member of the tail wagging media to call it what it is; not once were the words "domestic terrorist" ever mentioned.

The douchebags at the NRA even blamed the victims for not being armed, which it says could have reduced the number of dead. A real hypocritical move, since the NRA has always been totally against blacks owning or carrying weapons, even to protect themselves. A racist stand that was covered in my last book "Papa time" (Amazon. com/books.)

LAS VEGAS. On the night of October 1, 2017, white gunman Stephen Craig Paddock killed 58 people and injured another 489 when he opened fire on a large crowd of concertgoers at the Route 91 Harvest music festival on the Las Vegas strip in Paradise, Nevada. Between 10:05 and 10:15 p.m. PDT, 64-year-old Paddock of Mesquite, Nevada, fired hundreds of rifle rounds from his suite on the 32nd floor of the nearby Mandalay Bay hotel.

A Las Vegas police officer who was off-duty attending the concert is among the dead, police said.

A white man killed 58 people, including one cop and injured 489 others, yet the cops are still slaughtering unarmed negroes in the streets of America. It requires very little effort to hate a man whom you have wronged.

About an hour after the firing ceased, they found Paddock

dead in his hotel room from a self-inflicted gunshot wound. SWAT teams, using explosives, stormed the gunman's hotel room and found he had killed himself, authorities said.

"Las Vegas shooter Stephen Paddock had visited the Middle East during a series of cruises," police have revealed. Investigators remain stumped as to Paddock's motives but said he visited the contentious region on a cruise. He also took at least 11 other cruises to other destinations over the last several years, the AP reported. Using this kind of purposely detracting and inane logic, one can be sure that if one of his trips was to Colorado, they would remember white terrorist Stephen Paddock as a great skier.

His motive remains unknown, the police said, just like every single murder by a white person. There is still no motive for castrating, enslaving, lynching, incarcerating and shooting blacks, even today.

Trump congratulated law enforcement personnel who took a whole damn hour to locate the shooter with the help of an on- site injured security guard: "The speed with which they acted is miraculous and prevented further loss of life." Sheriff Joseph Lombardo said authorities believe it was a "lone wolf" attack. And the U.S. Homeland Security Department said there was no "specific credible threat" involving other public venues in the U.S.

Descriptions from the media included words like alleged, heartfelt, mental disorder, not one degrading word about a white thug, SOB, punk, POS, murderer, super predator, white supremacist bastard doing what white terrorists have been doing for centuries. Just another white man doing what white people do best. All the racist maggots, who usually come out to troll negroes, were nowhere to be found online. They must have been at their annual meeting in the cesspool.

Still waiting on one single courageous member of the tail

wagging media to call it what it is; not once were the words "domestic terrorist" ever mentioned.

He legally purchased the firearms, along with more guns found in his homes, in the states of Nevada, California, Texas, and Utah. They have not identified him as a terrorist because of his white status. They said they had no investigative information or criminal history, showing he was dangerous. His only recorded interaction with law enforcement was a minor traffic citation years before the shooting, which he settled in court. In other words, a perfect lily white man with no record, described as a lone wolf by law enforcement. His younger brother and others, who were in close contact with him, described him as an ordinary man with no apparent religious or political affiliation.

So they made the move to stain his girlfriend. Better place the blame on a Philippines native than a white man who, once more, did what white people are famous for. Long live white supremacy and the hallucinating utopia of a superior race.

Another article claimed: The Las Vegas gunman, behind the deadliest* (please see note below) mass shooting in modern U.S. history, spent decades stockpiling guns and living a "secret life" that investigators may never fully understand, police say. Clark County, Nev., Sheriff Joseph Lombardo said Wednesday that it was only logical to "make the assumption" that Stephen Paddock had "some help at some point" in pulling off Sunday's massacre. (That's after calling him a lone wolf, one day earlier). As evidence, Lombardo pointed to gunman Paddock's vast arsenal, explosive materials found in his car and his meticulous planning.

Failing to call Stephen Craig Paddock a white terrorist, Clark County Sheriff Joe Lombardo issued a statement three days after the shooting and said that there was evidence, which he declined to discuss, that Paddock intended to escape the scene, and that he may have had help from an accomplice. (That's again after previously calling him a lone wolf). Trying to sanctify the action of a white terrorist and blame someone else, anyone with dark-skin.

ONLINE CRETINS. A few days later, many ignorant keyboard warriors vented their opinion that the national focus should remain on black murders of blacks. Granted that many domesticated negroes have been killing blacks, it remains an undeniable historical fact that Aryan white supremacists have slaughtered 119 millions Native Americans, 800 millions Africans, with 60 millions blacks butchered just in the Congo by King Leopold II of Belgium. And a black man is the bad guy?

TESTIFY. Yet another great review came in. The gunman who opened fire on a country music show in Las Vegas killing 58 people before turning the gun on himself appeared to be "a rational man with a vanilla profile," according to a casino boss who knew him. Steve Wynn, who is also the RNC finance chair, said shooter Stephen Paddock had been visiting the city for 11 years and was known to staff as a regular guest. Wynn described Paddock as having: "The most vanilla profile one could possibly imagine."

IDIOTIC FALL-OUT. With all the gun laws already in the books and not enforced at any time, especially when it comes to white supremacists, the afterthought is always to ban whatever kind of weapon was used in the latest massacre. Therefore, it didn't come as a shock when someone proposed an outright ban on bump-stock devices.

Police said gunman Stephen Paddock fitted 12 of his weapons with bump-stock devices that allow semi-automatic rifles to operate as if they were fully automatic machine guns, which are otherwise already outlawed in the United States. Wayne LaPierre, the NRA's chief executive, accused the Bureau of Alcohol, Tobacco, Firearms and Explosives under Democratic former President Barack Obama of paving the way for the use of bump stocks and creating legal confusion about their usage.

Republican President Donald Trump was an outspoken advocate of gun rights during his 2016 campaign for the White House, and the NRA spent more than $30 million to support his candidacy.

Two-stepping as usual, the powerful U.S. gun lobby, the National Rifle Association, said on Sunday it would oppose an outright ban on bump-stock devices that the killer in the Las Vegas massacre of 58 people used to turn rifles into automatic weapons and strafe a crowd with bursts of sustained gunfire. Then the NRA, which has seldom embraced new firearms- control measures, stunned gun control advocates last week when it issued a new statement voicing willingness to support a restriction on bump stocks. A typical flip-flop for the NRA.

The next step will be a ban on windows, because people use them to jump to their deaths.

MY ONLINE POST. He was not a gun guy, he didn't have a criminal record, "a rational man with a vanilla profile," an ordinary man... Wow! All the wonderful words to describe a lily white killer doing what they do best and have been doing to the rest of the world since 550AD. Imagine if he was black, the countless of maggots who would type their venom online. It's a beautiful day in the USA when white people eliminate themselves.

The blame for gun violence rests squarely not on the NRA, Congress or the people responsible for enforcing the current laws, but on the citizens of this country who allowed their government to be hijacked by special interests.

How far will the white supremacy machine go to protect one of their own? Trying to find anything to deflect the blame from a white shooter. First, it was a woman from the Philippines, now it's another invisible accomplice. Ultimately, they might even blame Daffy Duck because he is black. It's time for the world to realize that white supremacy is an ignorant hallucinating utopia.

GLORIFYING MURDER. The Los Angeles Times resorted to the lowest denominator in trying to diminish the guilt of Stephen Paddock. Just like idiots jumping for joy when a black nation gets bombed, the LA Times published the following article, a proof of what the white supremacist media can do to glorify murder by one of their own:

"The trigonometry of terror: Why the Las Vegas shooting was so deadly. Arthur B. Alphin has a deep understanding of the trigonometry of terror. The retired Army lieutenant colonel and West Point graduate, who has a mechanical engineering degree and specialized in ballistics, has testified in many multiple-shooting cases. What he sees so far about Las Vegas shooter Stephen Paddock is a patient, well-trained gunner who did not pick and choose his targets, but held to a steady kill zone centered in the middle of thousands of concertgoers. Once the trigger was pulled, simple laws of physics and trigonometry sealed the fate of over 500 people who would fall wounded in the ensuing fracas, 59 of them fatally.

According to Alphin, he had a massive area equivalent to three, four, or five football fields packed with people standing side by side. He was not aiming at any individual person. He was just throwing bullets in a huge beaten zone.

Beaten zone is an infantry term dating to World War I. Shaped like the area a searchlight casts across a flat surface, it represents the area where bullets can strike, and moves substantially with tiny changes in the tilt of the gun. If the shooter shifted by about 1 degree, or the width of two fingers held at arm's length, Alphin said, the beaten zone would fall outside the crowd. That's all the distance you have to move and you aren't hitting anybody, Alphin said. So he had to be pointing or aiming at the very center of mass and then bouncing all over with the recoil.

From a perch 320 feet above ground in a hotel whose base was about 1,050 feet from the concert venue, Paddock was firing down the 1,098-foot hypotenuse of a right triangle, and would have to adjust his aim for the arc of the bullet over that distance. Alphin said there was 'no way' the shooter maintained such a steady kill zone by dumb luck. Steady nerves and planning are a better explanation for the casualty rate, he said. How did this guy get trained that well? Where did it come from?

"At least one of the 23 rapid-firing weapons authorities found in the hotel room had a bipod stand to hold it steady, according to law enforcement authorities. Paddock also may have fitted weapons with a device to make it cycle rounds more quickly into the chamber for firing, or converted some to fully automatic firing, potentially adding as many as eight rounds per second, Alphin said. There may also be expertise at work in deciding when to switch rifles, Alphin said. Gun barrels expand as they heat up, and the bullet can lose contact with the grooves that spin it and keep it point-forward. Without the spin, it will tumble. A bullet tumbling like that, good God, it will land on planet Earth but you don't know where, Alphin said."

All the fake news necessary to cover, muddle and whitewash a case of white domestic terrorism. Black Lives Matter, somewhat, ended up being mentioned and blamed for the violence of the white supremacists.

SAY WHAT? The white supremacy machine was running full throttle when several news outlets got it wrong by reporting that the Las Vegas shooting was the deadliest mass shooting in modern American history. Not only is that false, it's not even close. Basically, idiots are splitting historical facts in many compartments, to diminish their impact and hide their shameful past. Selective memory and destroying accurate history are other tricks, the hallmarks of white supremacy.

Here is a look back, through our ugly and painful history, at several of the deadliest American massacres that many wish they could sweep under the rug.

- The Bloody Island Massacre took place in 1850 in the Clear Lake area of California. The Pomo were a peaceful Native-American tribe that had been enslaved and abused by settlers, Andrew Kelsey and Charles Stone. Forced to build structures and do work as cowboys, the Pomo families were starving from the lack of food. After they killed Kelsey, the United States Cavalry exacted revenge by murdering 200 Pomo men, women, and children.

- The Fort Pillow, Tennessee, massacre in 1864 was one of the more brutal moments in the Civil War. The Confederate general Nathan Bedford Forrest received the surrender of between 500 and 600 Union soldiers. Traditionally, the troops, primarily African-Americans and Confederate deserters, would be taken as prisoners of war. However, the Confederate army and Forrest did not want to treat these men as regular prisoners, instead opting to slaughter them.

- In 1872, Louisiana was amid a hotly contested governor's race that was extremely split among racial lines. The state went to the Republican candidate, which angered many white Democrats. This frustration bubbled up in racial tension, and it came to a head in Colfax, Louisiana, on Easter Sunday in 1873. Over 300 armed white men, including members of white supremacist organizations such as the Knights of White Camellia and the Ku-Klux-Klan, attacked the Courthouse building. When the militia maneuvered a cannon to fire on the Courthouse, some of the sixty black defenders fled while others surrendered. When one of James Hadnot's own men accidentally shot him, the white militia retaliated by shooting the black prisoners. The white militia singled out those who were wounded in the earlier battle, particularly black militia members, for execution. In the end, the armed militia killed over 150 Negroes, with nearly a third of the victims being killed after the battle ended. Police from New Orleans were on the scene the next day and arrested 97 men, who were charged with breaking a law that would become known as the Ku Klux Klan Act. But eventually, the few men that saw prison time would be released less than two years later.

- On December 29th, 1890, pursuing their racist campaign to decimate the Native population, the US cavalry butchered 190 men, 400 women and children and wounded 121 members of the Lakota Pine Ridge Indian Reservation, at Wounded Knee, in South Dakota. Twenty soldiers received the medal of honor.

- The race riot in East St. Louis, Illinois, began in May 1917, and lasted three full days before they brought in the National Guard to mitigate the situation. It began when the primarily white workforce of the Aluminum Ore Company went on strike, leading to African-Americans being brought in across the picket line. That created the tension, but the violence began when rumors of a white man robbed by a black man at gunpoint popped up. That led to white people pulling African-Americans off trolleys and beating them, people firing guns at African- American homes, and homes being set on fire. The white mob murdered 40 Negroes and caused 8 millions in property damage.

- The September 30th, 1919 Elaine, Arkansas race riot began with a simple meeting of African-Americans inside a church. Mostly sharecroppers, the meeting was intended to discuss a way that they could get a higher wage for their cotton crops. But during the meeting, several white men showed up at the church and antagonized the black guards placed outside to protect the group.

A mob of 1000 armed white supremacists, supported by US troops, went "hunting Negroes" according to participating eyewitness H. F. Smiddy. 200 African-Americans lost their lives, while they jailed 385 in Phillips County.

On November 5th, 1919, they sentenced 12 black men to die on the electric chair.

- The 1921 race riot in Tulsa, Oklahoma, began with a young African-American shoe-shiner riding an elevator with a white operator, on May 30th. Some sort of incident occurred between the man, Dick Rowland, and the young woman, Sarah Page, leading to the man being arrested by Tulsa Police, for assault. We don't really know what exactly happened. The Tulsa Tribune printed a story saying that Rowland had tried to rape Page, with an accompanying editorial stating that they planned a lynching for that night.

Gossip spread through the white communities and the events became more and more extreme with each telling. Within days, large segments of Tulsa, heavily occupied by African-Americans, were burning, and mobs were out for blood. White rioters looted the area and attacked people that got in their way. The Governor of Oklahoma declared martial law, and sent in the National Guard, but by then, the damage had been done. The violence lasted only around 24 hours, but historians believe that, on May 31st, 1921, somewhere around 600 blacks were butchered in Tulsa, 1400 black homes and businesses were destroyed, with 10,000 black people left homeless.

We have relegated these deadly mob rampages to the "I don't remember closet" by a white supremacist society with selective memory, hell bent of ignoring accurate history. Déjà vu, if you read "World super predators" @Amazon.com/ books.)

ANOTHER EUROPEAN. After waiting for several minutes at a baggage carousel, Esteban Santiago, with a military ID, heard his name called over a public address system. Delta Airlines was paging him to come to a service desk to pick up his gun.

Minutes later, he killed five people and wounded six at the Fort Lauderdale airport on Jan. 6th, 2017.

Still waiting on one single courageous member of the tail wagging media to call it what it is; not once were the words "domestic terrorist" ever mentioned.

Where was the Department of Homeland Security? Should they have notified airport security or the local law enforcement agency of a customer picking up a gun? After all, there were many incidents of shooting at airports. The TSA will seize your toothpaste and invade every nook and cranny, every private crevasse of your body with a strip search for trying to bring breast milk for your baby, but what the heck, it's ok to pick up a gun at the service desk of Delta Airlines.

COLORADO On 11/02/2017, 47 years old white supremacist Scott Ostrem walked into a Walmart in suburban Denver, Colorado, shot and killed 3 people. The news media immediately went in a pathetic damage control mode by claiming he was suffering from financial duress.

Instead of calling Scott what he truly is, the media opted to goose-step over the facts and present his financial record as a defense. He filed for bankruptcy in September 2015, a whole 2 years before he acted out his confederate fantasy. They listed his debts at $86000 and credit card debt at $58000. They reported his year-to-date earnings as $23,637.

His stepsister ventured he suffered brain damage from taking LSD nearly 30 years ago, in 1988, and voices in his head have tormented him since then. She continued that Scott Ostrem was frequently counseled by a Catholic priest who placed a crucifix on his forehead, commanded demons to leave his body and asked God to silence the voices.

Of course, T. D. Jakes, one of the crooks and thieves fleecing the poor, came out to say it's not an act of God. How can he be so sure? In other words, T. D. Jakes admitted that his fairy God is not omnipotent and omniscient, otherwise, he would have the power and foresight to stop this violent act. According to the bible, his God created that killer and actually placed him in that store.

If Scott Ostrem had been black, the media would have described him as a thug, SOB, criminal, POS, murderer, welfare recipient or, in the words of Hillary Clinton, a super predator. This is the sad reality in the US, the greatest country in the world for white supremacists. Another example of domestic terrorism being swept under the confederate rug.

Still waiting on one single courageous member of the tail wagging media to call it what it is; not once were the words "domestic terrorist" ever mentioned.

GOOD OLE TEXAS. On 11/05/2017, white supremacist Devin Patrick Kelley, 26, of New Braunfels, Texas, which is about 35 miles from Sutherland Springs, entered a church, armed with a rifle and his military service.

Sheriff Joe Tackitt of Wilson County reported 27 dead and 27 injured in a mass shooting at the First Baptist church of Sutherland Springs, which is about 40 miles southeast of San Antonio.

The press used 40 words to describe the white shooter, and none of them included any derogatory word. If Devin Kelley had been black, the media would have described him as a thug, SOB, criminal, POS, murderer, welfare recipient or, in the words of Hillary Clinton, a super predator.

Still waiting on one single courageous member of the tail wagging media to call it what it is; not once were the words "domestic terrorist" ever mentioned.

Investigators even found a way to blame the shooting on family problems with his mother-in-law. Meanwhile, an idiot named Sebastien Blanc blamed the shooting on his atheism, because he ranted against God and the church on his social media pages. (Hey, Sebastien, atheists don't rant against God and a church.)

Once more, it was an occasion for certain people to skirt the issue by calling for more gun control laws to be enacted. A white supremacist domestic terrorist will find a weapon as surely as an addict will find drugs.

Not one word or advice yet from the NRA scumbags who blamed the black victims for not being armed and had plenty to say to Negroes after the Charleston, South Carolina shooting by Dylan Roof.

Texas governor Gregg Abbott said in a statement: "I want to thank law enforcement for their response and ask that all Texans pray for the Sutherland Springs community."

Texas Attorney General Ken Paxton said in his statement: "The thoughts and prayers of all Texans are with the people of Sutherland Springs, as tragic reports come out of First Baptist church. Please join Angela and me as we pray for those affected by this horrific shooting."

Paul Buford, a pastor at another church, told KSAT-TV that his congregants were in the middle of their service when they started getting calls about the shooting. Members of his church, who are first responders, rushed out while the rest of the congregation "immediately started praying." (What were they doing before that, collecting donations?)

Meanwhile, smart members fled the First Baptist church and took refuge at a safer gas station across the street.

Pastor Frank Pomeroy, who was in Oklahoma during the shooting, told his sheep: "Trust in the Lord with all your heart and do not rely, or lean, on your own understanding. You see, God's understanding is far greater, and there may be things that are taking place that you don't understand, but you still need to do what God's calling you to do."

So God wants his sheep to keep praying, and beg for his protection, while they are sitting ducks in a sty.

As usual in American society, when a white supremacist kills others, it was a simple task to figure out the race of the millions of ultra polite keyboard extremists who forgot all the right words to describe one of their own.

PRESIDENTIAL KLANSMAN. Trump's response to domestic terrorism was to cut funding to Life after hate, a group that helps people leave the white supremacist movement. And the president continues to embrace and delve deeper into his Klan and Nazi ideology, disregarding the fact that many black families have been destroyed, countless black men have been slaughtered, many black women have been raped, and many black babies have been sacrificed in pursuit of the delusional white utopia.

We should all observe a moment of silence, or take a knee, in respect for the dead brain of the president. Trump's racist agenda is very simple, and it is to undo everything a black president did before him. The crass ignorance of a white supremacist, 6000 years of dedicated inbreeding in the making, can be measured when he thinks that destroying the "legacy of Barack Hussein Obama" means it never happened. Just like the western world did and is still doing to Africa's glorious past.

Donald Trump is a "textbook racist whose words and behaviours show considerable prejudicial bias," a Duke University professor has claimed. The President's "insensitive, disrespectful and mean-spirited statements and actions" are consistent with several categories of racism including "insidious" and "symbolic" racism, according to Jay Pearson, an assistant professor at Duke's

Sanford School of Public Policy.

Prof Pearson wrote in the LA Times: "Throughout last year's campaign and his first eight months in office, the president has expressed his bias through government orders and the presidential bully pulpit (systemic racism)." Trump argued that as a Mexican, US District Court Judge Gonzalo Curiel, who was born and raised in the United States, could not fairly arbitrate lawsuits related to Trump University (structural racism). For years, Trump protested, falsely, that Barack Obama was not born in the US and was consequently elected illegitimately (symbolic racism)." These actions meet scholarly definitions of racist behavior, he said. Symbolic racism involves rhetoric that delegitimizes others, while structural racism assigns social value to people based on inherent differences, he added.

VINTAGE NAZI. A Florida congressional representative described President Donald Trump's phone call to the widow of a soldier killed during an ambush in Niger as insensitive after the president reportedly said the man "must've known what he signed up for."

Rep. Frederica Wilson (D-Fla.) was in the car with Myeshia Johnson, the pregnant widow of Army Sgt. La David Johnson, when Trump called her and spoke for about five minutes, according to South Florida's NBC affiliate. "Sarcastically he said: But you know he must have known what he signed up for," Wilson recounted to NBC6. "How could you say that to a grieving widow? I couldn't believe... and he said it more than once. I said this man has no feelings for anyone. This is a young woman with child who is grieved to her soul."

We all know the saying: leaders are made in times of crisis; well, this leader is creating crises at all times.

REALITY CHECK. While I reject, with all my being, the

white supremacist, callous and insensitive presidential phone call, I nevertheless can not bring myself to understand and accept the personal choice made by Army Sgt. La David Johnson. An American negro, in Africa, for the sole purpose of killing Africans and teach Africans to murder each other; and they branded this Negro a hero who was defending American freedom. Why and how? The US fought not one war for freedom and liberty. Not ONE DAMN war. They were all wars of aggression against black countries.

What the heck is a black American man, who can not freely walk the damn streets of this country without getting shot by the cops, what the heck is this black American man doing in 2017, 2154 miles, as the crow flies, away from his pregnant black woman and black children, upholding the right of the white supremacist agenda to dominate and control Alkebulan?

And many more facts are being swept under the carpet. Everyone is avoiding the obvious: they killed 4 soldiers during the attack, 3 whites and one black. They immediately retrieved the bodies of the 3 dead Caucasians, while the carcass of the negro had to wait 48 hours to be recovered. What else should be expected by negroes who volunteered to gamble their lives in defense and support of white supremacy around the world?

The official report is clear: "But it wasn't until two days later on the evening of Oct. 6, according to Dunford, that Johnson's body was found." The top general denied that the U.S. ever left him behind, arguing that French, American, or Nigerian troops were in the area at all times until his body was recovered.

Government officials and the public paying lip service to the fallen, and we all know very well, aside from the immediate families, no one gives a rat's ass about these dead American militants, especially the black ones.

FOLLOW UP. Frederica Wilson, D-Fla., has earned the ire of President Donald Trump and some of his supporters in recent weeks for criticizing his handling of a call to the widow of a fallen soldier. Federal authorities are now investigating an Illinois man who posted a meme that suggested lynching Rep. Frederica Wilson. Old habits die hard, and it requires very little effort to hate someone whom you have wronged.

The Chicago Tribune first reported that Tom Keevers was connected to the social media post, which called for "ten good men to help carry out a lynching." Des Plaines Police Department Commander Chris Mierzwa confirmed for ABC News that Keevers is the subject of an investigation. Mierzwa said we interviewed Keevers Friday night, and he currently faces no local charges.

The image at the center of the threat appears to be a Facebook post, with two lines of text below Keevers' name, photo, location and timestamp. The post reads, "Need ten good men to help carry out a lynching. Must have own horse and saddle. Rope will be provided."

No charges for threatening a black government official. Case closed.

NORTH KOREA. And, while Trump and his minions are busy posting daily threatening tweets and ignorant comments online, 50% of Americans believe that military action should be taken against North Korea, although 95% of Americans can NOT locate North Korea on a map.

As a public service, I would like to help the US military and all the pilots who will fly sorties, North Korea is located west of Germany and Switzerland, northwest of Italy, northeast of Spain, right south of London, below the UK. Drop everything there, within the borders of that rogue, out-of-control, misbehaving nation. That will teach Kim Jong-Un to comb his hair over.

Godspeed and c'est la vie.

COLUMBUS AGAIN. Tiptoeing his merry way on his white supremacist journey, President Trump criticized the idea of removing statues of Christopher Columbus and called for the preservation of history. "We believe we should preserve our history, not tear it down," Trump said Tuesday at the Heritage Foundation's annual President's Club gathering. "Now they are even trying to destroy statues of Christopher Columbus. What's next? Has to be stopped, it's heritage." Earlier this year, they defaced a statue of Columbus in New York, according to the New York Daily News. Protesters also called earlier this month for the removal of a Columbus statue in Manhattan. Columbus Day has become a point of controversy, with several communities choosing to instead celebrate "Indigenous People's Day." Trump earlier this month did not mention Native Americans in his first proclamation of Columbus Day statement.

There have also been debates across the country about removing monuments and statues of dead white supremacist leaders and generals of the Confederacy. Trump has in the past defended Confederate statues. In August, he said it was "sad" the "history and culture" of the U.S. is "being ripped apart" by the removal of Confederate statues and monuments.

"We believe we should preserve our history, not tear it down." Lynching Negroes is also part of your history. Surely, Trump would support displaying the bodies of blacks hanging from the Southern trees and that would add credence to his heritage as he goose-steps his way around the White House. No one expects Trump to know anything about history, or show any common sense; he barely understands why he should brush his teeth and take a bath.

SPECIAL LOVE NOTE TO SARAH HUCKABEE SANDERS. "To announce that there must be no criticism of the President, or that we are to stand by the President, right or wrong, is not only unpatriotic and servile, but is morally treasonable to the American public." Theodore Roosevelt.

KNOCK..KNOCK... President Donald Trump will be the first sitting president to address the Family Research Council's Values Voter Summit, which the Southern Poverty Law Center (SPLC) described as a rogue gallery of the radical right. Trump will be the keynote speaker at the event, which will also be attended by his former strategist, Steve Bannon. Other speakers include the founder of the anti-Islam group ACT for America and former Trump strategist, Sebastian Gorka. The anti-LGBTQ Family Research Council, labeled as a hate group by the SPLC, has hosted its annual summit since its inception in 2006.

YAHOO NEWS UK reported on 10/13/2017: "A special adviser to the UN has launched into an extraordinary outburst against Donald Trump, calling him a 'malignant narcissist, a sociopath and a racist.' Professor Jeffrey Sachs, an economist at Columbia University and special adviser to several UN secretary generals, made the comments on Radio 4's Today Programme this morning. Speaking about the President, he told presenter Sarah Montague: I believe on an individual level, he is profoundly psychologically ill. He is a malignant narcissist, and he is a sociopath, and he's a racist, so we've seen all of that unfold. It's hard to say it, but this is the grim reality that we face right now."

CHARLOTTESVILLE. On August 12, 2017, a group of heavily armed white supremacists, including neo-Nazis, skinheads, and KKK members, descended on Charlottesville, Va. for a Unite the Right rally. The city's plans to remove a Confederate statue of Robert E. Lee from a local park spurred the gathering on. Dressed in full camouflage, they were armed with large shields, wooden clubs, semi-automatic rifles and pistols. Chanting "blood and soil," Jews will not replace us, and "white lives matter", the inbred mob made its way around Charlottesville under the protective watch of local law enforcement.

Imagine, for a moment, how the police would have responded to a group of heavily armed negroes marching down any US city. They shoot unarmed black kids, even black babies.

One of the white supremacists, James Alex Fields, of Maumee, Ohio, rammed his car into the crowd, killing 32-year-old protester Heather Heyer and injuring 19 others.

Many lawmakers and ordinary Americans were shocked, but not upset, so was the president. In remarks from his golf club in New Jersey on Saturday, President Donald Trump said, "We condemn in the strongest possible terms this egregious display of hatred, bigotry and violence on many sides." On many sides? The president's implication that "many sides" were responsible for the violence didn't sit well with both a few lawmakers and private citizens who failed to remember that Trump's father was a member of the Klan. It didn't take long for the country and the world to understand that the president of the US is a blooming white supremacist.

The US is still a country where Blacks are considered commodities, not allowed to enjoy the freedom of expression guaranteed by the Constitution and the Declaration of Independence. Trump maintained Obama was NOT born in America, Trump was raised by a white supremacist father who was a member of the Klan, Trump still supports the white supremacists in Charlottesville, Trump made an explicit statement by pardoning his racist buddy Joe Arpaio. Ted Nugent's repeated calls for Obama's death didn't stop Trump from hosting him at the White House.

Many, however, continue to defend the stance of the president on confederate statues. Trump gets a free pass because one can not honestly expect him to know the difference between Robert E. Lee and George Washington, just as one can not expect a 1-year-old to know the difference between cocaine and baby powder.

TAKING A KNEE. In 2016, Kaepernick gained worldwide attention when he protested by not standing while the United States national anthem was being played before the start of games, motivated by what he viewed as the oppression of people of color in the United States. His actions prompted a wide variety of responses, including additional athletes in the NFL and other American sports leagues protesting in various ways.

Jerry Jones, the white supremacist owner of the Dallas Cowboys, said he would bench players who did not stand during the national anthem. His racist threat was publicized nationally and applauded on Twitter by President Trump, who summarized the two men's shared view: "Stand for Anthem or sit for game!" The president elaborated on his views, telling Fox News that the NFL "should have suspended" Colin Kaepernick for kneeling during the anthem because "you cannot disrespect our country, our flag, our anthem, you cannot do that." Proof positive that the idiot didn't even know the true reason Kaep would not stand.

Dozens of NFL players have knelt during the American National anthem before games, ever since Colin Kaepernick started the protest, which is not a protest of the national anthem, but rather of social injustice, over a year ago. The NFL protests became more widespread when President Donald Trump called players who knelt for the anthem "sons of bitches."

Fan backlash erupted as players kneeling in protest or simply not appearing during "The Star-Spangled Banner" mushroomed across the NFL, following President Donald Trump's repeated criticism of them. Negative reactions have included fans booing in some stadiums, the idiotic burning of "paid for" team apparel and season tickets, and two New Orleans Saints players being dis-invited as grand marshals for a Mardi Gras parade.

We need a first grader to explain to Dallas Cowboys owner Jerry Jones and the white supremacists that "kneeling" has nothing to do with disrespecting the flag, it has to do with how Negroes are mistreated and murdered in the US. No need to explain that to Trump because he hasn't reached the age of common sense yet. Trump enjoys the white supremacist hallucination that negroes are still on the plantations, 3/5 of a human, still not allowed, in his perfect Aryan world, to form their own opinion. Apparently, he thinks that his lunatic ideology can supersede the Constitution. If it was possible, Trump would hang Emmett Louis Till and Mary Turner, pump bullets into Martin Luther King Jr and kick Rosa Parks off the bus.

Rep. John Lewis (D-Ga.) praised NFL players who kneeled during the national anthem at games to protest racial injustice, saying he would kneel alongside them. "It is so inspiring to see these young men standing with their owners and standing with managers and coaches," the civil rights icon, who worked alongside Martin Luther King Jr. during the Civil Rights movement, said. "Some of these people would have said back in the sixties, don't go on the freedom rides, don't take part in a sitting at the lunch counter, don't march on Washington, don't march from Selma to Montgomery. You have a right to march. It's protected and shielded by the flag," he continued.

Lewis' comments came after President Trump said at a campaign rally last month that the NFL should fire players who kneel during the national anthem as a form of protesting. The NFL community responded in a show of solidarity through kneeling and linking arms before and during the anthem at games across the country.

WHITE LIE. (And the news continued.) Not much later,

former San Francisco 49ers they forced star Colin Kaepernick to counter a report that he would stand for the national anthem if they offered him a spot on an NFL team, deeming it a lie. Kaepernick, who refused to stand during the national anthem to protest police brutality towards African Americans, was previously a quarterback for the 49ers prior to opting out of his contract. On Sunday, he responded to a report that said he would stand if he was signed again, writing on social media: "A lie gets halfway around the world before the truth has a chance to get its pants on. Winston S. Churchill."

The goal and aim of white supremacy have always been to disperse false information: the Native Americans were called savages, the Africans were called cannibals, all that came from the real white genocidal murderers who were eating human flesh. John Garrison, the Donner Party, the Jamestown settlement in Virginia, Alfred Packer, Boone Helm, Jeffrey Dahmer, Hadden Clark, Marc Sappington, Otty Sanchez, Joseph Albert Oberhansley were white.

Now we are told by CBS Sports' Jason La Canfora that Kaepernick would stand for the anthem, if offered a contract. Just another installment of the white supremacy machine. All the illegal drugs and hard liquor in the world could not produce the level of stupidity enjoyed by Jason La Canfora, a category 5 moron who is probably raping women and little children.

In their delusional hallucination, the Zionist owned, dominated and sponsored media continues to claim that taking a knee is a disrespect to the flag, the country, and the Armed Forces. One can not expect the white supremacists to admit that the protest is about the treatment of Negroes in the US; they cannot understand anything that is not related to their close relatives. That's why they hated Barack Obama. He made the country prettier than their first cousins.

Stand for the flag, take a knee for humanity.

Vice President Pence joined the mix as he portrayed his walk out of a Sunday's game between the Indianapolis Colts and San Francisco 49ers as an act of patriotism. Pence's remarks followed President Trump's lead in trying to make the NFL players' national anthem protests of racial inequality in America about patriotism instead of race.

So, according to the lack of logic of the vice-president, when my dog walked out of the backyard, it was an act of obedience.

RACIST MEDIA. Fox News presented the following article on 11/13/2017. This has not been a good year for "The Star-Spangled Banner." And now things could get worse. The California chapter of the NAACP says the song is racist and wants Congress to find a different song to be America's national anthem. Sound crazy? It is. This is an example of political correctness on steroids and an attempt to rewrite history and deprive us of one of our most cherished national symbols. Things went badly for "The Star-Spangled Banner" when many football players around the country refused to stand for the anthem when it was played at the opening of their games, saying they wanted to protest racial injustice. In the challenging times our nation faces today, we need to focus on what makes us the United States of America and not be the Divided States of America.

I posted the following comment: "This is an example of political correctness on steroids and an attempt to rewrite history and deprive us of one of our most cherished national symbols." Black men, women and children hanged on trees are also part of your cherished national symbols. Stop being a cafeteria white supremacist going through the confederate buffet line picking and choosing what you want to be part of your heritage. It's all or nothing.

GERMANY. The players and staff of German Bundesliga team Hertha Berlin linked arms and knelt for about 12 seconds before their match against FC Schalke on Saturday, in solidarity with NFL players who have protested racial injustice and police brutality. As the players and staff knelt, a stadium announcer explained the gesture to fans. "Berlin is colorful", the PA announcer said. "Hertha BSC stands for diversity and against violence. For this reason, we are joining forces with the protest of our fellow American athletes to take a stand against discrimination. For a tolerant Berlin, both now and forevermore." (No comment from Fox News.)

JEMELE HILL is an ESPN host who tweeted that president Trump was a white supremacist who has largely surrounded himself with other white supremacists and is unfit to serve in the White House. Hill didn't mince words about her feelings toward the president or the impact she thinks he's had on the nation. "Trump is the most ignorant, offensive president of my lifetime," she wrote. "His rise directly results from white supremacy. Period." Jemele pointed to last August 2017 violent white supremacist rally in Charlottesville, Virginia, as an example of how Trump has empowered America's white supremacists. The president famously defended both those protesting and attending the white nationalist rally, saying, "You have people who are very fine people on both sides."

In a statement Tuesday, ESPN said Hill's comments about Trump "do not represent our position. We have addressed this with Jemele and she recognizes her actions were inappropriate," the statement said.

The ESPN's statement came even as they know it is no longer the time and days when slaves could not speak or even look at their white masters, a black woman can no longer be raped without recourse, Jemele Hill can no longer be muzzled by the will of the white plantation owners.

The US has the most concentrated amount of idiots per

square inch in the world. Of course, everyone expected idiots in the White House to counter, as they always do. They reserved the task for the sunny Sarah Huckabee Sanders who called Jemele's expression of free speech, a "firable" offense, despite the law of the land, which states:

18 U.S. Code § 227 - Wrongfully influencing a private entity's employment decisions by a Member of Congress or an officer or employee of the legislative or executive branch

- Whoever, being a covered government person, with the intent to influence, solely on the basis of partisan political affiliation, an employment decision or employment practice of any private entity

- takes or withholds, or offers or threatens to take or withhold, an official act, or

- influences, or offers or threatens to influence, the official act of another, shall be fined under this title or imprisoned for not more than 15 years, or both, and may be disqualified from holding any office of honor, trust, or profit under the United States.

Sarah Huckabee Sanders should be jailed for breaking the law and sued for violating Jemele's rights to freedom of expression. Once again, authorities are sending African Americans to jail for 10, 20 years for possession of marijuana under 20 grams.

Melody Hahm reported that Disney's Bob Iger had to explain why the corporation didn't fire or discipline ESPN's Jemele Hill over her Trump tweet, saying he needed to get involved in this instance, and ultimately decided that they should take no action against Hill. "I felt we had to take context into account."

Context included what was going on in America. What I felt, what we felt, was that there were many people who were outraged, particularly black people. They felt that the promise that was given to them, liberty and justice for all, during the Civil War or Civil Rights movement, was theirs. What they've seen in the last couple of months is the opposite", he said. Particularly in the wake of the Charlottesville protests, Iger said it was vital to understand where Hill was coming from, even if he did not condone the message. "It's not only disappointing, it's angered them. I've never experienced prejudice, certainly not racism. It's hard for me to understand what it feels like to experience racism. We need to consider what Jemele and ESPN were feeling during this time," said Iger.

Finally, a US corporation refuses to lynch a black woman on the advice of a white supremacist orange president. It's worth repeating: Enough black families have been destroyed, enough black women have been raped, enough black men have been slaughtered, enough black babies have been sacrificed on the altar of the racist, stupid, ignorant European ideology.

WHITE RAGE. It's not shocking to realize that not much has changed in the US since the silent parade organized by the NAACP, as about 10,000 people gathered in New York City on July 28th, 1917, to march in silence down Fifth Avenue to Madison Square. It was a response to the wave of lynching and white mob violence against black people across the country.

In the great US, it was entertainment, when thousands of white people in southern cities, including Waco, Texas, and Memphis, Tennessee, would gather to witness the lynching of black people.

"Just a few weeks prior to the march, racial tensions grew thick among the black and white workers in East St. Louis, Illinois. For 24 hours, white mobs burned homes and killed any black person they could find, regardless of age, gender or ability. The mob killed about 200 people while the remaining 6,000 black residents fled their homes to escape the violence." (Taryn Finley)

AMERICAN LUNACY. Dr Kenneth B. Clark explained: "The white backlash is a new name for an old phenomenon, white resistance to the acceptance of the Negro as a human being. As the Negro demands such status, as he develops more and more effective techniques to obtain it, and as these techniques come closer to success, the resistance to his demands rises in intensity and alarm. The forms it takes vary from the overt and barbaric murders and bombings to the more subtle innuendo of irritation and disparagement."

AMERICAN IGNORANCE. The history of the black man's protests against Aryan inhumanity began in 550AD, during the raid and kidnapping of able-bodied Africans off the coasts of Alkebulan. The first slave revolt in the US was in 1526 by the slaves owned by Lucas Vasquez de Ayllon.

In Maryland, in April 1775, governor Robert Eden requested arms and ammunition to put down any slave uprisings. And slavery has not yet ended today, in 2017. Blacks have exhausted all venues to escape the atrocities from the white people, from drowning in the ocean after jumping off the slaves ships, mutiny aboard the same ships*, unarmed slaves fighting the armed traders, later petitions to Congress, appeals to presidents, buying their freedom, court lawsuits, sit-ins of the 60s, etc...

(Note* It's worth noting that captain Harding compelled the rebellious slaves to eat the heart and liver of a terrorist sailor they killed.)

Between 1791 and 1804, Negroes finally found a solution that the masters could understand. The only clear and effective method to stop the racism of the white supremacists came from Jean-Jacques Dessalines, in 1804. The only thing the white American massa feared and still fears is a black insurrection. And much of that fear is in reaction to the Haitian war against slavery that could be exported and repeated. That's why South Carolina banned the importation of slaves in 1792 and Alabama enacted a law that would fine anyone who taught a negro to read, write, or spell, from $250 to $500.

At the convention of 1843, Henry Highland Garnet delivered the call: Brethren, arise, arise! Strike for your lives and liberties. Now is the day and the hour. Let every slave throughout the land do this, and the days of slavery are numbered. You can not be more oppressed than you have been, you can not suffer greater cruelties than you have already. Rather die free than live to be slaves. Remember that you are millions more! Are you men?

Where is the blood of your fathers? Has it all run out of your veins? Awake, awake..."There shall be no peace to the wicked." Frederick Douglass.

President Lincoln, who long endorsed the idea of colonization, promised government aid to colonization schemes in Central America, in a meeting with several negro leaders in 1862. He said: "There is an unwillingness on the part of our people, harsh as it may be, for you free colored people to remain with us... It is better for us both, therefore, to be separated." Meanwhile, Lincoln was trying to get rid of the problem of slavery by getting rid of the slaves. It's still ongoing today, in 2017, in the US.

A NEW DAY. Too long have others spoken for the negroes who are needed only when votes are wanted. We aim much of the actions of the federal government at keeping Negroes in a controlled, peaceful state. The same situation that existed between 1830 and 1861 is still prevalent today, in 2017, from the housing discrimination to the struggle for political rights.

Emancipated American Negroes don't have freedom, equality, the right to life, liberty and the pursuit of happiness.

Only the black American can put an end to the ongoing

slavery and abuses. In the end, Negroes in the US will have to choose. They must decide between following Marcus Garvey's movement "back to Africa" or Jean-Jacques Dessalines' simpler solution to "chop their heads off." Obviously, the nonviolence of Martin Luther King Jr is obsolete, as the planet is not big enough for Negroes and the parasitic feeble-minded white supremacists to co-exist. In the words of president Lincoln: "There is an unwillingness on the part of our people, harsh as it may be, for you free colored people to remain with us..."

Two thousands years of humiliation, abuse and deprivation cannot be expected to find a voice in a whisper

# KUBAKWA

Another delusional and hallucinating buzzword, making the rounds, claims the US is the greatest country in the world. Granted it used to be a beautiful land where peaceful people enjoyed a relaxed lifestyle. Lately it has become an aberration where miles of concrete roads lead from one shopping mall to the next.

A great country where clinically obese humans walk from food store to food store, inhaling everything in sight to maintain their sumo wrestling's figure.

A great country where 19 millions children go to bed hungry, every single night.

A great country where millions are over breeding and mass producing dogs and cats, in puppy and kitten mills, so they have a bit more money they need to make it to the end of the week.

A great country where online cretins, with less than two drunk brain cells fighting over the couch, are prompt to call anyone who does not readily agree with their idiotic comments: patsies and "snowflakes".

A great country where countless of the most crude and ignorant people in the world wander the streets to purchase illegal drugs and the crappiest products on the planet. 175 people die every day in the US from drug overdose. And the survivors seem happy and content to have worked 50 to 60 hours a week, so they can buy more drugs, get a Halloween costume for their pets, drink almond milk, eat baby carrots or pull up to a dumpster to order their fast food.

A great country where rich brainless idiots find it a status symbol to pay $50,000 for a Nike Air Force One so cals sneaker when they can not afford a $132,000 Buschemi 100 MM Diamond trainer.

What other country, on the planet, can claim this greatness? The toll on everyone is so high that 99.99% of the citizenry require medication for stress, anxiety, and high blood pressure.

They filled prescriptions for one-day old babies. Everyday life has replaced natural disasters as the principal venue for the people to get hurt, used and abused. Human suffering is now the most prolific product offered by the US worldwide.

CHICKEN HAWKS. This flawed system resonates all the way to the countryside. Take, for example, a chicken farmer who raises poultry for commercial in-store sales. To start with, the companies which distribute the birds to the stores are a monopoly, complete with lobbyists. They own the hatcheries, the feed mills and the packaging plants. The chicks are hatched, delivered to the farmer along with the premixed feed and picked up at harvesting time. Big corporations have a way to "legally" circumvent any law and this business is no exception. The feed is questionable at best, loaded with enough antibiotics, growth hormones, and assorted chemicals to take a day old chick from egg to the store in 46 days. Various useless government agencies, like the FDA and USDA, deemed this system legal and safe.

To qualify for the blessed opportunity to grow chickens for the companies, the farmer builds, maintains, upgrades a chicken house, pays for utilities, including rising fuel cost and labor, with money out of his own pocket. Each chicken house, built on his land, is about the length of a football field, equipped with expensive fans and heaters (day-old chicks require a 95 degrees environment, free of drafts), at the cost of 300 to $500,000 each. The poultry companies "facilitate" the approval of loans to farmers who received a contract from them. Besides that new mortgage, the farmer is responsible for keeping his tractors in working condition and providing for his family.

After meeting these conditions to the satisfaction of the companies, the farmer receives about 35,000 chicks per house, with the company approved amount of feed. The quality of different chicks and feed is also regulated and decided solely by the companies. After harvest time in 46 days, they pay the farmer 6 cents per pound, live weight. If the company is pleased with his performance, the farmer may also receive a bonus, otherwise he may be screwed in quality stock and feed the next time around. That's if the company doesn't cut him off completely, in which case, the farmer is left holding the mortgage payments and bag of associated loans to be paid to the bank.

Economists, heads of science departments, professors and researchers are all elated about a perfect system that benefits the companies and the farmers equally. All that false, skewed and unethical information was released to the public with no regard for honesty or even decency; not one of these geniuses apparently cared enough to talk to a farmer. If they did, they would have found out, like I did, that the great majority of chicken farmers are on the verge of tears talking about how badly they are getting screwed. I have met adult farmers with tears in their eyes, stressed to the limit in their everyday lives, trying to make sense of why and how they got trapped in such a business. Once they get involved, they can't quit for fear of losing more. I have seen farmers, dropped by companies, trying to sell metal roofing panels, ripped from their chicken houses, with nail holes in them, to raise money for food and mortgage payments. This is the true and honest story of the chicken farmers, and they are kept in total submission to the companies. They are not alone.

Once the chickens are collected from the farmer, they transport them in vented livestock trucks to the processing plant. There, many poorly paid employees work in shifts to kill, plucked, gut and bag the birds. It's worth noting that they abused the chickens at all levels of this process; it suffice to write that no one cares about the welfare of these animals. Time is money. After 46 days of ingesting antibiotics and steroids, the birds can barely stand up; then they suffer from broken wings and legs when they are violently collected and tossed in the trucks. At the slaughterhouse, many survive the automatic neck slicer until they meet the special bloodied employees in charge of putting an end to their misery. Once the carcasses have made it past the processors, they drenched the meat in chlorine to kill any bacteria and rid the smell of feces that splattered on the meat. The chickens are all dressed and ready for the stores and customers. Bon appétit!

MECHANICS. Most often than not, workers at automotive repair shops get a terrible reputation and reviews, and the saying goes that a talented mechanic is hard to find. Let's follow the process. A young man goes to a trade school and learns how to fix cars. He starts at a poorly paid minimum wage entry-level job at a garage, pays for all the tools needed to do the job and continues his education. After more advanced courses, they force him to move to another job with better hourly pay. But along with slightly better wages, come more demands of him. He will learn in many meetings that the company he works for has set goals, bills to pay and "numbers" that have to be reached. He also has bills to pay himself and a family to support. So he becomes a member of the team. (Déjà vu?) Several seminars, technical training, sales meetings, company indoctrination later, the garage starts to look more and more like a farm and the customers like cash cows. All the employee has to do is milk the cows, give the bucket to the manager or owner, who will give him a cup of milk that he can use to feed himself and his family. The best milkers make the most money, it's easy to figure out. It's that simple.

Or is it? Sometimes a good conscience has a way of tapping a few mechanics on the shoulder. Few, but just enough to maintain the proverbial exception. They are the smart ones, the ones who know not to kill the goose that lays the golden egg. They are not alone.

CAP AND GOWN. For a long time, the education business needed a financial boost, so they decided it among companies that they would hire no one without at least a GED. It was also a trick devised to deny employment to certain people of a certain skin color.

Countless of people flocked to community schools to pay a fee and learn to add 2+2. Then, the entire program was dropped, became obsolete when too many people knew the answers to the questions.

A number N is multiplied by 3, the result is the same as when N is divided by 3. What is the value of N? Which country put the first satellite in space in 1957? MLK and Malcolm X were both important figures in the American civil rights movements. Who is responsible for their deaths? (I rephrased and adjusted the last question for accuracy.)

Meanwhile, blacks failed to understand that they don't keep us out of a job because we are bad, lazy, uneducated. They shun us because we are too good, the very best. And they know it. Who were the teachers who educated and trained the so-called best European minds? Denying job opportunities is also about economic castration, something the establishment knows will create the anger seen among blacks. The science of criminology has determined that fewer jobs create more violence, and more jobs create less violence. Imagine a black man, kept from earning a living, frustrated at not being able to feed his family. The white establishment knows that. They can maintain white supremacy only when blacks are killing and destroying each other.

They made later a serious push to increase the GED job requirement to a college or university, associate or bachelor degree with a price tag of relatively $633 to $1,132 per credit hour. Why not try to entice and trap more people in the already successful scam of student loans? Regular tuition charges, online distributed learning tuition, technology, assessment and graduation fees could be collected by the Jewish dominated education mafia when re-arranged into student loans. These money laundering schemes and loan sharks were created to enslave students in a life of debts they will never escape from.

But the populace didn't budge; a GED is as far as they would go to get a job.

Getting an education, which is at best mediocre in the US, is made harder when students are being preyed on by teachers in heat. Here are the latest:

-They arrested a former middle school gym teacher in Georgia for the second time this year for having sex with a student.

Shawnetta D. Reece, 40, was taken into custody for engaging in sexual conduct with a high school senior in 2015, according to the Georgia Bureau of Investigation. They arrested the former Union County Middle School gym teacher at her Blairsville home.

Authorities realized the relationship while investigating allegations that the teacher was sexually involved with a 15-year-old student in 2013. They arrested Reece Aug. 14 for the relationship with the 15-year-old. They charged her with child molestation.

-A US teacher faces one count of first-degree sexual assault after allegedly having sex with four of her students, including two which took place in her apartment on the same day, according to police. The police affidavit about the charge against Art teacher

Jessie Lorene Goline states that the sexual acts happened between January and April 2016. The investigation into the schoolteacher started when parents accused the 25-year-old of having sexual relations with several students at Marked Tree High School, where Goline taught. Staff at the school intervened when a parent threatened to "do bodily harm" to the art teacher.

-A Brown County jury found a Howard piano teacher guilty of sexually assaulting one of his students in Green Bay. James Widiger, 63, will be sentenced Nov. 21 for two counts of repeated sexual assault of the same child. According to the complaint, a 14-year-old girl told police that Widiger, a Howard village trustee, would "grope" her under her shirt as often as five or six times per month during private piano lessons. The touching began when she was in fifth grade and continued through ninth grade, from August 2011 through March 2016, when she told her parents.

-A Beaumont Unified they have arrested a School District English teacher on suspicion of unlawful sexual intercourse and oral copulation with one of her students after detectives discovered evidence that the woman had an improper relationship with the minor for several months, authorities say. Samantha Lee Ciotta, 32, of Banning, who is also Beaumont High School's head cheer coach, was taken into custody and held at the Larry D. Smith Correctional Facility near Banning. Beaumont police detectives began investigating the alleged sexual abuse after receiving a tip. During the investigation, the victim disclosed to detectives there has been unlawful sexual intercourse.

-And there are many more accounts of teachers in heat.

GAMES WE PLAY. A subliminal message in conveyed thru the game of billiards. On the table which is the theater of operation, one white "cue ball" chases (pockets) and eliminates 15 colored balls, moving from solid balls number 1 to 7, and striped balls 9 to 15. It is a foul if the player accidentally pockets the white ball. The grand finale, the winning shot, the culmination of the game happens when the black ball (#8) is finally pocketed (killed). Do you wanna play?

Until the early 20th century, they made the balls of ivory from African elephants.

AMERICAN BRAIN. On 11/10/2017, Conservatives are publicly destroying their Keurig coffee makers in response to the company's decision to pull its advertisements from Sean Hannity's television and radio programs. Single-serving coffee- maker Keurig is in hot water with Hannity's fans. Users bitter the Vermont company has pulled its ads from Sean Hannity's TV show are calling for a boycott and even smashing their devices on video. "I pulled an 'Office Space' with my Keurig…" tweeted New Jersey Marines veteran and life coach John Angelo Gage, along with a video of him taking a hammer to his Keurig in a nod to the 1999 Mike Judge flick. "Would be a shame if everyone else joined me in the Keurig Smash Challenge."

Hannity retweeted some of the Keurig destruction videos on Sunday and hinted that he was purchasing 500 coffee makers of an unnamed brand "to give away" to those who made such clips.

The moral of the story is simple: destroying an appliance you paid for, because you are throwing a childish tantrum, is not only ignorant, it's a sign of mental masturbation. Besides, you already sent money to the company by buying it, so it's not a boycott.

All the drugs and hard liquor in the world could not produce this level of stupidity.

ORGANIC OFFERING, A few years ago, the definition of "natural" was changed to accommodate the agri-business giants and certain big food corporations. Many still know what "natural" means, as 99.7% of households in the US spent an average of $323 annually to purchase organic produce. The new organic food market craze has reached $65.8 billions in 2017. One can genuinely ask, "where was all that organic food production a few years ago, when companies were peddling GMO food?" It's safe to say that many claims of selling organic products, by most companies, are bogus. All that is needed is for a company to slap an "organic" sticker on a produce and idiots will pay double or triple the regular price.

THE NEW THREE AMIGOS. The government needed a clubhouse built for Congress, so they posted a public request for bids. A white man bided $50 million with a possibility of cost overrun, a black man's bid came at $20 million and a Mexican trailed with a $2 million bid. They awarded the white man the contract, which he quickly subcontracted to the black man, and pocketed $30 million. The black man sold his newly gained deal to the Mexican, and pocketed 18 millions. The Mexican built the clubhouse and was soon deported after the grand opening.

THE SMOKING CIGAR. How did we get to where we are now, was made possible by manipulating education and creating a system to dumb down people so the leaders would have the upper hand? It's a great country where a second to last place finish, in any competition, receives more trophies and accolades than the actual winner, just so their wussy feelings don't get hurt.

It will work for so long; then what? The answer is to return the old education system to the people to provide them with knowledge. Like the commercial said: an educated customer is our best customer... so, an educated citizen is our best national hope and asset.

Social activities promoting, benefiting the individual and humanity should be supported by a modern society, and shared in a group forum. Useless, parasitic, non sensical, mindless, absurd, foolish, insane, preposterous, implausible, screwy, farcical, laughable, strange, ridiculous, crazy, illogical, nutty, stupid, wacky, idiotic rubbish should never be allowed to be used to indoctrinate children, from birth. Decent parents should never allow their kids to be brainwashed. The BS that you do as I say and not as I do no longer rings true in our modern world.

We must ease the burden on the next generation.

This book is meant to be a comforting message to the downtrodden that they are not alone in their struggle. There are billions upon billions of abused and suffering people around the world. We don't have to get rid of our superfluous differences. All it takes is a concerted effort to make the world a better place for us and for all. Rectifying the dysfunctional of our world, ending the nightmare is within our capabilities if we just wake up. Together we can free justice, so it can be, once again, the finding of the truth.

# JUST A FEW THOUGHTS

"The cause of freedom is not the cause of a race or a sect, a party or a class, it is the cause of humankind, the very birthright of humanity. (Anna Julia Cooper)"

There is no difference between capitalism, socialism or communism, when people are only yearning for a natural desire for a better life. We have taken the simplest act and complicated it so much that life is no longer what it was in the beginning.

Because of sheer stupidity, humanity has passed the point of no return. What is corrupt has been corrupted forever, what is altered has been altered forever, what is untrustworthy can never be trusted again. It is very telling when people wish for their own extinction as the only hope and solution to reboot this nightmarish society. People are so hopeless that they believe only another Noah's flood or a new full coverage Sodom and Gomorrah can straighten up this planet that we messed up so badly. Billions of Christians everywhere are impatiently waiting and hoping for the Rapture. Millions more are yearning for a nuclear war against Iran, North Korea or Pakistan, totally clueless about the potential disaster from a nuclear weapon. Americans are that stupid. Mother earth will heal after she gets rid of all the human manure that has been heaped on her. We need to change our ways.

Humanity is like a dysfunctional husband who married a gorgeous, classy, sexy woman, leaves her alone at home, to cruise down the streets looking for a hoochie mama, waves a $20 bill to get the attention of a cheap street walker, or pays $10 for a bottle of beer so he can have the privilege of stuffing dollar bills down a gogo dancer's G-string. He is a family counselor. We need to change our ways.

Humanity is like the dysfunctional wife who married a

good, hardworking man, leaves him alone at home, to meet the next supermarket customer in line behind a dumpster, goes to a bar looking for the next stranger who will buy her a drink, gets on the dance floor to grind on a gigolo and whip her head like a windmill. She is a life coach who gives speeches on ethical conduct. We need to change our ways.

Anyone, outside of the immediate family, who pretends to love another person's children is a liar, and any legislator who kisses a baby on the campaign trail is a charlatan. In 2017, after millions of years of so called societal bonding, progress and technological advances, many are still incapable of showing any decent positive affection toward all humans. They murdered blacks for no other reason than the color of their skin. We need to change our ways.

The European world never misses an opportunity to blast militants factions which use very young children as war combatants. The western world even sets a minimum age when youngsters can join the military. The hypocrisy rests in the indoctrination imposed on young children of all ages at school. Part of their education apparently involves prepping, lying and brainwashing underage kids into thinking that it is patriotic to join the military when they come of age, to serve their country. The truth, which they will learn when it's too late, is that western armed forces are only used to enforce the ideology of the white supremacist elite who controls the world affairs. The kids grow up to be nothing but pawns, destined to be wasted on a foreign land, to enrich the already rich; and if they are "lucky", they come back home with mangled bodies, and will earn a living on a street corner, as homeless beggars. That's when they are not blowing their heads off, or killing the civilians they used to work with. We need to change our ways.

What good is it to make it illegal for a child under a certain age to consume alcohol, use tobacco products, yet carelessly throw them under the religious bus? The world should find a legal way to restrict the religious indoctrination until the age of 21, for the security of our children. We can no longer afford to remain silent, guilt free accomplices and allow children to be used as sex toys by Catholic priests, the Vatican or any other institution. No child is safe under Judaism, Christianity, Islam or atheism.

The Torah set the age of permissible sexual intercourse at 9 years old for girls, the Quran at 6 years old, Christianity at any opportunity a priest or evangelist is horny and Atheism wants to start the humping at the post-morula, modified blastula stage. It's time to prove our intelligence and show true love for the next generation. We need to change our ways.

The world should find a way to end the religious nightmare, educate the fools who keep financing the churches and save the countless lives slated for destruction. We must do it for the same reasons we can not afford to believe and build our lives around the "historical fact" that 3 cute little pigs built houses of straw, sticks and bricks in 1840. We can no longer afford to believe in a 400 lbs Aryan drunk sliding up and down a one foot wide chimney to deliver presents to little Negroes. The last time a white man visited little black children, he dropped tons of bombs on them. Because it may be only fairytales and mythology for some of us, but for many others, it's an invitation to murder. We need to change our ways.

The world should find a way to end the religious nightmare and free, not just emancipate the spiritual slaves. It is possible because it was done, more or less, for the physical slavery. As long as religious cartels are allowed to prosper and fleece the defenseless, there will always be genocides in the names of chosen fairies. The first step is to remove and eliminate the tax exemptions for religion. All businesses should pay taxes and there is absolutely no reason religion, which steals trillions of dollars from the uneducated poorest, should be given a free pass. We need to change our ways.

The world should find a way to end the political nightmare and restore the rule of law. If the national wish is for one country indivisible, a land where all men are endowed with certain unalienable rights, with equality for everyone, liberty and justice for all, the right to life, liberty and the pursuit of happiness, then one life should not be above the next, and no one should be above the law. We need to change our ways.

The world should find a way to end the European lies. As we get ready to celebrate Columbus' day on 10/09-2017, let's start by admitting that Christopher Columbus was NOT a navigator or an explorer. He was an idiot Zionist mass murderer who hitched a ride aboard the ships of the black Pinzon brothers. He didn't discover America and didn't open the "new world" to commerce. The time has come for accurate history to be taught to our children. We must stop honoring criminals and celebrating dead white supremacists. We need to change our ways.

Like branches on a tree, we all grow in different directions, yet our roots remain as one. In the words of Carl Sagan: "Like it or not, for the moment, the earth is where we make our stand."